The Devil's Carnival

Drawing by Lieut, R. A. Lawrence RA. 19th Battalion Northumberland Fusiliers for the "St, George's Gazette" April 1918

THE DEVIL'S CARNIVAL

The 1st Battalion Northumberland Fusiliers
The First Hundred Days of Armageddon
August-December 1914

QUO FATA VOCANT (Whither the Fates Call)

Based on the Diaries of Captain Beauchamp Tudor St John,
Lieutenant F. E. Watkins and Captain E. B. Gordon

Edited and developed by
John Mason Sneddon

Reveille
PRESS

Reveille Press is an imprint of
Tommies Guides Military Booksellers & Publishers

Gemini House
136-140 Old Shoreham Road
Brighton
BN3 7BD

www.tommiesguides.co.uk

First published in Great Britain by
Reveille Press 2012
updated, 2013

For more information please visit
www.reveillepress.com

A catalogue record for this book is available
from the British Library

ISBN 978-1-908336-35-4

Cover design by Reveille Press

Printed and bound in Great Britain by
CPI Antony Rowe, Chippenham and Eastbourne

Contents

This book is dedicated to the
memory of John Philips,
Heath House, Upper Tean,
County of Staffordshire.

Acknowledgements

This journey started in 1990 when Captain P.H.D. Marr, the then Honorary Curator of The Fusiliers Museum of Northumberland, introduced me to the diaries of Captain B.T. St John. During the many hours I spent in the Abbott's Tower, built into the great curtain wall of Alnwick Castle, transcribing the two hand-written volumes that made up the diary I absorbed from Captain and Mrs Marr, almost by a process of osmosis, the history and nature of the men of the Northumberland Fusiliers.

To the family of Captain Beauchamp Tudor St John my sincere thanks for permission to use his diary. I hope I have done justice to his memory, and the men of the 1st Battalion, who fought and died in the first 100 days of the Great War. Captain St John was a member of a family with strong military traditions and using his diary, and those of other members of the family, his great granddaughter, Emily Williams has produced an interesting book about those who served in both world wars. It is titled '*A Family at War* ', and was published by The London Press in 2001. I am grateful to Emily for an early draft of her book and our Email discussions concerning Tudor's experiences and other matters.

To Dr John Bourne, Professor Peter Simkins, Andy Simpson and the late Paddy Griffith for helpful comments and encouragement after reading draft chapters.

To my very good friend David Woodrow for many illuminating discussions and offering many textual suggestions that I believe much improved the text.

The origin of the photographs and diagrams are acknowledged when they are first listed. I would like to thank Mrs Lesley Frater, the current Museum Administrator, and the Trustees of the Fusiliers Museum of Northumberland, for permission to use the diaries and other material in their archives.

Finally to my friends who, aware of it or not, have been important in the preparation of this book. They listened to my chatter about the Northumberland Fusiliers and were interested enough to interject suggestions and seek clarification of technical matters, all of which I hope has made this a better book. Thank you.

Maps and Diagrams

Illustrations and Photographs

About this Book

My major interests in the First World War are the events of the first twelve months. Not for me the great attrition battles of 1916 or 1917 but the more intimate, and surprisingly more deadly, battles fought by the British army between August 1914 and August 1915. In pursuit of this interest I haunt regimental museums and archives for original material on the soldiers of 1914; diaries; letters; reports; and the like relating to the original British Expeditionary Force (BEF). Experience had demonstrated that such source material is thin on the ground when compared with the volume of paper relating to the Legions of the 'New Armies' that followed them to France and Belgium. But perhaps this is not surprising. The original BEF were to fight almost continuously for four months with most battalions losing about 90% of their original members as casualties of one sort or another. Sometimes however, in my search, it is possible to strike it lucky, and this book is a labour of love, and remembrance, arising from one such piece of luck.

In 1990, in pursuit of my interest, I arranged to visit to The Fusilier's Museum of Northumberland, situated in the Abbot's Tower in the great medieval fortress of Alnwick Castle to look at the archives of the Northumberland Fusiliers. To my surprise I found a rich collection of contemporary accounts relating to the 1st Battalion during the first four months of the war. Firstly there was a copy of the War Diary, complete with its appendices, listing the casualties killed in action, wounded or missing, all by rank, name and number. There was the diary of Lieutenant F.E. Watkins, the battalion machine gun officer who, before censorship throttled the flow of information from the front, sent his home to be published in monthly instalments in the "St Georges Gazette"[1]. Another was an unsigned typewritten manuscript

1 The St George's Gazette is the Regimental Journal of the Northumberland Fusiliers and at this time was published monthly.

entitled "European War 1914". Subsequent research identified it as an account of the experiences of Captain E.B. Gordon, Commander of "Z" Company, who joined his Battalion in France in October 1914. The greatest treasure however was two hard covered notebooks in which Captain Beauchamp Tudor St John recounted, in great detail, his experiences from the outbreak of the war on 4 August until he was severely wounded in the abortive attack of the village of Wytschaete on 1st November 1914.

My original intention was to publish St John's journal on its own but with the other diaries available it was possible to look at the experiences of the battalion from three different perspectives so this book has grown into the story of the 1st Battalion, and its trials and tribulations, as seen through the eyes of these three officers. The details contained in these diaries make the story of the 1st Battalion utterly absorbing for there are few other contemporary documents, perhaps with the exception of the 1st Battalion, Grenadier Guards[2], that survive to give us this level of insight to what it was like to be in a fighting battalion coming to grips with the reality of war.

Our three diarists cover all the fighting of the 1st Battalion: the Battle of Mons; Le Câteau; the Great Retreat; First Battle of the Marne; the Aisne and the transfer to Flanders in late September. Here they fought throughout the almost forgotten Battle of Le Bassée in which the British II Corps fought alongside the French Tenth Army to halt the German offensives along the valley of the river Lys and where they were to suffer grievously in the bitter fighting in and around the French village of Neuve Chapelle. After almost twelve days of non-stop combat the battalion was reduced to less than 200 and withdrawn from the battle to rest and re-equip.

That was not to happen. With less than twenty-four hours rest they were ordered to march to Kemmel to support the Cavalry defending the Messines ridge. When the British lost the village of Wytschaete on the night of 31st October, two companies of the Northumberland Fusiliers were ordered to support the 1st Battalion, The Lincolnshire Regiment in retaking the village. Neither battalion made any headway and lost heavily, including Captain St John who received a near fatal wound through his neck.

After three days rest the remnants of the 1st Battalion were ordered to Ypres where they came under the command of General Douglas

2 Craster, J M "Fifteen Rounds a Minute". The Grenadiers at War, August to December 1914. London: Macmillan 1976.

Haig, GOC I Corps. Here they fought in the dying weeks of the Battle of First Ypres, including beating off attacks by the famed Prussian Guard during the last great German offensive of 1914. By December, after rest and refitting, the ranks filled with older, poorly trained reservists and volunteers, they were in at the birth of trench warfare during one of the coldest, wettest, winters Europe had experienced in decades.

The popular media defines, and regurgitates, many of our common beliefs and mythologies about the First World War, as does the fragmented manner in which the war is dealt with in the National Curriculum in History for 11-16 year olds with its concentration on the perceived interpretation of the conflict through the eyes of a small number of war poets. After almost a century many still see the First World War only in terms of a grim hell of static warfare in which unwilling soldiers lived a troglodyte existence in deep trenches and dugouts sheltering from an unending artillery bombardment amid a forest of barbed wire. Here, surrounded by a landscape of mud and water-filled shell holes, the soldiers suffered, and grumbled, until finally succumbing to death, wounds or shell-shock.

Whatever grain of truth such descriptions may contain they describe a type of warfare totally unknown to the soldiers of 1914. In Flanders[3], during October and November, battles were fought in a countryside untouched by war, among villages, farms, fields, hedgerows and woods where, until the onset of winter, deep foliage obscured the view of attackers and defenders alike. When the infantry dug trenches they were not part of some elaborate field defences but temporary holes and scrapes, either dug for local defence, protection from enemy fire, or as a jumping off position for a renewed attack.

In such country the experience of the individual soldier is limited, and confined to actions within a few yards. As we will see in Captain Gordon's fight at Neuve Chapelle he and his men were fighting for their lives against sustain infantry and artillery attack while less than 200 yards away Captain St John's were sitting in their trenches in relative calm. It is this focus of individual experience that breaths life into these diaries for in the words of Georges Kimpflin "*The fighter has a short view but because his views are narrow they are sharp; because they are restricted they are clear. He doesn't see a lot, but what he does see he sees*

3 Although not historically, or geographically accurate, the term Flanders is used to describe those areas of France and Belgium, from Le Bassée to Ypres, in which were located the trenches of the BEF in 1914.

plainly. Because his own eyes, and not those of others, informs him, he sees what is." [4]

For my generation, who were born and grew up when many who fought in the war were still alive, our first encounter of the mythologizing of the 'lions led by donkeys' slant on military history was Joan Littlewood's musical *'Oh, What a Lovely War'*. Not the original stage production in Stratford East, seen by few, but the later film, which, with Alan Clark's polemic about the failed battles of 1915, *The Donkeys*[5] coloured the views of many of us. By contrast, but in the same vein, for my children's generation the Great War will always be seen through the jaundiced eye of Edmund Blackadder, the historically inaccurate, but brilliant doings, of successive Blackadders from the late Medieval period to the First Day of the Somme.

It is unfortunate that this "take" on the War, as expressed in these, and other popular works propagated through the medium of books, film, TV, is in danger of swamping our understanding of the events that constitute the history of the First World War. I hope this book will act as a slight corrective for it is a very personal account based upon the writings of just three men who were to write down their impressions of the chaos of war very soon after the events in which they participated.

These diary entries have sharpened my belief that the way in which the soldiers of 1914 internalised their experiences of war was very different from that of the men in the large armies of civilian soldiers that followed them. It is often forgotten that, in the opening months of the war, all armies were fighting with their best troops. For the British this was their small, long-service, professional army; for the Germans, Russians, and the French, it was their youngest, fittest and most recently trained conscripts backed up by a core of their professional soldiers, and all armies were supported by reserve forces composed of previously trained soldiers withdrawn from civilian life.

In addition they were fighting with weapons and tactics with which they were familiar through their pre-war training. This envisaged a war of movement and manoeuvre to bring the enemy to battle in which the infantry, supported by their artillery and machine guns, would strive to win the fire-fight and defeat the enemy by driving them from their positions. This form of warfare is recognisable in the fighting that

---

4 Georges Kimpflin. *Le premier soufflé*. P14. Quoted in Bryan miller "Drumfire. The Champagne Offensive. The French War Effort and the Death of Percée in 1915. MA Thesis. University of Colorado, Boulder 2001.

5 Alan Clark. The Donkeys. London Hutchinson 1961

occurred over most of the period covered by our story for continuous trench lines, from which the combatants shot and shelled each other, did not yet exist, or when they appeared, as they did by late December, they were in their very infancy.

The picture of the Northumberland Fusiliers that emerges from these diaries is one of a highly professional battalion, led by experienced officers who took their duties seriously, and went to war confident in their own abilities, and those of their men, to defeat the enemy. They were hardened to the dangers and discomforts of campaigning for many, particularly among the officers, NCOs and reservists, already knew what battle was like, either from the Boer War, or small actions against dissident tribesmen on the North-West Frontier or in Africa.

But we should not forget that 1914 was a year of great killing. One of the paradoxes of the war is that battle casualties were highest during the 'war of movement' in 1914 and 1918 rather than in the great attrition battles of 1916 and 1917 that so fixate the public imagination. In round numbers for 1914 the French suffered 300,000 killed, with many more hundreds of thousands wounded or prisoner. Germany, fighting on two fronts, suffered 840,000 casualties of whom 150,000 were killed in action. The British Expeditionary Force had about 96,000 casualties, dead, wounded, prisoner or missing, almost equal to the number of combat troops that landed in France just four months earlier[6].

By December 1914 most of the original members of the 1st Battalion, Northumberland Fusiliers, and their reinforcements, had been killed or wounded. Yet their sacrifice was not to be in vain for it was these almost forgotten battles of 1914, in which they fought so gallantly, that were to disrupt the German war plans in the west, leading inexorably to their defeat on the Western Front four grim years later.

6 A full count would have to take into consideration the casualties of the Austrian-Hungarian Empire; Russia; the Indian troops fighting in France; not forgetting the Balkan states such Serbia, invaded by Austria at the outbreak of war.

Prologue

It is my intention in this Prologue to give a little bit of the political and military background to our story. As far as the politics are concerned Captain St John, and his fellow officers knew little, and probably cared less, but politics, was the reason they were at war. The political compromises of coalition warfare with the French influenced, as much as the actions of the enemy, why they fought in a particular place at particular time, so politics has a bearing on our story and will perhaps be of some interest to the reader. As to the military background of 1914 the soldiers of the BEF, like the other armies involved in the conflict, fought according to their pre-war training and I have added a short section about the soldiers of the BEF in 1914 to give some idea of the 'working environment' of our three diarists.

The Politics

"The great thing to remember in dealing with them is that they are Frenchmen and not Englishmen and do not, and never will look at things in the way we look at them."

Sir William Robertson

Britain and France were not natural allies. They had been enemies for centuries and although warfare between them stopped with Waterloo, tensions continued to exist throughout the nineteenth century resulting from colonial rivalries in the carving up of Africa, Asia and the Pacific. The *Entente Cordiale* of 1904 resolved many of these tensions and this new friendship was strong enough for Britain to support France against Germany during the first Moroccan crises of 1905. It was also from this crisis that a pattern of tentative military co-operation began to emerge that would lead to British military support when war did break out between France and Germany in 1914.

Of course the *Entente Cordiale* did not make things perfect between the two nations. On both sides of the Channel, spoken and unspoken, were layer upon layer of prejudice and the worst kind national stereotyping. For example the French had a clear racial stereotype that appears in literature, cartoons and satire of the period that portrays the British as below average intelligence, dull, pedantic in their beliefs, and slow to adapt to changing circumstances; while the British thought the French unwashed, smelling of garlic, shifty and untrustworthy and all Frenchwomen were of easy virtue.

This all had a serious side for as Roy Prete has shown[7] many in the French army, particularly among senior officers, were completely Anglophobic, despising and discriminating against all things British. He further points out that in their military education, particularly the study of French military history, the curriculum was almost designed to reinforce the view that Britain was not to be trusted, and only meddled in European affairs to manipulate the balance of power, impoverishing her allies in the process.

Such prejudices ran deep in French society and were held even by informed observers, such as Victor Huguet, the knowledgeable and experienced military attaché based in London. After ten years living there he could still deliver a lecture to his fellow officers in which he argued that the English, as a race, were of mediocre intelligence; slow to see where their best interests lay; but once committed to a cause were tenacious in their determination to pursue it to the end. Applying this negative stereotype to the British army the French tended to view the British soldier as a valuable asset on the battlefield, steady and reliable, but lacking the dash and the superior *élan* of their own troops. Of British officers they had a very low opinion, particularly of senior officers, who were characterized by French visitors to peacetime manoeuvres as hesitant and indecisive, particularly when in command of large units. As Prete further notes "the image of the British as 'slow, late and unaggressive' was thus deeply entrenched in French military minds well before the first shots were fired".

In August 1914 both French politicians, and their military, were well aware how important British support was for their survival, but nobody said that they had to like, trust or respect them. The lack of a formal military alliance between Britain and France did not assist inter-allied understanding and co-operation. In their pre-war discussions

7 Roy A Prete: French Strategic planning and the Deployment of the BEF, in France 1914. Canadian Journal of History XXIV (April 189) pp. 42-62.

on military co-operation the British and French High Commands had only managed to reach an "understanding", which legally had no more status than a gentleman's agreement. This 'understanding' did not commit the British Government to any particular course of action but represented an undertaking on the part of the Army that in the advent of a war between France and Germany, Britain would mobilise her forces on the same day as the French. Brigadier-General Henry Wilson put flesh on this 'understanding' during his tenure as Director of Military Operations at the War Office. He developed, with the French, a mobilisation plan for the British army which assumed that sixteen days after mobilisation a British Expeditionary Force (BEF) of six infantry divisions and two cavalry divisions, with all supporting arms, would concentrate on the left of the French armies along the Franco-Belgian border.

With the exception of a small number of senior politicians the basis of this 'understanding' was unknown to the governments or parliaments of either nation and as it did not constitute a binding military alliance, upon which war plans could be based, the days leading up to the British declaration of war were a political and military roller-coaster for the French, confirming their prejudice that the British were always slow, late and unaggressive.

The British Dither

In late July, with Europe in free-fall towards war, Britain was undecided as to her course of action. She had spent most of her diplomatic capital trying to prevent war, but historical hatreds in the Balkans were proving too strong to be calmed by diplomacy. Yet the British government could not commit itself to the last act that may deter Germany's open ended commitment to support Austrian aggression against Serbia. This act would be to inform the Kaiser that if Germany went to war then she would have to fight the British, as well as the French and Russians. Even as late as 1st August, as the shooting war started to spread across Europe, and the French army mobilised, the British Foreign Secretary, Sir Edward Grey, reaffirmed Britain's lack of commitment to support France, echoing Prime Minister Asquith's statement of the day before.

Such public statements were predominately for home consumption for Asquith, and his closest advisors, had already decided that Britain could not stand aside if a major war broke out in Europe. Their difficulty, at the beginning of August, was that they were constrained by the strong anti-interventionist demands from a highly vocal public and press, combined with the delicate political necessity of holding the Government, and the Liberal Party, together by preventing the resignation of the anti-war ministers in Cabinet, including the powerful Chancellor of the Exchequer, Lloyd George.

In three days this would all change.

On August 2nd Germany issued its ultimatum to Belgium, demanding free passage for her armies, and when this was rejected Germany invaded Belgium. Asquith used Britain's obligations, as one of the signatories to the International Treaty that guaranteed Belgium neutrality and freedom from invasion, to convince his wavering colleagues that British honour could only be upheld by punishing the invading Germans by siding with the French.

At 4 pm on August 4th orders were issued for the British army to mobilise and at midnight, when Germany failed to respond to the British ultimatum to withdraw her troops from Belgium, Britain and Germany were at war.

For the British Government most of August 5th was taken up with futile discussions between the politicians and military about whether the agreement with the French to concentrate of their left wing was the best option, or whether the army should be sent to directly support the Belgians by landing at Antwerp as advocated by Sir John French, Commander-in-Chief designate of the BEF. Lord Kitchener, on the other hand, was in favour of supporting the French but concerned that the proposed concentration area designated by Henry Wilson was too far forward and could place the BEF in danger if the French lost the first battles. He suggested concentrating the army further back, around Amiens, to wait and see how events played out between the Germans and French before committing the BEF to the fight. The only decision made at this inconclusive meeting was to reconvene next day[8]

For the French High Command, unaware of these discussions, and impatiently waiting for news of the arrival of the BEF, only bad news trickled out of London. Kitchener had an unjustified fear of invasion, or at least raids in strength, and ordered the 4th Division to be dispersed to defend the East Coast[9], a troop movement that almost completely

8 Sir Henry Wilson, worried that his plans with the French may come to naught characterised the meeting as "An historic meeting of men, mostly entirely ignorant of their subject".

9 Including a Brigade of Infantry sent to Cromer to protect Mrs Churchill and her children who were on holiday.

disrupted Sir Henry Wilson's carefully worked out timetables for the dispatch of the BEF to France. In addition the Cabinet got the jitters about the Irish and ordered that another division should be retained at home to deal with any trouble in Ireland. The BEF was now reduced to four infantry divisions, not the six the French were expecting, and at the headquarters of the French Commander in Chief, General Joffre, his Chief of Staff, General Berthelot, on hearing of the reduction in the size of the BEF, wondered if they would ever be able to count on such unreliable allies. French confidence and trust was slipping away even before the first British soldier had set a foot on French soil.

Throughout August the French completely miss-read German intentions and their strategy turned out to be a disaster that nearly lost them the war. Believing that the main German thrust would be directed at central France, between Verdun and the Ardennes, Joffre concentrated his armies accordingly but the Germans were to make their main effort with their armies of the right wing, totalling nearly a million men, with the extreme right wing army, the *First Army*, of 300,000, commanded by General von Kluck, biting deep into northern Belgium before swinging south-west to invade France by the "back door", across the Flanders' plain

To his credit Joffre, in his pre-war planning, recognised that this manoeuvre was a possibility and proposed to move the bulk of the French armies into Belgium and Luxembourg as soon as war was

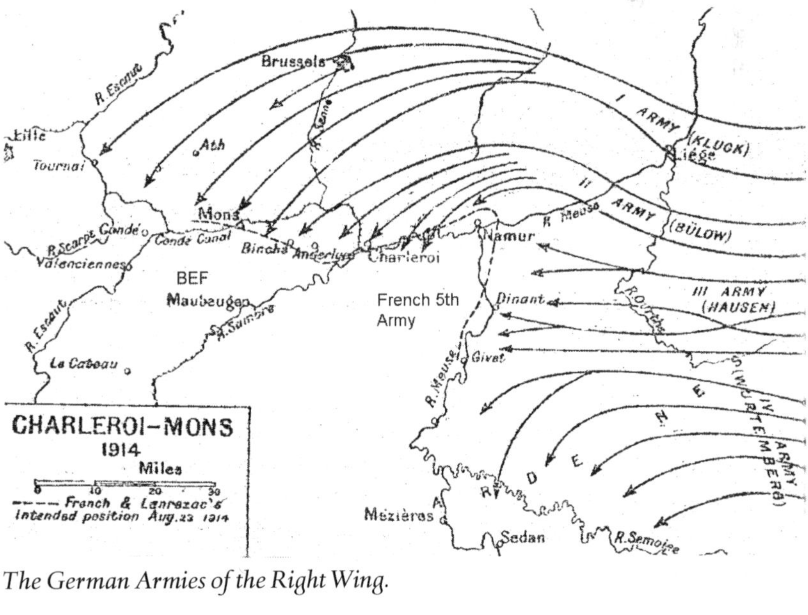

The German Armies of the Right Wing.

declared in order to invade Germany and destroy her armies while they were still mobilising. This was vetoed by his Government who did not want France branded as the nation that violated Belgium neutrality, or to be seen as the aggressor in a war against Germany. Under these circumstances the best Joffre could devise to counter any move by the German right wing was mobilise his Fifth Army west of the river Meuse where it would be in a position to support the French offensives in the centre, or launch its own offensive into Germany, through the Ardennes, depending upon the circumstances.

Joffre also assumed that the British would keep to their pre-war understanding and provide a force of 150,000 men, concentrated on the left of the Fifth Army sixteen days after mobilisation. Based upon that assumption he ordered General Lanrezac, Commander of the French Fifth Army, to begin his offensive against the Germans on that day[10] as he would have the newly arrived BEF available to defend his left flank as they moved up the eastern bank of the Meuse into Belgium. Unfortunately the dithering and delays on the part of Asquith's government forced Joffre to tinker with the details of Plan XVII[11] resulting in strategic decisions that increased the risks to the French armies, particularly the Fifth. With the no show on the part of the British Joffre had no choice but to delay Lanrezac's offensive, first to August 20th, then to the 21st, delays that increased the danger to the Fifth Army from the Germans pouring into northern Belgium.

While he waited for the British Lanrezac began to receive reports from Belgium that indicated that the German thrust through eastern Belgium was much larger than that originally anticipated by French intelligence and as a result Joffre give him permission to re-orientate the Fifth Army, making it easier for it to move up the Meuse valley to counter any German threat towards the important river crossing at Charleroi. This new orientation was to subtly alter the role of the BEF.

In keeping with his perception that the BEF was poorly trained for a European war Joffre had allocated it a minor supportive role as

10 That would have been no later than 18th August.

11 The French War Plan, known as Plan XVII as it was the 17th version prepared since the French defeat in the Franco-Prussian war of 1870-71. It was submitted by General Joffre in 1913 and, unlike previous plans, did not define a strategy for the French armies in response to a German invasion. Rather it was a plan of concentration placing the French armies in a position that gave the Commander-in-Chief the option of an offensive into Belgium, or Lorraine, depending upon whether the Germans were making their main thrust across the French frontier, or indirectly through the Belgian Ardennes.

flank guard to the Fifth Army, not directly participating in the French offensive, but perhaps playing a useful role in mopping up after a French victory. With the altered realignment of the Fifth Army the BEF now became an integral part of the strike force for, with the French continuing to assume that the major German penetration into Belgium would be limited to the western bank of the Meuse, the BEF, moving up the eastern bank, would be in the ideal position to strike into the flank of the Germany armies when attacked by the French.

Thus from Joffre's point of view it was more critical than ever that the British got themselves into position as quickly as possible. The concentration area for the BEF, on the left flank of the Fifth Army, was being kept free of French troops; obviously essential if the British turned up, but it created an undefended area that represented a grave danger to the French left wing if the Germans, pushing down the Meuse valley, arrived in northern France before the British. Furthermore, with the new orientation of his army, Lanrezac had to withdraw his troops from the eastern bank of the Meuse leaving that flank undefended until the British turned up.

It was August 14th before Sir John French, Commander-in Chief of the British Expeditionary Force, accompanied by his personal staff, crossed the Channel to Boulogne where he was enthusiastically welcomed onto French soil.

Their arrival in Paris on the 15th attracted a large cheering crowd as they made their way to their first official call on President Poincaré, recorded by some observers as a polite meeting without warmth or enthusiasm, an atmosphere not helped by Poincaré complaining that the British were not only late, but would not be ready for action until the 25th, jeopardising French plans for a knockout offensive against the Germans.

The next call was on Messimy, the War Minister. A short business like meeting from which the most important outcome was that Messimy would make all the arrangements for Sir John to meet General Joffre the next day. This first critical meeting with Joffre went better than anyone expected. Perhaps relieved that the British had finally arrived Joffre greeted his visitors warmly and with the aid of maps explained the general situation as far as it was known. He explained his ideas for a combined offensive involving the British, the Belgians and the French Fifth army to clear the Germans out of northern Belgium and asked Sir John to collaborate by moving the BEF as quickly as possible north of the river Sambre[12] so to be in a position to support the left wing of the French Fifth Army. In the absence of any British strategy Sir John agreed to fall in with Joffre's plans, promising that he would immediately contact General Lanrezac with a view to collaboration. He also undertook to speed up the movement of the BEF so that it would be ready to move by the 21st rather than the 24th.

The meeting with General Lanrezac was not a success. The tone of the meeting was set by General Hey D'Oisel, Chief of Staff to the Fifth Army, who greeted the arrival of Sir John French and his staff at Lanrezac's HQ with the words: *"Well here you are – and not a moment too soon. If we are beaten, we will owe it all to you"*. The subsequent meeting between Sir John French and General Lanrezac did not go well and no plans were developed for liaison between the two armies that were expected to co-operate to stem the German invasion of northern France.

The Army Available for War in 1914.
"That Perfect Thing, Apart" [13]

The Serving Regulars

It is often written that the BEF sent to France in August 1914 was the best trained and best equipped army the British Government ever sent to war. In some respects this is true but in my opinion the common interpretation of this statement is for patriotic, nationalistic consumption as almost half of the soldiers who landed in France that August were reservists, called up from their civilian lives, and of variable military effectiveness depending on how long they had been in the reserve.

On the other hand Britain probably did have one of the best-trained and experienced armies in the world, but her long-service, highly trained professionals, were serving overseas. The army "census" of 1st October 1913, showing that 77,130 of them were stationed in India, with a further 34,619 distributed throughout the other colonies, serving in part, to police the Empire, and so not immediately available to be shipped to France to fight the Germans.

12 The Sambre is a major river in Northern France and flows into the Meuse at Namur

13 A description of the 1914 British Professional (Regular) Army attributed to Generaloberst von Moltke Chief of the German General Staff

The situation of the Regular Army stationed in the United Kingdom and Ireland was entirely different. The census shows they numbered 125,209 but only 30-40% of these would be available to fight overseas. The others were new recruits undergoing training, young soldiers too young to be sent overseas, men waiting to leave the army and all the soldiers in training, administrative and other roles at Army Depots, Training centres, etc. throughout the country.

Under the Caldwell system for providing troops to serve the Empire the majority of infantry regiments in the British Army consisted of two front line Battalions numbered 1st and 2nd. One battalion was stationed in the United Kingdom while the other was stationed overseas, either in India, or one of the other colonies, for a period of anything between five to fourteen years before rotating its station with its sister, home based, battalion. It was rare for the two battalions that made up a Regiment to ever meet and unusual for officers and men to serve in a Battalion other than their own. For example, the two Battalions of the Royal Welch Fusiliers celebrated St David's day together when their troopships crossed paths in Malta in early 1914, the first time the two battalions had met in over 30 years.

Only the battalion stationed overseas was maintained at war strength with the home-based battalions, as an economy measure, maintained at about 40 – 50% of this. Their major role, in addition to being available for home defence or trouble in Ireland, was to recruit and train new soldiers. These were then sent out as drafts of trained men to the battalion serving overseas replacing the time-expired men and any casualties.

The Regular Army Reserve

The second class of soldiers available for call up on mobilisation, and more importantly could be sent to fight overseas, was The Regular Army Reserve. This was composed of time-expired regular soldiers who, on discharge from the Regular Army, were required to served a further nine years in the reserve. The 1913 census showed that there were 145,090 troops in the Regular Army Reserve, including those in the Regular Reserve of Officers. They attended an annual camp where a basic level of training was maintained, particularly in musketry, and the opportunity taken to measure and fit them out with kit, which was maintained in the battalion mobilisation stores at the Depot ready to equip and arm the reservists on mobilisation. In time of war the home-based battalions would be brought up to war strength by an influx of their reservists and the procedures for mobilisation were practised and reviewed each year as part of the Army's annual training cycle.

The degree of military preparedness of soldiers serving in the reserve, and the amount of training they would require to bring them back to military efficiency, was obviously related to the amount of time the individual soldier had already spent in the reserve. A soldier coming to the end of this period, that is one who left the Army in 1905, would, in 1914, rejoin a military machine that had changed almost out of recognition from the late Victorian Army in which he had learned his soldering and it is unfortunate that, due to the haste with which the British Expeditionary Force was sent to France, there was little opportunity to retrain these older men before they found themselves in action.

As we will see from St John's diary the degree of military unpreparedness was to give the battalion officers something of a headache as they sifted through the mass of reservists to select the best available men to bring their battalion up to war strength.

The Battalion

The unique historical nature of the British Army was that throughout most of its existence it served and fought overseas. These long periods away from home, cocooned in an environment of their own creation, resulted in each regiment developing a unique character or "persona" which developed and matured with the myths and traditions that grew up around each new campaign. Successive generations of officers and men passing through the ranks of the regiment were taught their regimental history and group memorises as an essential part of their training alongside the more usual military skills by the long-service NCOs and serving officers that were the backbone of the regiment. Serving soldiers, ex-soldiers and their civilian supporters were notorious for the intense pride and loyalty they exhibited towards 'their' regiment, behaviour very much like that seen today among the fans of a modern football club.

For most of the three hundred years of its existence the army was not popular among the civilian population. To serve in the army, or 'go for a soldier' was, for the majority of the working class the last resort of the desperate, or the scoundrel, and before the mass patriotism of 1914 swelled the ranks of the army with men from all social classes it was the experience of most young soldiers that joining the colours usually meant severance from family and friends. Sir William Robertson, the only soldier to rise from private to Field Marshal, recorded that when he wanted to join the army his mother said she would rather see him dead than wearing a red coat! For the sons of the middle classes, with so many new opportunities for advancement, a military career was equally uninviting. A glance at the list of officers killed in action in 1914, and whose biographies were printed in Bond of Sacrifice[14] quickly demonstrates that the majority were drawn from a relatively small section of society, predominately the land-owning gentry, or descended from them, the social class who traditionally provided their sons for the army. Captain Beauchamp Tudor St John's very name spells out his aristocratic lineage.

The backbone of any regiment were the NCOs, the long-service soldiers who may have served twenty years or more as they worked their way up the ranks. These were men of strong personalities, self confident and full of energy, and better educated than their Victoria counterpart. Their job was to teach the men their drill, musketry, physical training and field craft, as well as what the Regiment would expect from them when it went to war. The changes in infantry tactics introduced after the South African War placed great responsibility for initiative and leadership on the NCOs who were trained, like the junior officers, to grasp and maintain command of the troops around them in the rapidly changing situations on a battlefield. Officer's memoirs, Official Dispatches, and Regimental Histories are full of the names of this outstanding class of NCO who distinguished themselves with exceptional military skills. In our diaries the names of such NCOs are often recorded, along with their deeds.

Finally the common soldier who was to do the fighting in time of war and in peacetime all the rough and boring jobs. From the working class many joined because they wanted to be soldiers and have a bit of adventure and travel before they settled down; others because they were unemployed or unskilled for the industrial age. Requiring a relatively small number of new recruits each year the army was in a position to pick and chose and took only those that met the Army's standards as regards physical fitness, respectability and be able to read and write.

14 The Bond Of Sacrifice is an album that set out to honour the memory of those officers killed in action by recording, with a photograph, a brief biography of their life and military service. By late 1914 it became obvious to the publishers that the scale of officer deaths in this war was so great that publication could not continue as planned. It ceased after the publication of the second volume. The two volumes that were published contain details of the 2,500 officers who fell in action in 1914 and 1915.

John Baynes in his book '*Morale*[15]' describes the soldiers of the Scottish Rifles at the beginning of the war as having the nature of a child, physically a man, but mentally a boy. He suggests that most recruits had a mental age of about ten, which, with training and instruction would rise to about twelve or thirteen but few soldiers would ever developed a truly adult approach to life. Baynes, himself a serving officer when he wrote his book, saw this reflected in his soldier's simple gallows humour and their apparent inability to fully appreciate the seriousness of the danger in which they would often find themselves.

The Northumberland Fusiliers

It was widely recognised that Regimental pride and traditions were the mainstay of a soldier's morale and the army 'establishment' went to great lengths to cultivate this pride through inter-regimental competitions and the tolerance of small, idiosyncratic variations in the approved military uniform. In the status ranking of British regiments The Royal Northumbrian Fusiliers were a regiment with a formidable reputation. They definitely considered themselves a cut above most other infantry regiments in the British Army, being one of the oldest and, sharing with very few, the ancient privilege of marching through the City of London with bayonets fixed, drums beating and colours flying. They may not have had a monopoly of smartness and discipline but they had high standards to maintain and these were characterised in two of their common nicknames, "the Shinners" from their high standard of discipline and 'spit and polish', and 'The Fighting Fifth' for their prowess in battle.

But they, like most of the older infantry regiments, did not start life in the British army but in the service of a foreign ruler. Founded in 1674 as a mercenary regiment, known as "The Irish Regiment", they were part of the "English Brigade", raised and paid for by the Prince of Orange in his war against the French[16] but in 1675 the Northumberland soldier, and landowner, Sir John Fenwick, became Colonel changing the name to "Fenwick's Regiment". Sir John set about recruiting large numbers

15 John Baynes. Morale. A Study of Men and Courage. Cassel & Co. Ltd. London 1967.

16 The politics of this period was very complex. Charles II was technically an ally of King Louis of France in his war with the Dutch and had in turn just concluded a humiliating treaty with the Dutch to end the Second Dutch War but Charles II turned a blind eye to his subjects fighting in "English" regiments in the pay of one or another of these European Powers. As a general rule Catholics fought on the French side and Protestants for the Dutch but experienced soldiers were at a premium and were recruited by both irrespective of their religion.

of experienced soldiers who had "come on the market" as a result of the disbandment of the English army at the end of the Dutch Wars. With this influx of experienced men the Regiment soon gained the status as one of the best in the Dutch service.

For the next ten years it fought for its Dutch paymaster but in 1685 Monmouth's Rebellion rattled the government of the newly anointed Catholic King, James II, who seized upon the rebellion as an excuse to request the transfer of "his" regiments from the service of his Dutch brother-in-law. Three Scottish and three English Regiments came over from Holland, too late to take part in the Battle of Sedgemore, but were involved in the pacification of the West Country after Monmouth's defeat. This scare was sufficient for the King to desire an increase the size of the permanent army so the British Government agreed a purchase price with the Dutch and "our" Regiment became incorporated into the British Army as the 5th Regiment of the Line. In 1751 the Regiment became the 5th Foot, in 1782 the 5th or Northumberland Regiment of Foot, and in 1811 the Northumberland Fusiliers.

The original purpose of Fusilier regiments was to provide a bodyguard for the artillery, and to prevent the civilian transport drivers deserting their posts when the army came into action. Their name comes from the special musket, or "fusil" they carried in an attempt to reduce the number of accidental explosions that occurred when the sparks from the fuse cord or match on the more commonly used "matchlock" rifle landed on the open powder barrels stacked around the guns when they were in action. After the adoption of the flintlock rifle this function fell into disuse and Fusilier Regiments evolved into crack infantry regiments with many of the characteristics of modern 'storm troopers'. In recognition of this role Fusilier Regiments wore a distinctive (pre 1914) dress uniform, of a red coat and a grenadiers cap or "Busby" similar to the Foot Guards. However in keeping with English class distinctions the cap was slightly smaller than that worn by a Guardsman and made of seal or racoon skin rather than bear skin. The Northumberland cap was of racoon and worn with a scarlet over white Plume on the left hand side, the origin of the distinctive Fusilier plume worn by serving soldiers to-day.

It is now difficult, after a period of successive army reorganisations, which has resulted in the disappearance of many famous regiments, to comprehend the power of regimental pride in 1914 and how this helped to sustain and support the individual soldier through some of the most extreme periods of combat experienced by the British Army.

The engagements of the first four months of the First World War were fought by these 'original' highly professional regiments made up of serving Regular Soldiers or drawn from the Regular Reserve of recently discharged soldiers. These soldiers knew one another and were linked by the closest bonds of comradeship forged through years of mutual service to the Regiment and after the battles of 1914 they had almost all gone, both the regulars and reserves[17].

The Infantry Battalion

In 1914, at War Strength, a battalion consisted of 30 officers and 977 men, 9 pack horses, 13 riding horses, 26 draught horses, 8 heavy draught horses, pulling a one-horse cart, 12 two-horse carts, 3 two-horse wagons and 9 bicycles for reconnaissance and message carrying, all under the command of a Lieutenant-Colonel. It was organised into a headquarters, four rifle companies, one machine gun section equipped with two Maxim machine guns and the transport section. Each of the four rifle companies consisted of six officers and approximately two hundred and twenty men, commanded by a Major or a Mounted (senior) Captain, with a junior captain as second in command. The smallest unit in the company was a section of twelve to fourteen men under a section commander, who was a N.C.O. Four sections made up a platoon, commanded by a lieutenant, and four platoons made up the rifle strength of the company.

Battalion Headquarters

The headquarters company was the command and control centre for the battalion and consisted of the commander, the second in command, the adjutant, the quartermaster, the machine gun officer, the transport officer and the medical officer all of whom were mounted. There were also the officer's servants, the transport men, medical staff, machine gun crews, armourers, signallers and other specialised staff. In some battalions the headquarters company could number over a hundred officers and men who, in addition to their other duties, were all trained to the same high standards of musketry as the riflemen serving in the companies and provided the battalion with a useful tactical reserve in battle.

---

17 In three weeks of non-stop fighting the 7th Division lost (killed, wounded & missing) 364 out of 400 officers and 9,303 other ranks out of 12,000.

The Soldier

In 1914 the fighting strength of a battalion lay with the riflemen in the four rifle companies. On the march regulations stipulated that an infantry soldier should carry no more than 60 lb. Beside his clothing this included his rifle and bayonet, 120 rounds of ammunition, entrenching tool (grubber), water bottle and webbing from which his equipment was suspended. On his back a pack containing, greatcoat, spare clothing, rations and limited personnel possessions. The weight of the pack balanced the weight of the ammunition carried in pouches across the chest. When, during the retreat from Mons, soldiers abandoned their packs to decrease the weight carried they found difficulty in marching as the unbalanced weight of the ammunition pouches suspended on the webbing across their chests tended to pull their bodies forward. In the battle zone it was usual to add to the weight of the soldier's standard equipment by issuing an additional two days iron rations and two cotton bandoleers each containing 50 rounds of ammunition. Once trench warfare had become established in the winter of 1914/15 labouring tools such as picks, shovels and a wide variety of 'trench stores' would be added to the burden carried by men 'going up the line' for their tour of duty in the trenches.

The major firepower available to a battalion, both for attack and defence, lay in the rifles carried by the 884 riflemen. His personal weapon was the .303 Short Magazine Lee-Enfield Rifle Mark III. This rifle was 3 feet 8.5 inches long and weighed 8 lb. 10.5 oz. The magazine held ten rounds (two five round clips) which was twice as much as the German Mauser rifle and the bolt action for loading and extracting the spent round was the quickest in the world and a skilled marksman could accurately fire at up to 20 rounds a minute. Both officers and men were taught the fundamentals of good shooting, firing at least 250 rounds on the annual musketry course in addition to the normal shooting practice conducted as part of their individual training. In learning to use their rifles effectively they were taught how to pick targets at great distances and to fire at them using both slow and rapid fire in addition to "snap – shooting" at moving targets up to 600 yards range. They were also taught the "mad minute" of rapid fire where each rifleman was expected to fire 15 to 20 round into a two foot target 300 yards away within a minute. This was not the accurate shooting of individual marksmen but designed to put down a wall of fire through which the enemy infantry could not pass. Field Service Regulations 1909 describe ranges of 600 yards or less as close for infantry; 600 to 1000 yards as effective; 1,400 to 2,000 yards (the limit of the standard back sight) as long; and 2,000 to 2,800 yards as distant.

When under attack the officers and NCOs in charge of section of trench, or a line of rifle pits, exercised strict fire control over their riflemen either by verbal orders or by signalling with a whistle. When the attacking infantry were at long range they would only be engaged by the individual marksmen in the platoon but during the mass infantry attacks at short range, which were a feature of German tactics in 1914, they would be met by rapid fire from all riflemen. During such attacks there was no indiscriminate 'fire at will' on the part of the riflemen who maintained fire discipline by responding to instructions such as 'two rounds rapid', 'single fire', 'four rounds rapid' called by the officers and NCOs as they gauged the tenor of the enemy attack.

When fire control broke down, usually as the result of high casualties among the junior officers and NCOs, then there was a tendency for the men to fire off rapidly during attacks and alarms so that their rifles became overheated and the extractors broke leaving the empty cartridge firmly wedged in the breech[18]. If this occurred among sufficient men in a trench the attacking enemy could get close enough to overwhelm and massacre the occupants.

The Machine Gun Section

The complement of a machine gun section was fifteen men, commanded by a lieutenant, with a sergeant as second in command. The section were all well trained 'specialists' with interchangeable roles, and equipped with two .303 belt fed Maxim machine guns. This two gun establishment was identical to that in a French or a German battalion.[19]

Transport Section

The type, and number, of the transport required by an infantry battalion on active service was clearly set out in regulations and divided into two classes. The *First Line Transport* was an integral part of the war organisation of a fighting battalion and always accompanied the troops

18 This was known as 'brassing-off'.

19 The reason why the Germans appeared to have more machine guns on the battlefield was that they fought in regiments of three battalions instead of the British single battalion and their machine guns were organised as a single 'machine gun company' which allowed all six guns to be brought into action on the same part of the battlefield. Additionally each regiment had a reserve, or replacement gun, giving each German regiment seven guns and each German division 28 machine guns as opposed to the British division with 24 guns.

on the march and went into action with them. Without its contents the battalion would not be able to fight as its wagons carried the machine guns, reserve ammunition (185,000 rounds), tools, medical and technical equipment, water carts, a cook's wagon and the officers mess cart. The *Second Line Transport* consisted of the heavier wagons carrying baggage, stores, and supplies necessary for the general subsistence of the battalion and, as these were not required to support the troops in immediate action, travelled in the rear of the marching columns.

The Battalion on the March[20]

In order to help us to understand the difficulties facing the average regimental officer during the retreat from Mons and the subsequent campaign in Flanders it is worth looking at what they were expected to achieve in the organisation of a typical infantry battalion on the March. It is important to appreciate that the 'Great Retreat' from Mons was not a disorganised crowd of soldiers moving along the roads of northern France but an organised withdrawal in which battalions kept their formations and marched, as far as the stress of the retreat permitted, according to the methods developed during their peacetime training.

One of the most striking observations in the entries in unit War Diaries is the very early hour at which battalions were aroused from billets. It was typical for officers and men to be roused two, or even three hours, before the time when they actually started to march, which would normally be between 5 and 6 am. This early rise was not only required for the obvious need to put on equipment, and have breakfast (if any), but also to form the troops into their proper place within their companies, and then companies into their proper position, in relationship to the transport and machine gun section, in the line of March of the battalion. Additional time would be required to organise the line of March if the battalion was to travel as part of its Brigade when each battalion had to be assembled into its proper position within the Brigade order of March. This organisation was vitally important for a battalion on active service. The marching orders for the day, issued the previous evening, would specify which company, (or battalion in Brigade formation), was to act as advance guard, which troops were in support, and which were in reserve, for if these troops were not in their proper place within the column at the beginning of the March then, if they came into action, the chain of command would break down and

20 March with a capital M is used as a noun to describe a formed column of men and equipment that would then 'march' to their destination.

the effectiveness by which they could respond to a rapidly developing situation would be seriously impaired.

The importance of positioning units in their proper place is emphasised by the experience of the Northumberland Fusiliers on the morning of the 28th August. Still closely pursued by enemy units their retreat was delayed for an hour and a half due to difficulties in getting 9th Infantry Brigade's column assembled in its proper order due to a heavy dawn mist.

Time and Space allocated to the March

Once in line of March infantry, and other troops, were expected to cover ground at a steady calculated pace that brought to them to their destination within the allocated time. For troops marching in ideal conditions, that is on a flat clear road, soldiers marched with a 30 inch pace at a rate of 98 yards to the minute, taking 18 minutes to cover a mile. At the end of each hours march there was a short break of 10 minutes and a battalion would be expected to maintain an average march of 3 miles an hour including short halts. The battalion's wheeled transport could only maintain 2.5 miles an hour and normally started its journey an hour or so before the infantry. To relieve boredom and fatigue the men sang most of the time they were on the march.

In calculating the amount of road space a battalion required on the March it was assumed that infantry marched in columns of four and that 0.5 yards of road were needed for each man. Therefore each company of infantry required 125 yards of road, or 590 yards for the four companies, with an additional 60 yards required for the headquarters staff including mounted officers. The machine gun section required 30 yards of road to accommodate its two limbers. The battalion transport marched in single file; each of the 2-horsed wagons was allowed 10 yards of road; the 4-horsed wagons 15 yards. Each bicycle, or pair of bicycles riding side by side, was allocated 6 yards of road. The regimental first line transport required 210 yards, the second line transport, including the officer's mess cart, an additional 115 yards. When field kitchens were added to battalions an additional 15 yards of road were needed. When marching as a Brigade the four infantry battalions would require 1.5 miles of road for its fighting troops and 0.75 mile for their transport. When assembled into a Division, with all ancillary units attached, including artillery, 8 miles of road were required for the fighting troops, 5 miles for the transport and an additional 1.75 miles to accommodate the ammunition and supply trains and the field ambulances.

The Battlefield

The popular image of the First World War is the static post-1916 'industrial' warfare of extensive trench networks, huge artillery assets and poison gas and tanks but this was not the way of war in 1914. The armies of the three main protagonists, Germany, France and Britain, were trained for a war of movement designed to manoeuvre their enemy onto a battlefield of their own choosing where they could annihilate them with an aggressive violent attack. To that extent the armies of 1914 were to fight within a form of warfare that was recognisable from their training. Trenches, in the sense used to describe the Western Front after 1914, did not exist. To have a 'feel' for the experiences of our 1914 soldiers it is important to appreciate that when our diarists use the word trench they are referring to a variety of field defences the most common of which, to use a second world war term, were foxholes, a shallow pit holding one man, or as many as five or six. These were designed to provide some protection from the enemy but also to provide a steady fire platform for the soldier's personal weapon. These 'foxholes', and the more conventional trench in the sense of a deep narrow ditch, were seen as temporary refuges from the enemy, and places were the infantry could be reformed before renewing their assault. What they were not was a permanent field fortification behind which the soldier lived, fought and died.[21]

Most of the battles described by our diarists were fought over land untouched by war. The countryside, particularly in Flanders, was agricultural, reclaimed marshes of small fields surrounded by dense hedges and deep ditches, and broken up by many small woods with trees still in full leave. In such close country your enemy could not be seen until you almost stood on him and fields of fire were short so that infantry, advancing in the open, were very vulnerable to close range defensive fire from rifles and machines guns that were so well camouflaged that they were never seen.

Military Training

Battalion training followed a regular annual routine, During the winter months, when in barracks, the soldier was trained individually in physical exercises, route marching, bayonet fighting, musketry, signalling, fieldcraft, and scouting, with increasing opportunities for

21 When 'conventional' trenches first made their appearance along the banks of the Aisne in September 1914 they were immediately recognised as ushering in a new kind of warfare, moreover one that would require new doctrine and new tactics.

individuals to develop new specialist skills such as machine gunner, scout or signaller, as well as achieve the extra proficiency with a rifle necessary to become a marksman, all of which carried additional pay allowances. Company training took place in the spring, followed by Regimental training, then Brigade and Divisional exercises during the summer, the whole cycle finished off with the Army manoeuvres in the autumn. Although there were limitations on the availability of suitable amounts of the English countryside that could be given over to the army for several weeks in late summer these big manoeuvres usually involved several weeks of near-active service conditions and were held over the open downs of Wiltshire and Berkshire.

Battlefield tactics were based upon the principle of 'Fire and Movement' a manoeuvre common in all European armies at this time. When an enemy position had been identified the artillery, and the battalion's two machine guns, would open up on their positions with the aim of demoralising them and preventing him bringing up supports. Under cover of this bombardment the infantry would start their attack. Working in small groups, usually in sections of four men widely spread out to reduce casualties, each section would crawl forward taking any advantage offered by ground cover until they came within effective rifle range. The sections would then work their way forward in short rushes under the covering fire of the other sections until the first line was about 100 yards from the enemy. Here they formed a rough firing line by digging shallow fire pits with their entrenching tools while the second and third waves, acting as supports and reserves, moved up to 'thicken' the firing line. From this position the attacking troops would attempt to subdue the enemy with accurate rifle fire until the time arrived to take the enemy position with a bayonet charge.

Chapter 1

The Journey to War (4-21 Aug. 1914)

Beginnings

In the autumn of 1913 the two active service battalions of the Northumberland Fusiliers exchanged home and foreign postings. The 2nd Battalion moved to Ambala in the Punjab and a few months later the 1st Battalion returned from India to start its home tour of duty at Portsmouth as one of the four battalions in the 9th Infantry Brigade. It was here that Captain Beauchamp Tudor St John joined as 2nd Captain to 'B' Company.[22]

In the summer of 1914 world events were to conspire to disturb the settled routine of a battalion on home station for, as the 1st Battalion

Beauchamp Tudor St John as a Subaltern.

22 In 1913, just several months before going to war, a radical change was introduced in the structure of home – based infantry battalions. This was the replacement of the eight-company system with a new four 'double company' structure with the introduction of platoons and sections as the company's tactical formations in battle and a redefinition of the responsibilities and roles of the officers and NCOs. As a 'junior Captain' St John was appointed 2nd in command in a 'double company'. The impact of this change on the BEF has never been evaluated.

returned to Portsmouth from their summer training at Wool in Dorset, the newspapers were full of reports of the assassination of Archduke Franz Ferdinand, heir to the Austrian throne, and his wife Sophie, in Sarajevo. At first the possible importance of this tragic event barely touched the consciousness of the officers and men of the 1st Battalion for, having just returned from two months strenuous training, they had more pressing things on their minds. In the *St. George's Gazette*[23] we learn from 'The 1st Battalion Notes', dated 23rd July 1914, that 'the month of July has been used as a period of restful repose so far as training is concerned, the chance of a fortnight's leave has been seized by all those who could fit it in.' In the same edition we find that the sergeants are busy competing for a billiard cup when not engaged in confetti battles on the South Parade Pier! For the officers the highlight of the summer was the first weekend in August – the Bank holiday and Goodwood races – and throughout Southern Command as many as possible were taking leave, or otherwise arranging their military duties, to be able to attend. Not even the Government's declaration of the 'precautionary period' on 27th July, signifying the first steps towards the mobilisation of the Army for war, was allowed to upset well-laid plans to attend the races.

> *St John.* I can well remember the day that the idea of the probability of a European war came into my mind. It was on the day that the content of Austria's note to Serbia were made public in the English press and like many others I wondered what was behind this historic document. I remember that Haroldine Peck and Miss Blake motored over from Hamble on that day and the conversation turned somewhat light heartedly on the presumptuous tone of the note. I remember saying to Had something to the effect that I wasn't at all sure that it was a subject for light hearted treatment which led her to ask " Do you think England will really go to war with Germany? ". This question non-plussed me in a way for although I thought, and said, that if Austria persisted in her note and Serbia didn't knuckle under to her an Austria-Serbia war was inevitable which would drag in Russia and Germany, then France, and then England

23 The St George's Gazette is the Regimental Journal of the Northumberland Fusiliers and at this time was published monthly.

was bound to come in. Yet this idea of Armageddon was unthinkable to me. I can still clearly remember Had saying to me at parting 'If you do have to go and fight mind and kill heaps of Germans, they are a vile lot of people.'

From that date until the day that saw us actually on the sea en route for France events of great magnitude crowded one upon the other in such rapid succession that I find I have but a very confused impression of all that did happen. I remember a short period of very high tension and expectancy until Austria refused Serbia's reply to her note and Russia began to mobilise. Then a further period of nervous apprehension as to what our Government would do, followed by a curious mixed feeling of relief and despondency when at last the precautionary period was ordered. Relief that the Nation was not going to evade her obligations and despondency at the thought of what this war was to be like. I never had any illusions as to the war being a picnic though I likewise had no idea as to the pitch of " frightfulness " to which Germany would go.

29 July, Wednesday

Acting on prearranged instructions the battalion sent detachments to guard important local premises against possible sabotage by the hundreds of enemy agents that many believed Germany had planted in the country prior to the outbreak of war. As Captain St John was not on leave he was sent to guard the waterworks at Bedhampton.

St John. From out of this confusion of recollection one or two events stand out more or less vividly in my minds eye. First of these was the reception of the order of the precautionary period. I had been playing lawn tennis that afternoon at the United Services Club and at tea time there were rumours of the arrival of the order. There had been one or two similar rumours previously and at first I was inclined to be sceptical about this one but I noticed the arrival of several orderlies whose arrival synchronised with the hurried departure of most of the officers. About 5.30 I started off on my bicycle to barracks to find out what was going on. I was met on arrival with the news that the battalion was to parade at 6.0 in marching order. I dashed off to my house, which was about one and a half miles from Barracks, got into my uniform as quickly as possible and dashed back to parade.

I was not detailed, according to the scheme for the precautionary period for any specific duty, but owing to so many officers being away on courses of instruction, leave etc. I found that I had to proceed at 7.30 to Bedhampton by train and to guard the waterworks at that spot. I sent Sanders, my servant, with a hurried note to Madge with orders to collect some bedding and food for me and to come on to Bedhampton by the next possible train.

I found myself at Bedhampton with a inadequate force and a few sheets of typed orders and instructions which were a certain amount of assistance in enabling me to see clearly for myself how impossible it was to prevent a determined man from destroying the waterworks should he so desire.

I set to work at once to do what I could by getting hold of the manager and posting sentries as far as possible on the most exposed and venerable spots such as valves, exposed piping, power houses, etc. I also, with some difficulty, persuaded a curious crowd that I had not brought the men there as an illustration of " life in the army " for their edification and organised a system of passes signed by the manager and counter signed by myself for the use by men actually necessary to the works.

30 July, Thursday

St John. I then rang up headquarters and reported my arrival and told them what I thought about it all and then tried to get the RE[24] people to get me some materials for defensive purposes. It took me 24 hours or more to get through to the RE owing, as I learned afterwards, to the absence of the entire staff at Goodwood races.

31 July, Friday

St John. I spent until Friday trying to make bricks without straw when I handed the command over to its rightful owner

24 Royal Engineers

and returned to Portsmouth and my sorrowing family who had been out to visit me and bring me food.

4 – 6 August

St John. The next event which is still clear to me was the arrival of the order to mobilise. This arrived on Tuesday 4th August and we had been expecting it hourly ever since I returned from Bedhampton the previous Friday. During this interval of expectancy the men had been confined to barracks and officers were only allowed out for two hours at a time. I slept on my camp bed in Dick Vachell's room. There was very little really in the shape of work to be done. We did all we could but soon reached a point where we were stopped by not having the official order to mobilise. Dick Gatehouse, whose wife was to stay with us, and I used to go home for breakfast, spend the morning in Barracks, and then spent two hours at home and return to sign our names in the guard book and go back for another two hours. It was during one of these returns to barracks on the Tuesday that the long desired order to mobilise arrived. I remember I was standing talking to Colonel Anslie and one or two others when a telegraph boy gave the Colonel a message and he simple opened it and read one word 'Mobilise' on which we all quietly vanished and began the series of carefully planned 'jobs' which were required to be done in order to bring the Battalion from a peace footing to a war footing in both men and material.

The battalion had a very efficient plan of mobilisation and experienced officers and NCOs to carry it out. By 7.15 pm an officer and NCO had been dispatched to Newcastle to pick up the reservists flocking in their hundreds into the depot. These would bring them up to fighting strength in 'rifle and bayonet men' but the battalion needed horses for its transport and Captain H. B. Sandilands, with a list in his pocket, left the barracks early in the morning of the 5th to requisition suitable horses from their owners in and around Portsmouth, including some attractive draught horses from the brewery. By 8.30 am the horses already on strength had had their veterinary inspection and by 12 noon the medical inspection of the men was complete and at 12.20 pm, one sergeant and 24 men, deemed unfit for active service, left for the depot.

August 6th was a day of hectic activity. At 9.40 am the first party of 420 reservists arrived; followed by 18 draught horses from Army stables; another 221 reservists at 11 am and then Captain Sandilands with 39 horses at 3 am next morning. The movement was not all one way. They were required to send an experienced Captain, two subalterns and 15 NCOs to the depot to train the recruits in the new 8th (Service) Battalion, the first of forty-five New Army Battalions to be raised by the Regiment.

9 August, Sunday

> *St John.* It was calculated that we should require five days to complete the work and we did it in that time without any hitch and on the following Sunday we were again waiting, this time for the order to embark. We employed this period of enforced idleness in getting the thousand odd men who now made up the battalion as far as possible fit to march. Most of the reservists who rejoined the colours were soft and we were fully occupied hardening them, getting them used to their equipment, the pattern of which was new to most of them, and teaching them as much as possible a few of the principles of scientific warfare.

That Sunday, for the first time, the Battalion paraded at war strength in full service order to be inspected by Brigadier-General Shaw, Commander of the 9th. Infantry Brigade.

10 August, Monday

The sorting out of the reservists began. The officers had anticipated that the first to arrive would be those highly trained soldiers who had left the battalion immediately on its return from India but the first drafts were mainly of men coming to the end of their period in the reserve. They had been in civilian life for almost nine years and although they had attended the annual musketry course they had little experience of the modern army, or the revolutionary developments in infantry training that had been introduced in the last few years. The officers saw them as more of a hindrance than help in bringing the battalion up to full efficiency. The Colonel had already returned 201 of them to the Depot for further training along with the young soldiers, under 19 years of age, who were too young to be sent overseas and a hundred trained reservists, surplus to immediate requirements, to be sent to France, when required, as the battalion's first reinforcements.

Still at war strength following the departure of almost 400 men there were still doubts about the quality of some of the remaining reservists and the Colonel took drastic action. He sent an urgent telegram to the harassed Depot Commander in Newcastle instructing him to go through the reservists and select one hundred who had most recently left the regiment and dispatch them immediately to Portsmouth. In turn each Company was to weed out 25 of their most out of date men and return them to the Depot. Despite this action the Battalion went to war with a large proportion of its riflemen drawn from the older men, but they were not to fail the battalion for they were to demonstrate that they retained the endurance, bravery, and devotion to duty that had characterised British Infantry down the centuries.

13 August, Thursday

> *St John.* I do not propose to dwell on the pains of parting. I dislike saying good-bye to people I like at any time and so I found the wrench of parting from my family a very severe business. I never said goodbye to the boy at all. I left the house at 6 am and bade farewell to Madge and my Mother in barracks just before we marched out. We waited an hour at Portsmouth station before our train departed and then through to Southampton.

The Regimental History contrasts their departure from Portsmouth in 1914 with that of 1899 when they left the same barracks to fight in the South African War. On that occasion the streets were thronged with cheering masses, whereas on the 13th August 1914 only the curious lined the street and, but for the presence of a few relatives saying a tearful farewell, it could have been a normal regimental move taking place rather than a battalion leaving to fight the most powerful Army in the world. When they arrived at the station, perhaps in an attempt to mislead any German spies who may have been around, they found that the two trains which were to take them to their 'unknown port of embarkation', predominately displayed 'Woking' on their destination boards. But they were Southampton bound and embarked on the *SS Norman*, an old boat belonging to the Union Castle Line, which was so overloaded with both the 1st Battalion The Lincolnshire Regiment and the 1/Northumberland Fusiliers that, as soon as it entered the open sea off Southampton, it developed an alarming list. Luckily, such a trivial matter was not allowed to impede the voyage to France.

They arrived off Le Havre about midnight and, as they entered the outer harbour, excited troops crowded along the decks and rails to experience their first sights and smells of France. For two hours they slowly steamed through the locks and basins and along waterways so narrow that the ship almost touched the quays on both sides until they moored alongside an inner wharf close to the boat carrying the 1st Battalion, The Royal Scots Fusiliers and the 4th Battalion The Royal Fusiliers, the two other battalions of the 9th Infantry Brigade.

The total strength of the Battalion was 1016 officers and men. This included the Medical Officer, 1 Corporal and 4 Privates attached from the RAMC, an Armourer Sergeant, 1 Officer and 9 other ranks from the Divisional Cycle Company and 4 Army Service Corps drivers attached to the transport

The Officers, of the 1st Battalion Northumberland Fusiliers, who embarked for France 13 August 1914:

Lt. Colonel H.S. Ainslie — Commander.
Major C. Yatman. DSO — Senior Major.

Captains

H. S. Toppin (wounded 26th Aug. kia. Sept. 14th 1914).
H.R. Sandilands (wounded 24th Aug. 1914).
R. F. Gatehouse (missing in action 14th Sept. 1914.).
J. H. Matthews (kia 15th Sept. 1914).
B. T. St John (wounded. 1st Nov. 1914).
E.L.D. Forster (wounded 14th Sept. 1914).
B. H. Selby (wounded 20th Sept. dow. 21st Sept. 1914).

Lieutenants

R.M. Booth
H. L. Ovans (wounded 26th Aug. & 14th Sept. 1914).
G.O. Sloper (wounded 14th Sept. 1914).
C.T.S. Cogan (wounded 9th Sept. 1914).
F.E. Watkins. Machine-Gun Officer (invalided Sept. rejoined in Oct).
H.O. Sutherland (missing in action 14th Sept. 1914. Wounded and POW).
R.T. Vachell (wounded 20th Oct 1914. rejoined 6th Dec. 1914).
B.G.C. Hobbs (3rd Batt. wounded Oct 20th 1914).
C.L. Hodgson. 3rd. Batt.

2nd. Lieutenants

L.A. Barrett
E. F. Boyd (kia. 20th Sept. 1914).
B.G. Gunner. Transport Officer
E.E. Dorman-Smith (wounded 26th Sept. & 9th Dec., 1914).
A.B. Surtees. 3rd. Batt
A.F. Geddes. 3rd. Batt (wounded).
E.S. Swaine. 3rd Batt. Divisional Cyclist Corps (wounded).

Captain. W.N. Herbert, Adjutant (wounded 13th Oct. 1914).
Captain. A Landen, Quarter-Master
Captain. M. Leckie, RAMC (wounded and POW 24th Aug., dow 29th Aug. 1914).

14 August, Friday

The first British troops, who arrived at Le Harve the day before, found the town decorated *en fête* with flags and banners welcoming *les brave Anglais*. Their march, from the docks through the old town of Harfleur to the Base camp being erected at Espremensil above the town, was like a Royal procession but remembered by many as the hottest march they ever did, even when compared with the worst days of the retreat from Mons. They had not eaten since the day before and weighted down with pack and equipment, the sun blazing on their backs, they struggled through the narrow, steep, cobbled streets densely packed with the cheering crowds. The air was stifling, but succour was at hand.

As the crowds pushed around, and even through the marching columns March discipline broke down and it became impossible for the officers and NCOs to prevent the well-meaning populace giving some relief and comfort to the men by pouring cider, beer, wine, and even spirits down their throats. But the worst part of the march was still to come, the final two miles to the plateau above Harfleur. It was a long, steep, sandy road that proved too much for many of the reservists who, still soft and unfit from civilian life, simply collapsed, unconscious, face down on the road to be pulled unceremoniously out of the way and left in any available shade to be looked after by the bystanders. For the others, still trudging up the hill under the blazing sun, the temptation to drop out must have been very strong as they passed exhausted men them being fanned, bathed in eau de Cologne, and even being revived with brandy, all administered by pretty French girls!

In the evening, with nothing much else to do, large numbers of soldiers collected on the road outside the camp and fraternized with the inhabitants. These included large numbers of young women, not all of whom were respectable.

British troops arriving at a French harbour.

The 9th Infantry Brigade had a more sober welcome next day.

> *St John.* At about 4 am we disembarked and formed up inside the shed, which by its smell appeared to be the summer residence of some tonnes of putrefied meat and fish. We sat here for two hours during which time some of us got coffee.
>
> Shortly after 6 am we proceeded to our rest camp led there by two diminutive French boy scouts. The road to the camp lay for the first few miles through the slums of Le Havre. It was rather early for demonstrations by the natives, but there was evidence of great welcoming to those who had arrived before we did. Bunting was plentiful everywhere, and of the few natives we did see many of them bore evidence of frequent libations to the glory of the allies.
>
> After an hour's march, the sun, which had been shielded behind mist, began to make it's presence felt. Also the route began to climb up rather a trying hill and the road became

sandy and badly metalled. At first a man here and there sat down by the roadside but soon they fell out like flies. We tried every means to urge them on, but soft words and harsh and even hard actions failed to move them. The truth was that they were done. Being soft and not having any breakfast are not good as a combination on which to perform a trying march. We eventually reached our camp, and with one or two exceptions who were taken to hospital, all the men turned up fairly soon after we had arrived. Our camp, which was supposed to accommodate 4,000 troops, was pitched on a high stubble field. There was no shade and the sun was very powerful. We lay about for several hours waiting for the arrival of our transport with food but none came. At about 3 pm having had nothing in the shape of meat or drink except water since the previous evening, I boiled some water and made soup with oxo cubes. This helped a little but by seven o'clock I was ravenous. We had tried the farm nearby to see if anything could be got from there but they were cleaned out. At about 7 pm I went down the hill to the village and got what to me tasted better than any meal I have eaten – a large omelette and some cold ham with a bottle of red wine at a little wayside cafe.

We got back to camp at 9 pm and an hour later some of our transport rolled up and I got my valise and turned in[25].

15 August, Saturday

About midnight the fine hot weather broke with a spectacular thunder and lighting storm followed by rain that settled into a steady downpour which lasted throughout the next day, converting the field into a sea of mud in which everyone floundered and slipped, soaked to the skin. In the afternoon they received orders to proceed to Harve station and entrain for an "unknown destination". This short journey was difficult from the start. The horses could not move the wagons from the quagmire on which they were now parked and large fatigue parties, working ankle deep in liquid mud, were detailed to push and pull the wagons across the field to the road. The next difficulty was to get down the hill; it was dark and the horses, unable to see their way down the steep slippery slope

25 Of the four battalions of the 9th Infantry Brigade the Northumberland Fusiliers were the only one billeted in Bell tents.

jibbed and plunged in their harness. Once again large fatigue parties were detailed to help but both water carts overturned, one damaged beyond repair.

> *St John.* The march down to Le Havre took us four hours with constant halts to deal with jibbing horses, but we reached the railway station at last and made much quicker work of putting the horses and wagons on the train. We then found a café which opened for us, and we got some much appreciated coffee at about 6 am and went to our seats in quite comfortable 1st class carriages where we soon fell asleep through sheer weariness. At about 7.30 am I half woke up and found we had begun to move but I was soon asleep again and didn't really wake up till near 10 am when we found we were dawdling through some peaceful part of the French countryside. We didn't know where we were or what was our destination and neither did the guard or the engine driver; at least so they said. At lunchtime or thereabouts, we got to Rouen where we fed the men and ourselves and changed the engine. The new driver seemed to think we were going to Amiens and his supposition turned out to be correct as we reached Amiens at about 5 pm. From Rouen to our destination our journey was a triumphal procession.

At every station the train was greeted by large crowds of girls, women and old men (France had mobilised almost all men of military age), who, amidst loud cheers and cries of "*Vive L'angleterre*" and "*Vive La France*", pressed gifts of tobacco, food and wine into the willing hands of the troops who, in return, gave away their cap badges, shoulder plates and even uniform buttons as souvenirs and who, by noting the other badges proudly worn by the women and children, could easily work out which battalions were ahead of them down the track.

As the train slowly wound its way through northern France these joyful receptions were frequent and the senior officers began to worry about how much beer and wine was being consumed by the troops riding in the box cars along the train, a concern not shared by the junior officers who seemed quite content to supplement the contents of the Mess hamper with wine and fruit pushed through their carriage windows.

At Amiens they learned that their destination was Busigny which was reached at 9.55 pm and, looking forward to getting out of the cramped train, were disappointed to learn that their billeting arrangements had been changed and they were to go to Landrecies, which they reached at 11.30 pm. Here the men were billeted in the town barracks, which to their disgust were not very clean, having just been evacuated by French battalions sent north to join the French 5th Army. The officers fared slightly better in the girl's dormitories in the convent school, but the beds were very small and already arranged to serve as a hospital to receive casualties from the fighting in the north.

Next morning the 9th Infantry Brigade marched 6½ miles to Noyelles and for the next five days billeted in the village, and along its lanes. In this rural backwater the realities of war seemed a long way off and for many of the survivors of the BEF these last four, peaceful days, before Mons, were to be remembered more like a training exercise in an exotic land rather than preparation for battle. In such an atmosphere it is perhaps not surprising that Lieutenant Watkins[26], who was orderly officer on that first evening, found that the outpost sentries were carrying out their duties with unloaded rifles!

17 August, Monday

> *St John.* We got turned in at about 1 am and I was early astir next morning. After a rather indifferent breakfast in a cabaret I went up to barracks and was told I was to go on a WD bicycle to a place called Noyelles to take over billets there. Accompanied by the cyclist section I got myself and all my Xmas tree equipment on to the machine, which was much too low for me, and proceeded on my journey which, was fortunately only 10 kilometres long. I got to the village of Noyelles without mishap and proceeded to find billets for the Regiment. This was no easy job as I am not a good linguist and had not been given an interpreter but I managed it just in time before the battalion got into them.
>
> We had collected our two interpreters at Le Havre, although to the uninformed they appeared to be just two private soldiers in the 114th Regiment, they were really

26 The battalion machine-gun officer. Lieutenant Watkins kept a diary that he sent home at monthly intervals to be published in the St George's Gazette as "A First Battalion Diary". He was killed in action 3/1/1915.

two quite interesting personalities. One of them was a big jeweller in the Palais Royal in Paris and the other was the lawyer who defended Mme. Stendhal in her famous trial.

17-21 August, Monday-Friday

St John. We stayed at Noyelles from Monday August 17th till Friday 21st during which time, except for the foreign language and the unusual comfort of billets instead of the more economical bivouac under a wet hayrick, we might have been doing easy manoeuvres at home. The weather was glorious and as we got no newspapers we had very little to remind us of the war.

We passed the days in mild company training or route marching while bathing in a deep and sluggish stream in the afternoon. This same stream was the cause of our first causality- a death by drowning[27]. We had few of the old fashioned sorts of orders too, one of them being no one was allowed to go outside his billeting area without a pass, and if he did go outside then he must be fully equipped and armed. This meant that to go to the only shop in the place, which was 200 yards outside our formal area, I had to don my war-like garb, though the officers and men in whose area the shop was situated, visited it in shirt sleeves and slacks. I remember an amusing incident in that shop. I was buying some soft-shoes for my sore feet and there was a considerable crowd in the shop and a great hubbub. Presently I was appealed to for help. It appeared that some men wanted to buy some castor oil for their boots and no one knew the French for it. The only aid was a French-English dictionary, but all references to 'huile' failed to get us out of the difficulty until I had the brilliant idea to demand of the M'mselle some 'huile pour le stomac du bebe.' At once came the reply 'Ah oui Monsieur, je comprends, c'est la Ricin'!! and what is more, the necessary oil was produced not from the shop but from a neighbour's nursery.

27 9495 L/Cpl William Barraclough.

Chapter 2
The Battle of Mons

The War Plans

At the heart of the conflict between France and Germany were the consequences of France's defeat in the Franco-Prussian War of 1870-71. Germany was aware that, in some manner, France would seek revenge and the worst nightmare of her military planners was an alliance between France and Russia that, in some future war, would compel Germany to fight simultaneously of an eastern and western front in a long drawn out conflict with an uncertain outcome. For over twenty years Bismarck's diplomatic skills were employed to prevent such an alliance but when the new, young, Kaiser, William II, dismissed him in 1890 his carefully constructed web of alliances began to fall apart. With a desire to rule as sell as reign, William II, much influenced by Prussia's part glories, took German domestic and foreign policy down a more nationalistic and militaristic road that increased the suspicion, and fear, of her European neighbours concerning Germany's long-term ambitions.

Following the creation of the Triple Alliance between Germany, Austria-Hungary and Italy, signed in 1892, France and Russia both felt increasingly vulnerable and entered into their own treaty in 1892 in which France agreed to provide loans and expertise to expand industrialisation in Russia and modernise her army. After 1905 this Alliance began to be consolidated into a military alliance that contained secret clauses in which each country agreed to support the other if either were attacked by Germany, or one of her allies. Furthermore the General Staffs agreed that both countries would mobilise their armies on the same day and co-ordinate military actions against Germany starting between on the 15th day after mobilisation.

France undertook other precautions. Between 1875 and 1900 her military engineers built a strong line of fortified areas, of which Verdun is the most famous, along its common border with Germany. In their war plans the German High Command came to consider that this fortress line was too strong, and would take too long, to reduce by direct assault and developed an alternative strategy, which was to attack France indirectly through Belgium.

This plan, often referred to as the *Schlieffen Plan* after its originator, was to concentrate seven Armies, numbering almost four million men, along the border with French and Belgium. The four Armies along the eastern border were to hold the French and absorb the attacks they were expected to make to regain their lost provinces of Alsace-Lorraine. While the French were so occupied three massive German armies, the 1st, 2nd and 3rd, would cut through Belgium and western France, sweeping south to swing around Paris, to trap and crush the French armies against the eastern German armies; a classic encircling manoeuvre.

The Germans had a strong suspicion that some sort of military agreement existed between France and Russia and accordingly their war plan was predicated on two critical assumptions. The first was that Russia would be slower to mobilise her armies than France; the German estimate was that she would take about forty days longer. The second premise was that if the German armies attacked France (and Belgium) with speed and violence the French armies would be destroyed within this forty-day time frame. With France defeated, or at least suing for an armistice, the threat of a two-front war was removed and Germany could then turn her military might eastwards to deal with Russia.

The French also made war plans to deal with a German invasion. The current version was called Plan XVII, as it was the 17th developed since the Franco-Prussian war, and was simplicity itself. Of all the European armies that went to war that August the French Army attached most importance, in its training and doctrine, to the cult of the offensive. Following the declaration of war the French army would mobilise more quickly than the Germans and, with over one and half a million men in its 1st, 2nd, and 3rd Armies, launch a pre-emptive attack into the heart of Germany, neutralizing the great German military complex at Metz, disrupting the mobilisation of the German armies and liberating Alsace – Lorraine. This, the French believed, would force Germany to sue for peace. Unfortunately such an unrealistic plan was doomed to failure and almost lost France the war within the first few weeks for it seriously underestimated the strength of the German army, and the effectiveness of its artillery and machine guns when deployed against French infantry attacking in the open.

The British did not have a plan to fight in Europe. Instead the General Staff had their 'understanding' with the French that in the advent of war troops would be sent to northern France to strengthen and lengthen the French defences along its common border with Belgium[28]. It was in fulfilment of this undertaking that, between the 12th and 17th August, the BEF, numbering approximately 120,000 men, was shipped to France and concentrated close to the old border fortress of Maubeuge ready to support the French Fifth Army in its offensive against the Germans invading Belgium. As we have already noted the strategy of the French High Command was for General Lanrezac to advance up the Meuse valley and secure the river crossings at Charleroi to form a bridgehead from which to attack the Germans. The role of the BEF was to protect Lanrezac's right flank, advancing into Belgium as far as the town of Mons where, after crossing the Mons-Condé canal, pivot westwards to be in a position to attack the flank of the German armies as they retreated in front of the victorious French.

Unfortunately the French High Command had so little insight into the movement of the three German armies that made up the right wing of the invasion that they were unaware that the army approaching Charleroi, and the French Fifth Army, was General von Bülow's *Second Army*, while the German *First Army*, commanded by General von Kluck, was swinging through Belgium far to the east and it was he, as he began to swing his army westwards to penetrate into northern France, who would collide with the BEF.

21 August, Friday

The first day of the British advance was swelteringly hot and to their disgust the troops found themselves marching along roads where only the centre part, just broad enough to take a single vehicle, was cobbled. The wide sides of the road, where they were marching, were covered in layers of dry earth and animal dung through which they trudged

28 In a discussion on cooperation between the British and French in 1910, Sir Henry Wilson, then Commandant of the Staff College, asked General Foch, Commandant of the *Ëcole Supérieure de Guerre in Paris* "What would you say was the smallest British military force that would be of any practical assistance to you…?" "One single private soldier and we take good care that he was killed" replied Foch in the certainty that if Britain committed even one soldier to fight with France against Germany thousands more would follow.

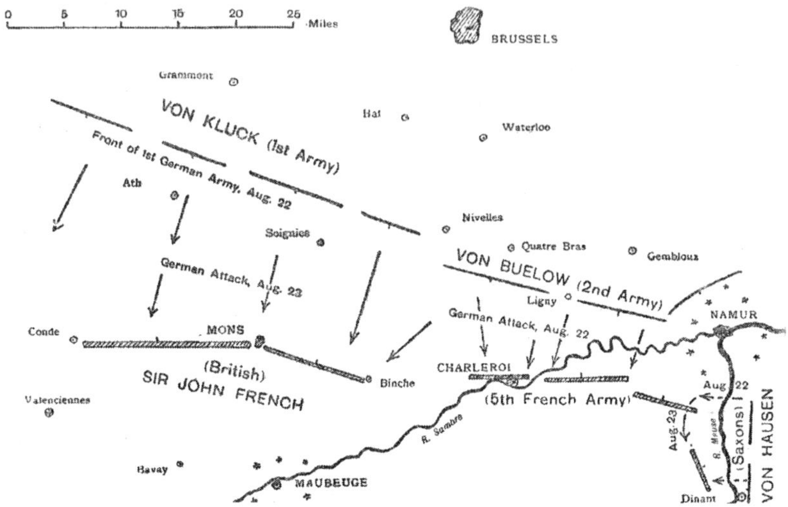

The German attack on the French and British August 22 and 23.

shrouded in clouds of dust churned up by the transport. It was a relief to all when they reached their billeting areas about mid-day.

> *St John.* We marched for some miles to a place called La Longueville where we went into billets. Toppin and I were in a cottage with a bed each and the other boys dossed down on the floor. I was kept busy all day paying the company, and was not finished doing so when an orderly came to me at about 7 pm to say that the CO wanted all Captains at once. I left the pay sheets etc to Sergeant Laws to settle up and finish, and went off to Headquarters where I found a collection of serious faces. As soon as we had all gathered the Colonel gave us a short lecture on the situation which he illustrated on a map by the aid of a solitary candle stuck in a bottle. In fact the whole scene was not at all unlike the pictures one sees in the illustrated weeklies usually under the title of 'Council of War' or something of that sort.
>
> It appeared that the Germans had crossed the Belgium Frontier and were marching west and we were to march at day break with the idea of meeting them and checking their advance and finally (this quite a special idea for peace field day) driving them back to Berlin and so home for Xmas!!

On the March in France.

That night, for the first time, they threw out an outpost line to provide early warning of the enemy and for the 3rd Division this was found by the 1/Lincolns who, by chance, overlooked the battlefield of Malplaquet where in September 1709 Marlborough defeated the French in what he described as a 'very murdering battle'. Two battalions in the 9th Infantry Brigade had been here before and the 1/Lincolns (10th Foot), and the 1/Royal Scots Fusiliers (21st Foot) both carried battle honours won at terrible cost that day. Next morning as they marched past the obelisk that marks the battlefield the 1/Lincolns gave three cheers to the memory of the men of their regiment who had fought and died on that ground two hundred years before.

The rumour in the ranks was that they were marching to support a successful French offensive and would soon come to grips with the enemy. Unfortunately, although the BEF were supposed to be collaborating with General Lanrezac, the liaison between the British and French armies was so poor that there was no direct communication between the two Army headquarters. Therefore it is not surprising that the British were totally unaware that earlier that morning, and less than forty miles away, von Bülow's *Second Army* had launched a pre-emptive attacked on the French and captured the bridges at Charleroi. Von Bülow renewed his attack on the 22nd and Lanrezac fearing for the safety of his army started to retreat leaving the British, who by noon had reached the Mons–Condé canal, dangerously exposed to the German Armies massing around them.

Late in the evening of the 22nd Lieutenant Spears, the BEF's liaison officer at Lanrezac's headquarters, managed to report to Sir John French on Lanrezac's decision to retreat. Sir John immediately gave orders to withdraw from the exposed position at Mons but, before these could be issued, he received an urgent request from Lanrezac asking him to relieve the pressure on his army by attacking the flank of the *Second Army*. Sir John was unwilling to risk his army in such a manoeuvre but, believing the French intelligence reports that the bulk of the von Kluck's *First Army* was still in bogged down fighting in northern Belgium, he agreed keep his troops in position for a further twenty-four hours to prevent the leading elements of the *First Army* crossing the canal and adding their weight to the attack on the French. This decision was to be of great help to Lanrezac, who managed to withdraw most his army intact from the clutches of von Bülow, but it almost sealed the fate of the B.E.F. at the very start of the war.

The Battlefield

The canal runs in a straight line from Condé to Mons suggesting that it could form a good position from which to fight a defensive battle but this is misleading for any serious defence along the canal was compromised by a number of disadvantages, both natural and man-made.

Firstly, the land on the northern (German) side of the canal sloped upwards not only giving them the advantage of observation but it was also covered with numerous small, dense, fir plantations that came right down to the canal bank in places and would provide useful cover. On the British side, between Condé and Mons, the land was flat and swampy, cross – cut with drainage ditches, some as deep and wide as small rivers, and all lined with dense stands of pollard willows. These were a serious barrier to the movement of reinforcements and made it impossible to bring artillery close to the canal except where they were substantial bridges over the wider waterways. An additional complication for the BEF was that as the canal approached the town of Mons it swung north in a loop, about two miles long and one and a half miles across, forming a pronounced salient. It was within this salient, containing the densely populated industrial and mining area of Mons and its surrounding villages that the troops of the 8th and 9th Infantry Brigades were to fight throughout Sunday 23rd, much of it close-action street fighting for which they had little training.

The British plan for Saturday 22nd August was for II Corps, with I Corps on its right, to advance into Belgium as far as the Mons-Condé canal and halt for the night behind an outpost line centred on the road and railway bridges across the canal. Somewhere ahead were the enemy but as GHQ did not anticipate anything more serious than encounters with cavalry, or other advance units of the German *First Army*, the defences prepared along the outpost line were neither extensive nor in depth. In fact GHQ were so confident of the outcome of the Lanrezac's offensive, and their role in it, that they did not even take the precaution of laying demolition charges on the bridges.

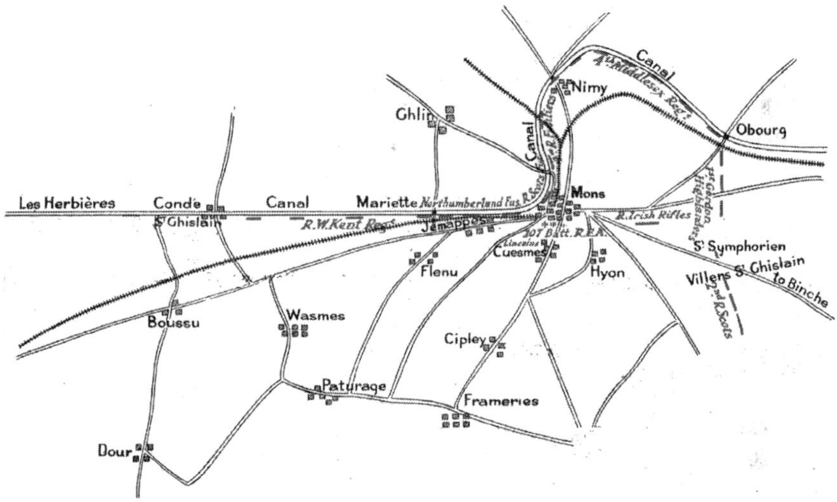

The 3rd Division's defence of the salient.

The 3rd Division had the most difficult area to defend, about eight miles of canal bank, including Mons and the salient north of the town. The right hand section was the responsibility of the 8th Infantry Brigade, who placed the 4/ Middlesex along the canal bank from Obourg to Nimy with its other three battalions positioned across the base of the salient. The left hand section, about six miles of canal bank, was the responsibility of the 9th Infantry Brigade. The 4/Royal Fusiliers defended the bridges at Nimy and the canal bank to the northern suburbs of Mons. Next the 1/Royal Scots Fusiliers held the complex of locks and bridges in the industrial suburb of Jemappes while to their left "B" and "C" Companies, 1/Northumberland Fusiliers, defended the road bridge at Mariette.

This whole sector consisted of rows of tightly packed cottages intermingled with numerous coalmines, factories and other industrial complexes, such as gas and chemical works, that stretched for more than a mile inland from the canal.

22 August, Saturday
On crossing the border the BEF left the pleasant French farmland behind and entered the 'le Borinage', the Black Country of Belgium, a typical coal mining area familiar to many of the reservists marching in the ranks of the Northumberland Fusiliers. Throughout the morning they tramped along the streets of a large, sprawling, built-up area criss-crossed by a maze of streets and alleyways that were in turn bisected by railway lines leading to and from pit heads, coal dumps and factories. The whole area was dominated by large spoil heaps of mine waste, some hundreds of feet high, that cascaded into the streets in places The only redeeming feature of this grim landscape was the ecstatic welcome of the inhabitants who milled around the marching soldiers and showered them with flowers and small gifts while cheering themselves hoarse.

> *St John.* Ready to move off at 3.30 am. Filled with suppressed excitement which in my case was mixed with a certain amount of apprehension. However these feelings wore off

A Battalion resting in a Mons street.

as we swung along in the early morning haze of what turned out to be a brilliantly fine day. We crossed the battlefield of Malplaquet with its war memorial and were soon in Belgium. Our route lay along the 'Route pave' that we found very trying to our already tired feet. Shortly after crossing the frontier we were halted while the Field Officers went to confer with the Brigadier. The result of this conference was that B & C Coys. under Major Yatman moved to the head of the column and the march was resumed.

At the next halt we were told that we were to proceed to and hold a portion on the railway and canal to the west of Mons. For the rest of the way our route lay through a series of mining villages in each of which we were greeted with enthusiasm the inhabitants crowding about us and pressing on us gifts of eggs, chocolate, tobacco, fruit, matches, cigars etc. I noticed that the signallers who were in front got most of the swag and so greedy were they that I should estimate each signaller got a dozen eggs and 2 lb. of chocolate with other things in proportion. At last I sent up to tell them to behave themselves and let some of the men behind then get a chance threatening with company punishment the next signaller I caught taking anything even if it were pressed on him.

About a mile from our objective we halted and threw out an advance guard of our own. B and C Coys. were now out alone and we proceeded more quietly. After going for half a mile we were halted by our point and a long pause ensued. I went on to see what was up and found the point was refreshing itself in a bar.!! I promised them a court martial and kicked them out and we went on. The court martial did not come off as by the time we had a chance to hold it the men who were to be tried were missing and the NCO dead.

The Defence of the Mariette Bridges

The industrial area of Quaregnon- Mariette was densely populated and the village of Mariette was divided in two by the canal, which at this point was about 60 feet wide spanned by a steel framed cantilever bridge raised and lowered by a hand winch situated on the northern (German) bank close to the bridge-keepers cottage. On the Northumberland's side, in addition to the main canal, was a flood aqueduct, about 15 feet wide, that took excess water from the main canal, and was separated from it by a central bank, 45 feet wide, along which ran the southern towpath. The road from the village crossed the flood aqueduct by means of a fixed iron girder bridge with a stone parapet and continued across the central bank to the canal bridge. Along this short stretch of road were three houses that would have to be taken into account when preparing the defences.

After crossing the main canal bridge the road traversed about 60 yards of open space before reaching the level crossing of the railway that ran parallel with the northern bank of the canal. It then entered the northern half of the village, bending northwest to form the main street, which was about a quarter of a mile long, before open country was reached.

On the Northumberland's side of the canal there was no open spaces as the houses, outbuildings and sheds of the village came right down to the bank.

The task of holding the bridges was allocated to "B" Company, while "C" provided support from rifle pits and garden walls to the right of the bridge, as well as manning the two barricades built across the street between the bridge and Quaregnon station where Major Yatman had established his headquarters. Captain St John's first job was to set up an advanced post on the Baudour road, beyond the northern outskirts of the village, to give early warning of any enemy advance and then start his men on the barricades and other defence works.

Bridge at Mariette. This photograph was taken in 1927 when the north bank was more built up than in 1914. The centre cottage, facing the bridge is the site of the bridge-keepers house.

> *St John.* In the open space by the bridgehead (on the north or German bank) was an enclosed wood yard fenced with old rail sleepers. This we speedily demolished leaving the ground open. Some 500 yards to the west of the bridge, one came to a long shed close to the canal bank filled with coal. Running from the bridge keeper's garden in a NE direction was a narrow lane apparently leading nowhere in particular and not marked on the map. As time was short a thorough reconnaissance of it was not possible but it debouched into an open space after a 100 yards enclosed on both sides by high brick walls. As soon as possible we began to prepare the bridgehead for defence. Having demolished the fence of railway sleepers we made an entanglement from the end of the houses on the North side to the level crossing gates with some barbed wire I requisitioned from an unwilling native and the wire fence that guarded the railway line. We jammed the iron gates of the level crossing closed and also created an obstacle on the north side of the bridge itself. Altogether we made it very unpleasant for anyone attempting to advance to the bridge by the main road or deploy along either side of the main road or debouche into the open space. We left a small opening easily closeable for the return of our advanced post that had orders to retire as soon as a determined advance on the post by the Germans became evident. I also notched and loop-holed the walls of the bridge keeper's house and garden and arranged for a post of 12 men under Sgt. Panter to be there.
>
> The next defensive works were in the houses on the bank between the canals. One of these houses we demolished altogether as it seemed in the field of fire of the detachment we had entrenched in the garden on the E. side. The other we loop-holed and barricaded.

Sergeant Panter's section had a clear field of fire over the open ground between the houses and the level crossing, as well as good views up the main street, so could seriously interfere with any enemy advancing from that direction. Although they appeared isolated on the German side of the canal they were not unsupported for any enemy approaching across the open ground in front of the gate-keepers cottage would be exposed to fire from the troops on the south bank. In addition the three

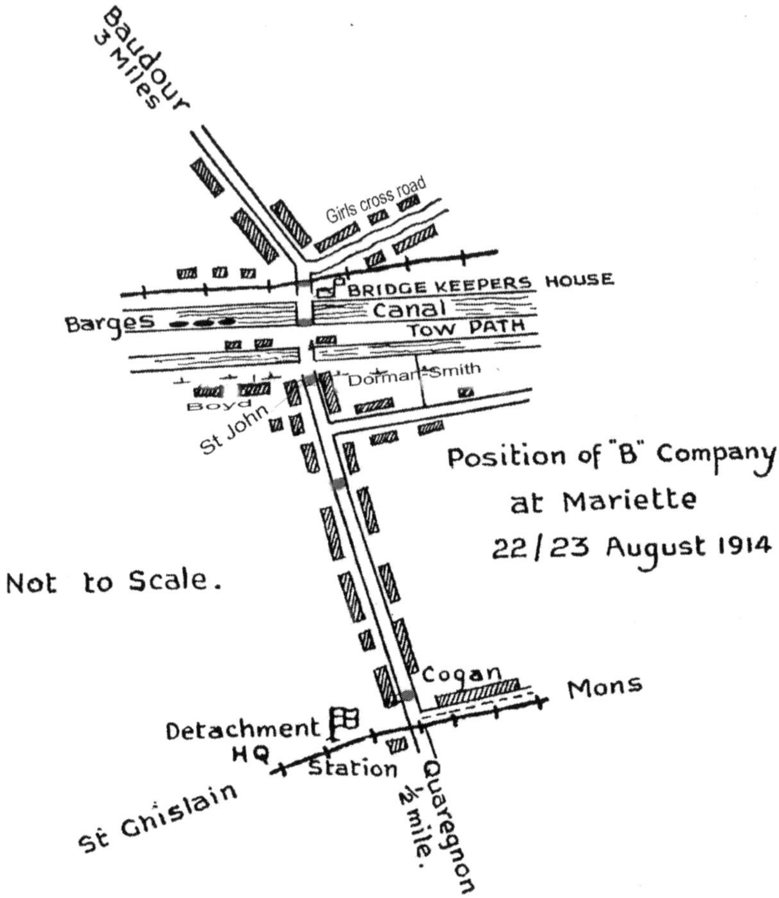

The defences at Mariette.

men in the house on the towpath would provide additional fire support when the time came for Panter and his men to withdraw.

Unfortunately, in spite of these precautions for their safe return, most of Panter's men were to retreat back across the canal as soon as the enemy appeared in force. This allowed the Germans to reach the northern bank early in the battle and eventually the coal sheds west of the bridge, moves that made "B" Company's fight to deny them the bridges all the more difficult and dangerous, and almost brought disaster in the late afternoon.

> *St John.* The inhabitants of all houses near the bridge were cleared out bag and baggage. Some went gladly and others

had to be coerced. One family we evicted three times from a house close to the bridge and each time they sneaked back to it by a back entrance. At the time I was terribly sorry for these poor people but in the light of after events I came to the conclusion that many of them were of German sympathies. I am quite sure that the Bridge Keeper was a spy, but though I suspected him at the time I had not time enough to watch him carefully. The people I was most sorry for were the owners and inhabitants of the 5 barges on the canal.

At first I was contented to shift these barges from the north to the south bank but later, as it seemed such a simple matter to get them back again across the canal, that we decided to sink them and got the RE officer who was preparing the bridge for demolition to blow a hole in the bottom of each one of them. The wretched owners had to depart in a hurry taking with them such of their more treasured possessions as could be carried in a small bundle. The weepings and lamentations were loud and sorrowful. The menkind wept more bitterly even than the women, who no doubt shared in a lesser though quite appreciable degree

Barricades at Mariette.

Building barricades at Mariette.

> with the children the excitement of the prospective picnic-like existence they were so suddenly called upon to assume. The work of preparation kept us busy till darkness put a stop to it. We were much hindered by the crowds of curious sightseers who looked on with amazed delight at the unusual sight of strangely garbed soldiers destroying someone else's property and now and then I had to use sufficiently strong measures to scatter them to permit the men to work.

The Brigade Reserves at Cuesmes

When the 9th Brigade reserve arrived in Cuesmes they were greeted by cheering crowds who showered them with fruit, tobacco, beer and other small gifts. This festive mood continued throughout the day and, once settled into their billets, and with strict orders about behaviour, the troops were allowed to walk about the town. Some were given medals bearing the image of Saint Barbé, the patron Saint of miners by children from the local school while others received, as good luck tokens, small pieces of ribbon in Belgian national colours from Nuns at the convent gate.

Throughout the evening most enjoyed the unexpected pleasures of free beer and admiring young women who hailed them as their saviours from the dreaded 'Bosch', but for some there was work to do.

Lieutenant Watkins was sent to reconnoitre the road back to Frameries in case the Brigade was forced to retire in the dark and importantly, for the events of the next day, officers from the Lincolns closely examined the three miles of road leading from Cuesmes to Mons and planned how and where, they would build their barricades to support the troops on the canal if they were forced to withdraw.

23 August, Sunday

With the Lanrezac's Fifth Army in retreat Sir John French was increasingly concerned about the threat posed by the *First Army* and at 5.30 on the Sunday morning met with his Corps commanders, Smith-Dorrien and Haig, to gave orders for the outpost line on the canal to be strengthened and the bridges prepared for demolition, but it was too late. By the time these orders had passed down the chain of command to the junior officers who would execute them the infantry in the salient were already in action.

The destruction of the bridges in the 9th Brigade sector was the responsibility of the 57th Field Company RE but by the time they reached Mons only No 3 section remained, the other two having been hived off to work elsewhere in the 3rd Division area and, not knowing what tasks they would be asked to perform, had taken most of the unit's equipment with them. The consequence was that when the order to prepare the bridges for demolition was received by No 3 section they were short of everything; men, detonators, fuses and explosives. They had only one electrical detonator and the instantaneous fuse, which was part of their standard equipment, had been withdrawn just before mobilisation and not replaced. This meant that some charges would have to be exploded with the temperamental No 9 safety fuse that had a tendency to burn unevenly making the simultaneous explosion of the several charges required to destroy a bridge a matter of luck.

The Battle

The 'structure' of the battle is best understood by appreciating that the canal was actually inside the great wheeling movement of von Kluck's *First Army* as it swung south-eastwards across Belgium. It was the troops in the 'axle' of the wheel that first made contact with the BEF north of Mons early on Sunday morning and throughout the day the fighting progressively 'jumped' along the canal, east to west, bridge by bridge, as the infantry of the 'spokes' of the wheel moved down the roads that brought them to the canal.

On Saturday afternoon small parties of troops had been sent across the canal to form an advanced outpost line and it was these that encountered the cavalry screen in front of von Kluck's *IX Corps* soon after dawn on the Sunday morning. The most bizarre of these brief encounters was when six Hussars suddenly appeared out of a nearby wood and charged the 4/Royal Fusiliers guarding the Nimy Bridges. They naturally opened fire, killing four and wounding the others, one of whom was their young officer Lieutenant von Armin, son of the commander of the Kluck's *IV Corps* who later in the day would be attempting to force his Corps across the canal west of Mons. After these initial encounters there was a lull as the enemy withdrew into the woods and settled down to gather as much information as they could about the disposition of the British. They had time for it would be at least another two to three hours before the main body of their infantry and artillery reached the canal and the assault on the British could begin.

This started about 8 am with an enemy artillery bombardment on the positions of the 4/Middlesex and 4/Royal Fusiliers in the salient and, about an hour later, under cover of this bombardment the infantry of the *18th Division* began their attack.

Throughout the morning, while this violent battle raged for control of the salient, the 1/Northumberland Fusiliers at Mariette seemed immune from attack.

> *St John.* I slept that night on the floor of a butchers shop with a mattress off one of the beds under me. At daybreak we continued the work of defensive preparation making a strong barricade across the road at the bridgehead and loopholed every available wall and house.
>
> I lost all sense and count of time but it was well in the day before fighting began. We had reports of the approach of the dreaded Uhlans but we had not seen anything of them ourselves.
>
> The attack by the German artillery began first on the two main bridges about a mile away to the E of us and the other about the same distance W. On the previous evening our position had been well reconnoitred by a Taube aeroplane at which I had a sporting shot and for doing so I got badly hauled over the coals by our second in command who had drawn a blood curling picture of our position being given

> away and the lot of us massacred all owing to my absurd lightness of heart.
>
> As a matter of fact I stood on our bridge for quite a while watching the fight going on at the other two bridges. As we found out later on the troops at both these bridges had a very bad time of it and were badly cut up.

They received their first news of the advancing enemy from an unexpected source. At Quaregnon railway station Major Yatman was using the local telephone service to maintain contact with brigade headquarters at Cuesmes and in the middle of the morning he was called to the telephone and when he picked it up a strange voice identified himself as a British agent who wished to make a report to the officer in command. He said he was in the neighbourhood of the Bois de Baudour, (about four miles north of Mariette) and started to give details of the German units that had passed through the village that morning when the line suddenly went dead and all contact north of the canal was lost.[29]

The first visual sighting of the enemy was made soon after by Sergeant Panter's detachment, which was surprised to see enemy infantry enter the top of the village in columns of fours, without scouts or skirmishers, and march steadily down the hill towards the bridge. Waiting until the head of the column was well down the street they opened rapid fire scattering the enemy and littering the street with his dead and wounded. Unfortunately some of Panter's men, either thinking they had done their job, or unnerved by the increasing intensity of the German return fire, retreated back across the bridge to join the main body at the barricades.

It must have been about this time that the Royal Engineers turned up to deal with the bridges.

The destruction of the bridges defended by the 1/Royal Scots Fusiliers and 1/Northumberlands were the responsibility of Lieutenant Boulnois. He had left Cuesmes at 7.15 am riding on the company forage cart stacked with packs of explosives, a drum of electrical detonator leads and the single electrical detonator. He was accompanied by his section of 4 NCOs and 4 sappers, all riding bicycles and carrying their rifles and ammunition. There were five bridges along the densely built

29 According to the Regimental History Major Yatman attempted to find out the identity of his mysterious spy after the war but could find no record of a British agent operating in that part of Belgium at that time.

up canal bank from Jemappes to Mariette and, as moving the wagon through the maze of streets and alleys was not easy, it was late morning before Lieutenant Boulnois had finished his survey. All the bridges were identical, steel-framed drop bridges with a 40 to 50 foot span and raised and lowered by a winch and counterweights positioned on the northern [German] bank. He calculated that it would take twenty-five of his 15 oz slabs of gun-cotton, placed in the angles of the girders, to destroy each bridge. Starting from Jemappes he moved back along the canal towards Mariette dropping off at each bridge the required explosives, long lengths of detonator lead cut from his drum and an NCO and sapper with instructions to place the charges and attach and run out the leads ready for his return with the detonator.

It would appear that Lieutenant Boulnois and his men arrived at Mariette soon after 11 am when the battle was in its early stages and the enemy prevented from approaching too close to the bridge by the fire of Sergeant Panter's depleted section keeping the bridge sufficiently clear of direct enemy fire for Sergeant Smith and Sapper Dabell to fix the explosive charges and run out the leads out as far as the edge of the towpath. While this was going on Lieutenant Boulnois occupied himself sinking the canal barges at the request of Captain St. John.[30] With the first stage of their work was completed Lieutenant Boulnois sent Sapper Dabell back to Cuesmes with the forage cart. He mounted the drum of electrical leads on the carrier of a bicycle taken from one of the houses and, accompanied by Sergeant Smith, now loaded with the detonator as well as his rifle and ammunition, started back toward Jemappes to see how the work on the other bridges were getting on.

It was soon after they had left that the situation down at the bridge began to change.

> *St John.* The weakened detachment did not dare remain for long in so exposed a position though Sgt. Panter remained as long as he safely could and handled all through it with great coolness and good sense. His action certainly checked the German advance for a time and evidently sent them back for artillery for the next thing that happened was the arrival

---

30 Capt. St John states in his Journal that the bridge was prepared for demolition and the barges blown up early on the Saturday evening. However given the crowded events of these days in is not surprising that his recollection of the timing of events is astray. As noted above the 57th Field Company did not start work on the bridges until the Sunday morning.

> of a high explosive shell on the bridge. This was followed by a steady rain of shell, mostly high explosive.
>
> One of the houses between the bridges got badly treated. I thought the detachment inside were done for and did not see any of them again for a fortnight when three of them turned up and reported that they had stopped in the cellar of the house and watched the Germans pass along all that night and most of the following day.[31]

Following the withdrawal of Sergeant Panter's party the enemy brought infantry and artillery close to the canal and attempted to reduce the barricades by a combination of artillery and small arms fire.

> *St John.* The detachment to the west of these houses came in when the first shell arrived. My barrier across the road was getting rather crowded with the incoming detachments who all seemed to desire to be near an officer and disliked the idea of going into any more houses. However I got some of them away into the prepared houses in rear of the barricade.
>
> On the other hand one or two men on the barrier were convinced that it was nice to be in a house with all these nasty shells flying about in the open and the house on the right of the barrier was getting quite full when a high explosive crumped right into it doing a lot of damage. The nervous ones came tumbling out of it again. Under cover of the artillery fire the Germans had occupied the house at the end of the main road and when it stopped for a bit they sniped at us out of the windows making the barricade rather unpleasant though most of the shots were going high. We were doing some damage too and any German who showed

---

31 This was the house between the canal and the aqueduct that St John had garrisoned with Corporal Johnson and Privates Green and Batton to provide covering fire for Sergt. Panter's men when they withdrew. When the German shells struck the house Corporal Johnson was killed but Green and Batton took cover in the cellar, which had a window looking onto the bridge. Here they were stuck and unable to join the rest of the Company. Late in the afternoon, ten minutes after Captain St John and Sergeant Lewis had withdrawn from their barricade, the Germans started to cross the bridge. Green and Batton lay hidden in their cellar watching the German infantry marching across the bridge in columns of fours continuously for over 3 hours. At dusk they made their escape, and, following the retreating BEF while keeping well clear of the Germans, rejoined the battalion 5 days later.

himself got a very warm reception. Not many did show themselves and for a time there was quite a lull in the fighting though the periodic shell kept coming along. One of these burst on the road a yard or two in front of our barrier but except being covered in dust and debris no harm was done.

Early on in the proceedings my Sergeant got very excited shooting at some Germans on the canal bank. I could not see them from where I was and the man was very keen to point them out as they showed themselves. After having knocked out 5 of them he called out to me " Can't you see them sir, another of the buggers over there quite plain in his red breeches and blue coat. bang! there 'e is sir dead as mutton now ". I never found out if they really were Frenchmen we had been shooting but I don't think they could possibly have been and more likely were Germans in French uniform.

After an hour or so of this sort of game (I lost count of time altogether) a new diversion was created. We were waiting ready for some Germans we had noticed trying to get around the corner of the street opposite to us when, all of a sudden, 3 or 4 little girls dashed out of a house. They were across the street in another house and the back again and then backwards and forwards once more. I called out to cease fire, which was done at once. The lull only lasted for 2 or 3 minutes during which time I could hear these children crying but it was long enough to enable the Germans to cut some of my barbed wire and get round to the coal sheds to the west. At that time we could not believe it was anything more than a lucky coincidence for the Germans but in the light of what we heard afterwards there can be no doubt it was a neatly arranged ruse for the carry-out of which they counted on our (to them) idiotic chivalry. Anyway it was most successful from their point of view and the men who got into the coal shed made themselves very objectionable to the right flank of our barrier. One of their bullets hit my sword and tore away the scabbard so that I had to discard the weapon to my great relief.

The incident with the children had allowed the enemy to reach the cover of the coal sheds and, bringing cross-fire to bear on the barricades, forced "B" Company to keep their heads down. This allowed small groups of enemy infantry to filter across the open space and occupy the dead ground where the canal bank was high enough to provide cover. They also manhandled a field gun to within 400 yards of the barricades and, although it was so close, the defenders could not see it through the thick pall of smoke from the burning houses and the dust thrown up by the exploding shells. However its discharge could be clearly heard and, taking a bearing, a detachment fired steady controlled volleys in the general direction of the noise which soon slowed its rate of fire.

It was now about 3.30 pm and the position of the 1/Northumberlands was deteriorating by the minute but to appreciate the full extent of the danger we need to look briefly at what had happened to the rest of 9th Brigade during the morning.

The Fortunes of the 9th Infantry Brigade

By late morning the situation in the salient was reaching a climax. Some of the assault groups of the *18th Division* were across the canal east of Obourg where they established a bridgehead through which poured large numbers of infantry, accompanied by artillery and machine guns. Finding the country behind the British line weakly defended they began to drive their way across the base of the salient towards Mons and, to avoid being trapped, the troops defending the canal started to withdraw at about 2 pm.

The fighting in the salient now became vicious and at close quarters as a running battle developed through the suburbs of Mons as the survivors of the 4/ Royal Fusiliers, the 4/ Middlesex and the 2/Royal Irish Regiment, who had been sent up in support, fought their way out of encirclement. The enemy's advance was slowed by the rearguards who, fighting from street corner to street corner, covered the retreating infantry as they worked their way towards safety on the other side of the town[32].

For the 9th Infantry Brigade reserve at Cuesmes there was little news of this fighting and, although the noise of artillery could be distinctly heard from the direction of Mons, it did not appear to raise any alarum in either soldiers or civilians. With no orders the troops were permitted to leave their billets to mingle with the inhabitants who, in their Sunday

32 There were many acts of bravery that went un-recorded. At Obourg railway station D Company 4/Middlesex lost very heavily defending the railway bridge and when the order came to withdraw an unknown rifleman climbed on the station roof shooting any of the enemy who ventured onto the bridge. He lived long enough for the survivors of his company to make their escape

best were out and about, either going to Mass, visiting friends and relatives, and even boarding the train to Mons. It was not until late morning that reports on the extent of the enemy attack on the canal reached 9th Brigade HQ making it clear that their battalions on the canal were fighting for their lives. If there were to an orderly withdraw, the 9th Brigade reserve would have to go forward and support them.

Orders were quickly issued and within minutes the peaceful Sunday stroll of residents and soldiers alike was rudely interrupted by the wild galloping of officers and mounted military police as they rushed through the streets shouting at the troops to return to their billets immediately. Within thirty minutes they had fallen in fully equipped and ready to move.

The 1/Lincolns were to cover the withdrawal of the 4/Royal Fusiliers and 1/Royal Scots Fusiliers. As these battalions were expected to pull

Sunday afternoon: The Lincolns build their barricades.

back along the main road from Mons the Lincolns quickly marched the three miles down the road and took up a position astride the Rue La Chausse, a long straight avenue that ran towards the centre of the town. Here they tore up paving stones, chopped down trees and used anything else that came to hand to build four strong barricades across the avenue, ably assisted by civilians, including a young woman who impressed the soldiers by working 'like a Trojan'.

By mid-afternoon the 4/Royal Fusiliers had retreated through Mons into the Grand Place, the market square, where they rested for about fifteen minutes while the officers and NCOs sorted the men out into their companies.

4/ Royal Fusiliers rest in the Grand Place. Mons.[33]

As soon as they left the square troops of the *84th Regiment* from the *18th Division, IX Corps* entered and rounded some of the civilians, including the Burgomaster, and drove them in front as human shields as

33 This picture is usually captioned as the 4/ Royal Fusiliers *on their way to* Mons. However, I believe that it was taken on Sunday afternoon during the battle. Most men do not have their packs, are carrying extra bandoliers and their rifles are beside them, not stacked. They also have the look of men who have been in action and, although there are civilians around, there are no signs of the ecstatic crowds that turned out to greet the troops on their arrival on the Saturday. Both the Regimental History and the War Diary describe the battalion marching through Mons directly to the canal on the Saturday but the survivors of the fighting on Sunday did briefly halt in the Grand Place to reorganise before continuing their retreat. This photograph is sometimes captioned "A Company" if that is so they were the reserve Company on the canal and the rearguard during the withdrawal.

they started after the 4/Royal Fusiliers. Along the road the 1/Lincolns waited, the rattle of machine gun and rifle fire growing louder as the battle moved towards them, and soon the survivors of the 4/Royal Fusiliers were passing through the barricades. A few minutes later a crowd of enemy infantry and civilians swarmed around the corner at the bottom of the avenue to be met by a fusillade of rifle and machine gun fire, supported by shrapnel from a section of the 109th Battery RFA unlimbered behind the barricades. In the ensuing panic most of the civilians escaped although seven were left dead on the road along with many of the enemy. Searching for cover the enemy infantry broke into the houses and started sniping at the barricades and it was beginning to look as if it would be a long afternoon for the 1/Lincolns but after about ten minutes of half-heartedly shooting the Germans, perhaps exhausted after their hard days fighting, and in no mood to sustain any further causalities by attacking another well-defended British position, withdrew. The 1/Lincolns spent the rest of the afternoon unmolested and started back towards the 9th Brigade rallying point in Frameries at 6 pm.

It was also about 2 pm when Lieutenant Boulnois and Sergeant Smith, cycling back along the canal, ran into Captain Wright, adjutant to the 3rd Divisional Engineers driving up from Lock 2 where he had been wounded in the head. He informed Lieutenant Boulnois that there were no orders concerning the destruction of the bridges but, as they discussed the worsening situation facing the infantry, a dispatch rider cycled up searching for the headquarters of the 1/Royal Scots Fusiliers. He told them that he had orders for the troops on the canal to retire at 3 p.m. and immediately Captain Wright realised he had a problem; how to blow all the bridges between Nimy and Mariette with only one detonator in less than an hour.

Wasting no time he ordered Lieutenant Boulnois to start on his bridges that had electrical detonator leads while he set off by car to Nimy to order the destruction of the other bridges. Now accompanied by Sergeant Smith, and the dispatch rider, Lieutenant Boulnois took the detonator to the main road bridge close to Jemappes station, which had been successfully mined by Lance-Corporal Wiltshire, and who had ran the detonator leads out to relative safety behind one of the infantry barricades.

At first Lieutenant–Colonel Douglas Smith, Commander of the Royal Scots Fusiliers, was reluctant to allow them to blow the bridge, but after reading the orders to retire agreed and Lieutenant Boulnois successfully blew the bridge. Of the nine bridges on the 9th Brigade front this was the only one to be totally destroyed.

It was now about 3 pm and with the withdrawal of the infantry imminent Lieutenant Boulnois knew he had run out of time and decided that, of the four remaining bridges, the most important was the one at Mariette as it carried a road along which the Germans could bring artillery. Accompanied now by Lance-Corporal Wiltshire, as well as Sergeant Smith, he started to cycle rapidly back towards Mariette keeping away from the direct line of the canal where they could be fired upon by the enemy. They had no gone very far when Captain Wright overtook them in his car and, after a brief discussion, it was decided that he would take the detonator and drum in his car to Mariette while Lieutenant Boulnois and Lance-Corporal Wiltshire went to the bridges east of Jemappes to see if anything could be bone to blow them up. On arrival they found these bridges were still held by the infantry, but only just, as they were preparing to leave. Dodging enemy fire Lieutenant Boulnois found the detonator leads and connected them to the electricity supply in one of the houses close to the bridge hoping that when he switched on the lights the current would detonate the charges. Unfortunately, at the critical moment, a salvo of high explosive landed around the house and the power failed.

The last of the infantry were now leaving and grabbing what gear they could the sappers ran from the canal and up the street full of retreating soldiers and terrified inhabitants all running and pushing to escape the enemy infantry now pouring across the bridges. Further along the canal Corporal Jarvis, running back from Lock 2 through the alleys, caught glimpses of both soldiers and civilians falling dead and wounded as the Germans fired volley after volley from the hip as they ran up the narrow streets in pursuit of the retreating infantry.[34]

The planned, orderly, withdrawal of the Royal Scots Fusiliers was breaking down. The enemy were quick to cross the canal which preventing the scattered Companies coming together to reform the

---

34 Most accounts of the battle of Mons seem to accept that Corporal Jarvis managed to detonate his charges and destroy the bridge at Lock 2. This is mentioned in the citation for his Victoria Cross. However Jarvis, like the others in Lieut. Boulnois' section, attached electrical detonator leads to his explosives expecting Lieut. Boulnois to return with the detonator and set off the charges. He did not have time and Capt. Wright took the detonator to Mariette so it is difficult to see how Corporal Jarvis could have detonated his charges. If the bridge at Lock 2 was not destroyed this would not detract from the extreme bravery shown by Corporal Jarvis in placing his charges and the award of the V.C.

battalion. Moving forward with speed and determination the enemy fell upon 'B' Company, who had the furthest to go, isolating it from the rest of the battalion and dozens of sharp close range fire-fights developed among the slag heaps and cottages as 'B' Company, heavily outnumbered, fought for its life. In less than half an hour over a hundred were killed or wounded and the survivors were losing their uneven fight when the enemy were suddenly driven back by the impact of a flank attack delivered by 'A' and 'D' Companies, Northumberland Fusiliers, sent up to rescue them.

Everywhere south of the canal confusion and anarchy reigned. As the German infantry pushed forward through the suburbs they became mixed up with the retreating British who often found themselves behind the 'front line' as did Lieutenant Watkins, shepherding the battalion's first line transport, and his machine gun section, towards the battalion's assembly point in Frameries.

> *Lieut Watkins.* Left with transport and M.G. and ordered to meet C.O. at nearest dumping heap. Found open bit of road being shelled and sniped whenever anyone went near, so stopped and reconnoitred. Shortly afterwards decided to send men, under Regimental Sergeant Major, and to take transport myself, over open beside the road. Just starting when near horse slipped, caught its foot in front wheel, and could not get it out. Shell came over and landed near one of D Company's platoons[35] and shortly a second shell landed in the house on the side of the road ten yards away, blew out the roof and covered us with glass and brick. A lyddite, so must have been one of our own. Dismounted and got hold of horse whose leg had got caught and managed to get him free. Harnessed horses with help of the men I had collected. No casualties. Took limber and transport at trot across open. Germans had apparently ceased firing at road then. Saw Colonel who said we had better get on over railway as liable to get cut off. Crossed railway at level crossing and found D Company retiring. Went up hill and at top found cemetery found lots of wire had to be cut and had to chose between right and left of cemetery. Chose left where D Company

35 These shells were probably from the German artillery supporting the attacks on the 1/ Royal Scots Fusiliers who were still engaged in their withdrawal about a mile down the road from Lieut. Watkins's position.

were going and found small passage through houses. Tried to get limber through and failed. So pulled up six posts and broke one doorway with help of local saws, much assistance from a dispatch rider who had lost his way and joined us. D Company had gone on leaving us alone. Sent men out on flank to reconnoitre as inhabitants said Germans were approaching on our right. Adjutant came and told me where to go and went after D Company. Went over bridge into centre of town and found platoon of A company. Stayed there till dark.

The Retirement of Major Yatman's Detachment

Throughout the fighting at Mariette the 1/Northumberlands had no contact with the troops along the canal to their left or right. During the morning there had been visual communication with the 5th Division on their left through a signaller posted on a gasometer, but soon after the attacks started he was shelled off his position and all contact was lost. The telephone at Quaregnon station had also stopped working so the order to withdraw (issued from 9th Brigade headquarters at 2.30 pm.) failed to reach them and the bicycle dispatch rider with the written orders became so completely lost in the maze of streets that he did not find them until late afternoon after they had started their own withdrawal.

During the lulls in the battle they could hear that the noise of the attacks on the bridges on either side of them was increasing in intensity until, suddenly about 3.30 pm, it stopped. To Captain St John and his fellow officers down at the bridge this meant that the enemy had probably taken the bridges and cut off their line of retreat. They were about to send patrols along the canal bank to find out what exactly had happened when the Germans suddenly opened fire with another field gun that they had brought right forward and this new attack seemed to be the prelude to an infantry assault on the bridge for in an attempt to subdue the barricades it was firing shrapnel at point blank range. Luckily it had a poor field of fire and, although the continual hail of shrapnel bullets rattling around the barricades made life very uncomfortable, casualties were light but given the rapidly worsening situation Major Yatman decided at 4 pm that they had done enough. He ordered Captain St John to start withdrawing his men in small detachments down the side streets and alleyways out of view of the enemy. It was just as the last of the infantry were leaving the barricades that Captain Wright drove up to Major Yatman's headquarters and informed him that he had come to blow up the bridge. He also brought the unwelcome news, confirming their worst fears, that the enemy were already across the canal on both flanks. Although this made it imperative that they withdrew as soon as possible Major Yatman decided, as they still held the bridge, to have at least one attempt to destroy it.

By the time Captain Wright and Sergeant Smith had worked their way down to the canal everyone had gone except Captain St John and CQMS. Lewis. They, along with Sergeant Smith, agreed to provide covering fire while Captain Wright made his attempt to blow the bridge.

> *St John.* When most of the men had gone in fact only the Q.M.S and myself were left the RE officer and a staff Sgt. arrived to blow up our bridge. He reported to me that the Germans were over the bridges on both our flanks so the things did not look too rosy. However he got to work on his job but found that the man who had been laying the charges had only provided leads for the main canal and had not taken the 2nd waterway into consideration. Nothing daunted he went out in front of the barrier and got under the bridge of the near canal and dragged himself through the water to the centre tow path and wriggled about trying to find the leads that connected the charge. Unfortunately he could not find them and so he returned. It was a plucky action particularly as he was wounded at the time. I reported this instance and was glad to see that the officer got the VC for it although poor chap he was afterwards killed.

In spite of this head wound Captain Wright[36] swung himself hand over hand underneath the bridge that crossed the flood channel and dropped into the water to slither along the side of the towpath searching in the soft mud for the detonator leads. When he found them he saw that they had been cut too short so he swung back under the bridge and, dogging

36 Captain Theodore Wright, Royal Engineers accompanied the B. E. F. to France with the 56th and 57th Field Companies attached to the 3rd Infantry Division. *Citation in the London Gazette Nov 17th 1914.* Gallantry at Mons on August 23rd 1914, in attempting to connect up the lead to demolish a bridge under heavy fire; although wounded in the head he made a second attempt. At Vailly on September 14th, he assisted the passage of 5th Cavalry over the pontoon bridge and was mortally wounded while assisting wounded men into shelter. Capt. Wright is buried in Vailly British Cemetery. His Victoria Cross was awarded posthumously on 16th November 1914.

Captain Theodore Wright VC.

enemy fire, ran up the bank to the barricade where he cut longer leads from the drum and wrapped them around his body before swinging back across the flood channel. By now the enemy had worked out what he was trying to do and were determined to stop him. As long as he was in the water Captain Wright was protected by the height of the canal bank, but each time he raised his hands up onto the towpath to feel for the leads he was splattered with mud and stones from the hail of rifle and machine gun bullets fired from less than thirty feet away. He made several attempts before he eventually found the leads again but they were still too short to pull down the bank to splice with the lengths wrapped around his body. As it would have been suicide to expose himself by climbing up onto the towpath he had to give up the attempt and, as he swung back under the bridge, weak from his wound and exhausted from his efforts, he fell semi-conscious into the water. Sergeant Smith, seeing him fall, leapt over the barricade and running the gauntlet of intense enemy fire ran down the slope and into the water to rescue his officer.

Captain Wright's attempts to blow the bridge had taken almost ninety minutes. It was 5.30 pm, and they should have left the canal almost three hours earlier

> *St John.* Meantime the Q.M.S. and I had been doing what was possible in the way of covering fire and our barrier was getting most unhealthy so as soon as he got back we cut and ran for it, luck being with us we got away without being hit. I got round through gardens and back ways until I reached the railway line. Along which I went until I found the rest of my Coy under the command of Maj. Yatman. We began to retire being joined by small detachments of different companies on the way. That retirement was one of the most exhausting things I remember so far as I was concerned. We had no time to waste and my job was to post covering parties. We

had to defend every street corner and the result was that by the time I had placed one post I had to run and catch the column up and tell off and place the next. I would have given my kingdom for a horse and no mistake.

Luckily for us the Germans did not press their attention onto us too closely and after doing about a mile of streets in this way Yatman gave the order to close up and push on with only a small moving rearguard to protect us. A staff officer met us and told us where our rendezvous was and said we could get back quite easily across country. We marched on and turned into more or less open country. As we crested a small hill we saw about 500 yards in front of us quite a large body of Germans resting. It was a great temptation to give them a few rounds rapid fire but their presence showed us that we must be in a pretty nasty position and we came to the conclusion that as Providence had so far been kind to us in keeping the knowledge of our situation from the enemy we had better continue in the endeavour and so we turned about[37] After much weary marching we reached our rendezvous at Frameries by a circuitous route as dusk was falling. Find Batt. headquarters and two Coys anxiously awaiting us.

The Battalion suffered its first casualties in the Mons' fighting.

Killed: *'B' Company*: 1592 Pte Grey, 8658 Pte Hughes, 1188 Pte Thompson, 755 Pte Will, 1247 Cpl. Johnson, 1496 Pte Vines, and 898 Pte Tucker.
'C' Company: 1931 Pte Neave.

Wounded: *'B' Company*: 8766 L/Cpl Hitchens, 9376 Pte. Addams, 9489 Pte Hurst, 2446 Pte Nicholson, 3340 Pte Monohan, 9924 Cpl Quinn, and 1278 Pte Collins.
***'C' Company*:** 2352 Sgt. Gammon, 5183 L/Cpl. Betmead, 3716 Pte Richardson, and 9281 Pte Gould.

37 Although their first temptation was to open fire they appreciated the significance of such a large body of Germans sitting and resting *in front* of them and apparently feeling so secure that they had not bothered to put out flank guards or scouts.

Chapter 3

Frameries and Le Câteau

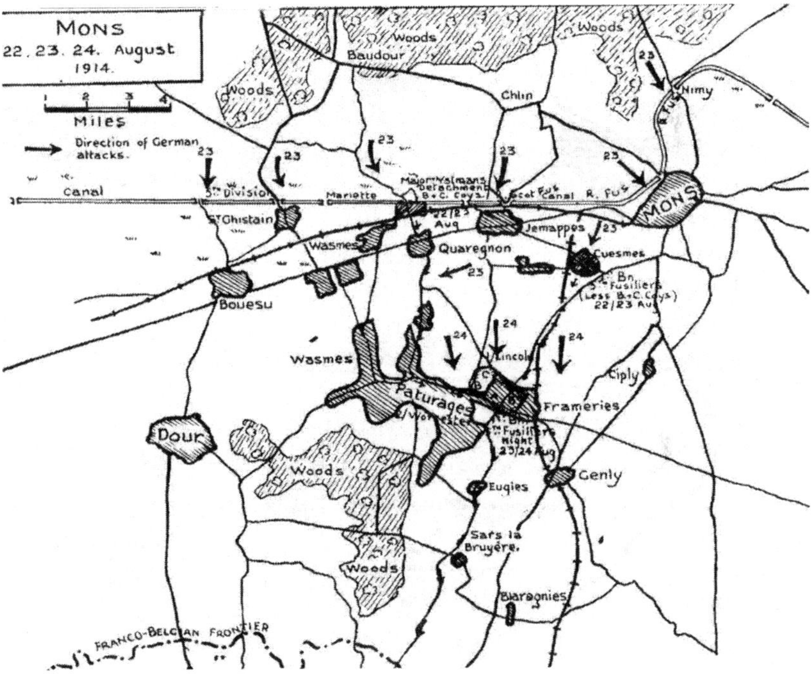

The retreat from the Canal.

Throughout the afternoon the 1/Northumberland's remained widely scattered. "D" Company arrived at the rallying point in Frameries sometime after midday, but then followed a long anxious wait for the rest of the battalion. "B" and "C" Companies arrived exhausted at about 7 pm, having made a wide detour to avoid the masses of German infantry spreading across the countryside like a plague. As the battalion transport had been sent away there were no rations to issue and the men were put in billets to rest while their officers waited upon events.

> *St John.* We were halted in a small street composed of the houses of the citizens who worked in the neighbouring factories, and we sat down on the kerb where we halted after sending out one platoon (Cogan's) to barricade and hold the Mons road. The retirement had made me hot and tired and, as I had not had any food since breakfast I was also pretty hungry but there was no food to be got as we had no transport. However I soon got cool and got a little sleep too lying in the gutter with my head on the kerb but I woke up after half an hour feeling very cold and stiff and went into a cottage where I begged a chair and sat by the stove. The cottagers were most kind although they were obviously afraid and knew that things were not going well. They provided me with coffee for which they refused payment and were most interested in examining all my belongings and equipment. A photograph of Roger delighted them beyond measure and all the family from Pere to Babe were called in to kiss it. Not being much of a linguist I missed a lot of their ecstatic compliments but Toppin translated some and being the old campaigner that he was seemed think that producing the photo would be a good stunt to ensure the production of fresh victuals etc. on future occasions.

"A" Company almost did not make it to the rendezvous. After their dramatic rescue of the 1/Royal Scots Fusiliers they were covering the rear of the battalion as it retreated towards Frameries when a passing staff officer, apparently pleased at finding a formed body of men, ordered them to barricade and entrench the Cuesmes road to cover the retreat of the men still drifting up from Mons. Here they waited throughout the hot afternoon as small groups, and even individual soldiers, passed through their barricade to be directed to Frameries. They saw nothing of the enemy, but the rattle of rifle and artillery fire all around them told them of the mopping up operations of the German infantry.

As soon as it was obvious that no more troops were coming up the road, and fearful of becoming cut off, they were preparing to leave when intense rifle and machine gun fire broke out somewhere behind them and the enemy artillery began to shell the road along which they planned to retreat. Reacting quickly before the light faded, scouts were sent out to fan out across the countryside to find an alternative route and one party struck it lucky. It was a deep railway cutting going in the direction of Frameries and in the gathering gloom the Company quickly assembled and, with riflemen placed along the rim to guard against surprise, silently made their way along it to join the rest of the battalion after dark.

The 1/Lincolns were also late having been waylaid to support the 8th Infantry Brigade, heavily engaged in fighting off a strong enemy attack. Fortunately they did not come into action and when the enemy discontinued their attacks at dusk they continued their journey to Frameries, arriving sometime after 10 pm.

With their arrival of the organisation of the 9th Infantry Brigade, as a fighting unit, was as complete as it was going to be. The 1/ Northumberlands and 1/Lincolns were the only intact battalions, the 1/Royal Scots Fusiliers, who had lost heavily in the fighting on the canal, were placed in reserve and went into billets. The survivors of the 4/Royal Fusiliers never arrived, having been forced by the presence of large numbers of the enemy to take refuge around Mons hospital with the 7th Infantry Brigade.

For the men of the 1/Northumberlands and 1/Lincolns there was to be little sleep that night. "B" and "C" Companies were set to dig a trench in a field situated on a slight ridge overlooking the roads from Jemappes and Quaregnon along which the enemy would advance; "A", the support company, built three strong barricades blocking the cross roads that formed the town centre while "D", with the machine-gun section, were in reserve. They spent the night in the power station on the outskirts of the town where a less than happy Lieutenant Watkins spent a restless night convinced that the tall chimney was too good a ranging point for the enemy artillery to ignore in the morning.

The battalion tool cart had been lost during the withdrawal from the canal and the men digging the trenches had to dig with their small entrenching tools or 'grubbers' and with the certainty of an attack in the morning, the officers and NCOs worked them in relays throughout the night to make holes deep enough to provide some protection. When on relief the exhausted men dropped to the damp ground and slept until shaken awake to do another stint, still reeling with fatigue.

During the retirement from the canal the 3rd and 5th Divisions had been forced apart creating a dangerous gap in the British defences, which if discovered by the enemy, would provide them with the opportunity to split II Corps in half. Realising the danger General Smith – Dorrien had twice asked GHQ to provide troops from I Corps to fill this gap until, frustrated at a lack of a reply, he drove over to Haig's headquarters and 'borrowed' the 5th Infantry Brigade, which moved to Paturages to plug the gap. One consequence of this move was the 1/Northumberland's surprise when they found that the troops holding the line to their left were not from the 5th Division as expected, but were the 2nd Battalion The Worcestershire Regiment from I Corps.

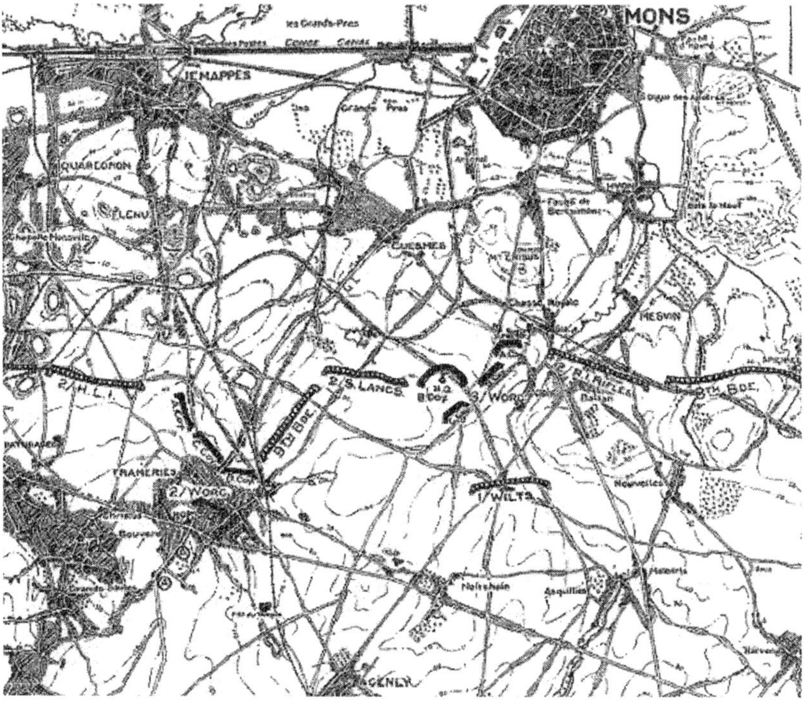

The British positions around Frameries.

Like most of the defensive line taken up by the 3rd Division for the night of the 23rd/24th the position around Frameries was far from ideal. They were still in the main industrial complex and in the densely build-up area their field of fire was severely limited and there were several large slag heaps that gave a commanding view of the village and the surrounding area, but were outside the British defence perimeter. With two battalions missing the 9th Infantry Brigade had too few men to form a continuous defence line so the Lincolns, who occupied the most exposed position, had only a tenuous link with the 2nd Battalion South Lancashire Regiment (7th Brigade) on their right and with "B" Company, 1/Northumberlands on their left. They in turn were separated by several hundred yards from the 2/Worcesters.

At this early stage of the war, when information was scarce and rumours abounded, most British officers were gripped with spy mania and, for whatever reason, many were convinced that the Belgian population harboured a large number of German spies, or at least enemy sympathisers. These beliefs were reinforced by the late and chaotic arrival of the British infantry among the mining villages south of the canal, and their failure to confine the inhabitants to their houses so that late into the night many civilians wandered about mixing freely with the troops, even those preparing the defences. Captain St John was typical in his suspicions that some of the population were quite prepared to act as spies and this belief was reinforced by many inexplicable events that occurred during the night.

The troops in the village reported suspicious characters wandering about the streets including 'drunken men' whose friendliness towards the troops building the barricades was embarrassing. Out on the trench line groups of hysterical youths appeared from the enemy's direction to tell stories of having run the gauntlet of the Germans to reach safety but then melted away into the darkness when questioned. Elsewhere parties of men approached the officers to beg permission to pass through the defences to retrieve wounded soldiers reported to be in a house on the Cuesmes road close to the German positions. Whether any of these individuals were French or English speaking enemy soldiers in civilian clothes, or even Belgian spies, cannot now be determined, but it would be a serious mistake to underestimate the professionalism of the German army who, given the confusion that existed throughout the night, did not find the means to determine what the British were doing, and the nature of the defensives laid out in front of them.

> *St John.* At about 9.30 all of the officers were called out and we proceeded to a field about half a mile away where we were to dig ourselves in. On our way across the field to choose the site of our trenches we suddenly came on a man lying prone in the grass. He appeared to be drunk and our interpreters assured us he was drunk but both Toppin and I thought he was only acting drunk. We said so, but it was considered to be a waste of precious time to take him back to headquarters and so he was allowed to go free. We sited and marked out our trenches and by midnight had the company up and at work at digging them. The men were tired and it was a heart breaking job to be constantly having to almost kick them to

do work that was to protect them from death. During the night on looking behind on one occasion I noticed that in a row of houses some 500 yards away there was one house with an unblinded upper window with a lighted lamp in it. I again called Toppin's attention to this, but we came to the conclusion that it was no good to take any action in the matter.

24 August, Monday

The Battle of Frameries

The enemy opened the battle before dawn with a heavy bombardment against the right wing of II Corps and by 5.15 am the whole of the 3rd Division line was under fire; a sure indication of the effectiveness of the enemy's night-time reconnaissance. All the signs indicated that the enemy infantry would soon attack but the 3rd Division was no longer in a position to stand and fight for its defences was unravelling by the minute. When General Haig agreed to move the 5th Infantry Brigade to Paturages it became an integral part of the 3rd Divisions defences, guarding the gap between it and the 5th Division, but as a consequence of sloppy staff work, the *command* of the 5th Brigade remained with Haig's headquarters and this was to have severe repercussions in the morning.

During the evening of the 23rd Sir John French summoned the Chiefs of Staff from I and II Corps to his headquarters at Le Câteau to review the situation and, after a brief conference, it was decided that the BEF would retreat to a new defence line being prepared along the Roman road from Le Câteau to Cambrai. At 1 am Brigadier-General Gough, Haig's Chief of Staff, telephoned the order to I Corps HQ but, as there was no direct telephone link between II Corps and GHQ, Forestier-Walker, Smith-Dorrien's Chief of Staff, had to drive 30 miles along roads congested with refugees to inform Smith-Dorrien of his new orders. In the meantime Haig issued orders for I Corps to resume the retreat at 5.30 am and, probably assuming that Smith-Dorrien had received the new orders at the same time as he did, saw no necessity to coordinate his actions with him. As Haig's orders included the 5th Brigade the gap on the left flank of the 3rd Division was re-opened. It was imperative that the 3rd Division moved quickly for the enemy would soon discover the unprotected flank and by attacking along it "roll-up" the line.

Orders were issued for the retirement to begin at 6 am, starting with the 8th Infantry Brigade on the right. They had been under fire for over an hour but the bombardment was poorly aimed and doing surprisingly little damage so it was a simple matter for them to disengage, form up outside artillery range, and march off. For the 7th Infantry Brigade dug in at Cipley, and the 9th Infantry Brigade at Frameries, escape was not so easy. At Frameries the enemy artillery had the range and their shells fell in and around the trenches and barricades for over two hours. This was not the continuous bombardment common later in the war, but one of intense bursts of shelling, mainly shrapnel, fired at irregular intervals so that on the whole the men were generally safe providing they kept under cover.

Nor were the 1/Northumberlands subject to an infantry attack. In front of their positions was a stretch of 'dead ground', out of sight of the trenches, where, at about 6 am, large numbers of enemy infantry began to assemble. Fortunately the artillery observers from 109th Battery RFA, who had two guns just behind the trenches, spotted them and firing over open sights the gunners decimated the densely packed enemy infantry. Other than the sudden increase in the rate of firing from the guns the men in the trenches were unaware that they had been the subject of an impending infantry attack or that the guns would continue to protect them from the unwelcome attentions of the enemy throughout the rest of the morning.

> *St John.* As soon as it was beginning to grow light I went down to our right to locate exactly the trenches, which were on the far side of some farm buildings, and to try and find out some means of fairly safe inter-communication. This took me about 10 minutes and I had a few words with Dick Gatehouse whose Company were manning those trenches. On the way back I stopped to light my pipe as it was now quite light and to have a good look around the country generally. I had just got my pipe lit when a regular inferno of shell fire burst upon us and around us. I made rapid tracks for my trench and got safely into it. I have no doubt that our friend the drunken man had been a spy and had given the enemy the line by means of the light in the house. All that morning the Germans shelled us with short intervals of quiet. During these respites I tried to get a look around as we had a bad field of fire, but it was no good and most unpleasant as someone was sniping me from behind all the time.

> After two or three hours of this game Gatehouse walked round to us and said that the enemy had guns right on our right flank and that troops on his immediate right were retiring. We had got no orders and did not want to go back but Dick said that if his right was left in the air he must retire and would let us know. Shortly after he reported that he was retiring and most reluctantly Toppin gave us the order to go.
>
> We got out in good order though the men were somewhat over eager to go and got back about 1000 yards into the village which was being shelled. There we were met by a staff officer who ordered us back again to our trenches, so back we went without any hurry or confusion but it was jumpy work walking over that field. Fortunately we were not expected and were able to reach our trenches without being molested though a heavy shell fire opened on us very soon afterwards. We found some men of the (I think) Worcestershire Regt. occupying our trenches and it galled me horribly to return under these conditions and I swore terribly at who ever it was who had originated the order to retire.
>
> An hour or so later we got a genuine order to retire through a factory yard and form up on the road beyond. This order reached us before it got to the Colonel who found us on the road and asked what the **** were we doing there. However he got the official order shortly afterwards.

It is surprising that "B" and "C" companies could withdraw, and then return, to their trenches relatively unmolested in the middle of the battle but the main enemy thrust was directed at the junction of the 1/Lincolns and the 2/South Lancashires over to their right. It was when the seriousness of this attack became apparent that "D" Company was sent forward to support the 1/Lincolns. For the next three hours they were to be involved in severe fighting and as a result suffer the highest casualties in the battalion.

> *Lieut. Watkins.* Woken about 4 am by shells bursting within 50 yards, aimed at chimney. Took limber down road parallel to trenches. Germans shelled road heavily all morning, had several narrow shaves with shell bursting in houses close by. Noise of shell deafening, as high explosive used. Our own guns could not locate the enemy. B and C Company had very

bad time in orchard as Germans had exact range probably through spies with telephones. 109th Battery brought two guns up near chimney stack, but they got roughly handled. Went down with Commanding Officer and Adjutant near trenches. Commanding Officer did not use M.G. as no suitable place available. Sappers made barricades across two roads by which our men had to retire. Reconnoitred a road for D, B and C to retire that led into main road. Telegraph wires all cut up, and Convent which had been turned into a hospital very nearly shelled several times. Brigade staff shelled out of their place and went a little higher up main road towards Frameries.

General Shaw directing the battle in the street after his HQ had been shelled. One of the barricades can be seen at the top of the street.

As the casualties mounted the small hospital in Frameries was overwhelmed and the Convent was pressed into use. Seeing that more medical help would be required an elderly lady approached one of "A" Company's barricades and demanded to be allowed to go down the street to fetch a doctor who lived there. Captain Sandilands, who was in command, explained to her that it was unsafe as the street was under shell fire and could be full of German infantry at any moment but undeterred she said that she had come to fetch the doctor, and that is what she was going to do. Worried about her safety Sandilands somehow managed to get hold of a megaphone and, between the intervals in the shelling, shouted for the doctor who appeared at the door of a house about twenty yards down the street. Just at that moment a shell burst on the roof opposite and the terrified doctor jumped back into his house. This was to happen twice more before he screwed up his courage and ran down the street to the shelter of the barricade to be scolded by the old lady for being so slow in coming.

By 9 am the German infantry broke off their attacks and, taking advantage of the lull, the 1/Lincolns, having lost four officers and a hundred and thirty other ranks withdrew, covered by "D" Company. But the enemy had not gone away. With the noticeable slackening of the British fire they rushed forward and mounted a machine gun on a large slagheap over-looking the British positions. Once the 1/Lincolns had withdrawn it was the turn of the 2/South Lancashires who were acting as rearguards for the 7th Infantry Brigade. Instead of filtering the men back from the firing line their officers, perhaps believing that the German infantry had given up, paraded the battalion in an open space prior to marching them off providing the enemy machine gun on the slag heap with the prefect target. Within a few minutes nearly three hundred men lay dead or wounded on the ground, the worst casualties suffered that the day in the whole 3rd Division.

By 9.30 am a general retirement was under way. "A" Company was ordered to hold the barricades until all the troops were clear of the built-up area and by the time the remnants of the 7th and 9th Divisions had pulled back through the town large numbers of the enemy were infiltrating the streets and alleyways where some sharp street fighting took place as they attempted to dislodge "A" Company from its position. It was time to go so, as the enemy broke into the houses and hammered at the walls to make loopholes, "A" company, using techniques perfected on the hill tops of the North-West Frontier, filtered away in twos and threes, silently and unseen, until only four men were left at each of the three barricades and they, with their two officers, slipped way before the enemy even knew the withdrawal had taken place

> *St John.* We were given orders to cover the retirement of the Brigade and the information that the Germans were already in the trenches we had vacated. There was some confusion on the road and we had very little field of fire in any direction and it looked like the end. We built a very hasty barricade

> across the road and lined up behind it with drawn revolvers expecting every minute to be rushed. Why the Huns failed to come on I still cannot imagine. For about half an hour we hung on there listening to the roar of battle all around us, and getting occasional bullets splattering on our barricade. We, or at any rate I myself, expected every minute to be the last. The confusion behind us, caused by troops of every unit going back, made seemed things even more hopeless. But presently the confusion cleared away and, seeing no sight of the oncoming enemy, we went back about 200 yards and took up a position where we had a rather better field of fire.

The attack on Frameries was carried out by the *6th Division, III Corps, First Army*, and there is no doubt that they had suffered heavily, particularly in their attacks against the 1/Lincolns and 2/ South Lancashires. Hauptmann von Brandis of the *24th (Brandenburg) Regiment* reported that in the initial assault six companies of his regiment had been practically wiped out, and Captain Liebenow of the *64th Infantry Regiment,* wrote after the war that at Frameries his battalion lost every fourth man and most of its officers. With the capture of Frameries, and the surrounding villages, discipline broke down and the exhausted and dispirited German infantry went on a looting and drinking spree that lasted the rest of the day. This allowed the British to escape with relative ease.

The casualties in the Northumberland Fusiliers at Frameries were relatively light, but without their transport they could not evacuate their wounded. These were left in the Convent, or on the battlefield where they fell.

Killed: Captain M Leckie. Medical Officer.
'D' Company: 174 Pte Smart, 1071 Pte Seage and 1368 Pte Smith.

Wounded: ***'B' Company***: 9184 Pte Wildman, 8815 Pte McCarty, 4898 C.S.M. Hone, 1729 Pte Bradley.
'C' Company: 9822 Cpl Buck, 3255 L/Cpl Calvert, 2841 Pte Atkins, 2383 L/C Page, 1672 Pte Cain, 9736 Pte Patterson, 398 Pte Pennison, 9642 Pte Kennedy, 99 Pte Nicholson, *9267 Pte Crouch.*
'D' Company: 6658 Sgt Fenemore, 782 Pte King, 8240 Pte Robinson, 9542 Pte Walker, 1001 Pte Wood, 1400 Pte Dale, 737 Pte Wilcox, 1122 Pte Turner, Sgt Samuels, 1011 Sgt Groves, 3746 Pte Durham,

9309 Pte Cairns, 91 Pte Holland, 8814 Pte Thorley, 9181 Pte Towle, 1372 Pte Farmer, 60 Pte Knowles, 9967 Pte Cowle.
Captain H.R. Sandilands:

The Battle of Le Câteau

The withdrawal of the 3rd Division proceeded without any serious interference but this was not true for the 5th Division on their left. During their withdrawal they were almost trapped by the inward swing of von Kluck's *7th Division* and only extricated themselves after fighting a sharp rearguard action at Elouges-Audregnies which resulted in the virtual annihilation of the 1/Cheshires, and the severe mauling of the 1/Norfolks. Unaware of these difficulties the 1/Northumberland Fusiliers were annoyed when, on reaching the village of Sara La Bruyére, they were told, without any obvious reason, to turn around and march back up the road towards Frameries and take up defensive positions where, unbeknown to them, they were to cover the right flank of the 5th Division and plug the gap that still existed between the 3rd and 5th Divisions. As it happened they saw nothing of the enemy and took the opportunity to get some much needed rest

> *St John:* We got orders to clear right back for about a mile into open country and dig ourselves in. I shall never forget the feeling of relief when we got into the open country again and were able to see something of what was happening. On the way we passed General Shaw who congratulated me on being the last person to leave the canal at Mons and said we had all done splendidly. Being very sick at having to retire and being also very hungry, hot and tired I thought he was being sarcastic and thought it in very bad taste on his part and it was not until some days later that I realised the dear old boy meant every word he had said. He must have thought me very ungracious.
>
> We dug ourselves hasty entrenchment's and lay in them for about an hour and then went back another mile and formed up with the rest of the Battn. in a stubble field where we made ourselves some protection in case we were shelled and lay down for a three hours rest. We could see sights of the enemy and occasionally they threw shells pretty near us but not into us. I got a wash at a farm and some kind person gave me a biscuit and a bit of chocolate (I had given all I had

on me to the men) as we were not allowed to light fires to cook ourselves some soup cubes.

At about 4.0 p.m. we fell in again and marched out of Belgium crossing the frontier at Rinette. When we got to Hons, which is about two and a half miles from the border, I was sent on ahead on a bicycle to a place called Houdain to take over billets for the Battn. and to meet the transport there. I got to the village and found Gunner there with the transport and with him got a sup of ale from a priest, but the inhabitants were full of reports of the much feared Uhlans who it seemed were all around us and sure enough we soon got word of them from some of our own cavalry. Also received orders to leave Houdain and to go to a Div. bivouac at a place called Bremeries. Once again therefore I mounted the old push bike and peddled slowly into Bavai. From this place to Bremeries bicycling was almost impossible as the road was blocked by regiments, guns, transport and fleeing natives with their cares and penaters packed into every kind of cumbersome vehicle.

They did not reach Bavai until after dark and found the town completely blocked by troops converging from all directions, many separated from their units and wandering aimlessly along with the general mass. As a battalion still in formation it was to take them a good couple of hours of pushing and shoving, none too gently, to force their way to the other side of the town where to their anger and frustration they were told that they had to march a further two miles to Bermeries before they would reach their transport. No rations had been issued so Captain St John had the cooks prepare a meagre meal from soup cubes, their first food for thirty six hours.

St John. On arriving at Bremeries I found some staff officers with lanterns (it was quite dark by now) and went up to one of them to ask where was our bivouac. To my joyful surprise I found I was speaking to an old friend in Col. Roger Boyle late of the Munster Fusiliers. He told me where about we were to bivouac and once more I plodded along in the dark. I fell into one ditch and had one or two minor accidents of that sort but eventually found our field. I also picked up the transport again and the Quartermaster, We got a fire going

> ready for the Battn. when it came along, which it did about midnight most of it tired and cross as I was myself. I got rid of my soup without any persuasion and had a sup of it myself and was quite ready for it too having had only a biscuit since breakfast on Sunday. We lay down on and under the corn stooks where we halted and got some sleep, but it was a cold night and our field was damp.

25 August, Tuesday

At 5 am they left for the village of Inchy on the Le Câteau-Cambrai road. It was to be the first of many long trying marches for, except for the regulation ten-minute halt, they had no opportunity to rest as their progress was slowed by the crowds of refugees who obstructed the road with every kind of vehicle from farm carts to dog carts and perambulators. Sometimes they would side step them by marching off the road, but going across ploughed fields was difficult and tiring but by the afternoon, as the number of refugees thinned, the road ahead was cleared by French Gendarmes and Territorials who pushed them roughly aside into the ditches and fields so as not to impede the marching infantry. The only excitement of the day was a grandstand view of their first battle between two aircraft in which both pilots were in mortal danger, not from one another, but from the heavy volume of small arms fire resulting from indiscriminate shooting by the excited troops on the road below.

> *St John.* I woke up at daylight and found that a certain amount of rations had arrived. Got some breakfast and also a tin of bully and some biscuit to go with it. We fall in at 5.30 a.m. and continue our march through Fombray Quesnoy to Le Cateau and Inchy which we reached at about 6.0 p.m. On the way we heard shooting behind us now and again and we saw a very pretty fight in the air. This fight, which was between a Taube and two of our aeroplanes, lasted for quite an hour. Time and again the Taube would try and get back to its own lines but each time one of our fellows would lead him away while the other manoeuvred for position above him. Eventually our men were successful and forced him to land in a very crippled condition. He came down about quarter of a mile from us and as he came over us we gave him a welcome from our rifles too. Our mounted

people rode up to where he fell but when they got there they found the Taube in flames and no Germans to be seen. We continued our march and passed some excited members of the French Territorial Guard. There were five of them and they informed me with much pride and much gesture that 'Andre', who looked benightedly sheepish, although he pointed to himself remarking that he had himself shot and brought to earth the 'aeroplane Allemande'.

When we got to Le Câteau a heavy thunderstorm broke and we all got drenched. Again I was sent on to take over billets and rode from one village to another on beastly greasy roads and a rather flat tyre. At each village we found other troops and eventually returned to the village of Inchy where we got quite cosy billets in a big barn. We also got into the local schoolmasters house where we were given hot water to wash in and a bang up supper too with some much appreciated wine and beers.

We got to bed at 10.0 with orders to turn out at 2.0 and to sleep in our equipment, which we did.

They were to have a very disturbed night as everyone was on edge with the enemy so close. At about midnight the outposts reported that they could hear cavalry approaching and the Lincolns were ordered to stand at arms and send two platoons to reinforce the outpost line; but it was a false alarm as it was our own cavalry withdrawing through the infantry's positions. As they passed they shouted unwelcome news of the closeness of von Kluck's Army and that the 7th Brigade, the 3rd Division's rearguard, had been in action at Solesmes and had not yet made it back to Le Câteau.

26 August, Wednesday

They were up before dawn and paraded along the streets of Inchy while the cooks worked their way along the ranks dispensing the latest rumours with a chunk of bread and a mug of hot tea. The word was that they were going to stand and fight and as dawn broke they marched up the steep hill south of the village to take up their positions.

The 3rd Division's line was on the ridge above Inchy, running between the villages of Troisvilles and Caudry, roughly parallel to the Le Câteau-Cambrai road. The 9th Infantry Brigade was almost in the centre and their short lengths of trench ran from Troisvilles to Audencourt and overlooked Inchy. To their left the trenches of the 8th Brigade ran from Audencourt to Caudry, and Caudry itself was defended by a very weak and incomplete, 7th Brigade which still had much of its infantry strung out on the roads having become lost while retiring from Solesmes. The Division was so short of infantry after three days of fighting that it could not spare a battalion to form a Divisional reserve and one had to be cobbled together from men taken from the transport, signals and other support units.

The 1/Northumberlands started their defensive preparations by having the men stack their rifles and parade in line on the hillside to march backwards and forwards across the slope to flatten a large field of standing corn in order to deny its cover to the enemy. While this was going on the officers examined the trenches started by the French civilians and found them both shallow and badly sited and selected a new line further down the hill. "A", "C" and "D" Companies would man the firing line supported by the machine guns on their left. "B" would be in reserve.

The 9th Infantry Brigade was to have a relatively uneventful battle. Situated as they were in the middle of the Divisional line they never came into direct contact with the enemy and, with their trenches half way down the hill, the enemy artillery was directed over and above them, searching for the British guns on the hill above. The only threat was when the enemy attempted to occupy Inchy and Beaumont at the foot of the hill but as soon as they were spotted they were driven out by a storm of artillery and rifle fire from the slopes above. It was fortunate that they could be discouraged so easily for above the British trenches rose several hundred yards of hillside devoid of cover and if the enemy had occupied the villages their machine guns would have had a clear line of fire as the British made their withdrawal up the slope later in the day. By the same token the bare lower slopes were a major disincentive to the German infantry to attack up the hill into the teeth of the rifle and machine gun fire from the best shooting army in the world.

Their only casualties in the battle were to be suffered by "B" Company, in reserve and concealed in the sunken road that ran along the top of the ridge.

> *St John.* We fell in at 5.0 and began by flattening a cornfield by marching over it. We then went to our digging area and took over the site of our trenches but before we had begun to dig we were told our Coy. were to be in reserve that day so

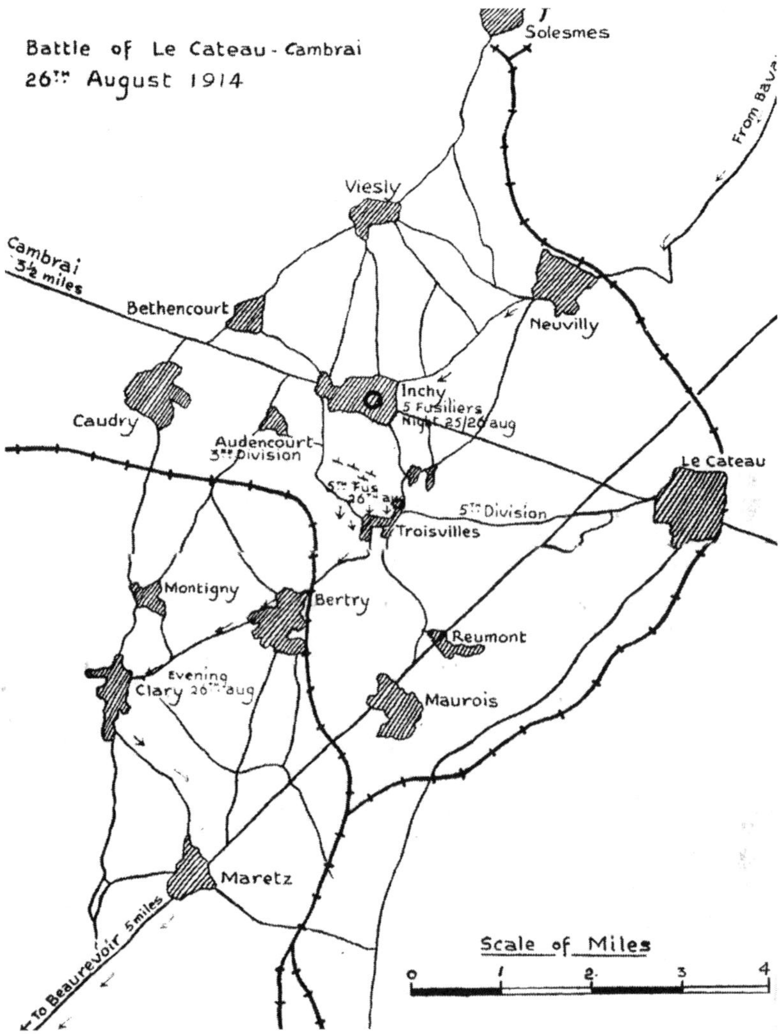

The Battle of Le Cateau.

we retired to a sunk road some 300 yards in the rear where was gathered the front line transport. We lay down under cover of the embankment and I went to sleep again but was woken by the explosion of a shell. Apparently a Taube had found the sunken road and the enemy were shelling it. I clung very close to the ground and got off the road but we had several casualties in the company including Dorman-Smith who got a bullet through his arm. We bound him up and sent him and other wounded away and buried the dead.

The transport shifted from our neighbourhood to a safer place. When we had done all this Toppin informed me that he was hit too and asked me to bind up his arm. He had quite a nasty wound by his elbow and I bound it up as well as I could. Later on he got a RAMC man to fix him up better. We lay there for most of the day, nothing much seemed to happen where we were except the occasional burst of rapid fire from our own trenches and a shell or two from the enemy; but there was much commotion away on our right and a hot fight seemed to be going on there.

Lieut. Watkins. Cup of coffee at 3.30 am Marched out at 4 am to about ¾ mile outside town to the south. Did not know quite what was going to happen. After some delay found we were going to take up a position which had more or less been prepared for us in front of village. This position was found to be not much good, and it was decided to dig further back up the rise. Line finally chosen, but hardly any big tools to dig with. Selected position for machine guns on the left of line with A Company, protected on left flank from view by a field of maize, and firing straight into the village. Had my own tools and dug as hard as possible circular pits with high enfilade bank on the right, as was told to expect enfilade fire from that direction. Got fairly well dug in in an hour when the first shell came over us, aimed probably at farmhouse about 300 yards in rear, behind which were some of our own guns. The ground sloped gently from the farmhouse to the first line of A Company's trenches, then steeply down to the Royal Scots Fusilier's front trench, so the M.G's. could fire over their heads into the village, a distance of about 800 yards. Two guns of the 109th Battery were placed about 100 yards slightly to my left rear in open ground, and were only concealed by brushwood. They were not discovered by the enemy and did good work to cover our retirement. The remaining guns of the Battery were placed behind the farmhouse and the sunken road, with an observing station about 100 yards in front of the farmhouse. The standing stacks of corn had been laid flat by our men whilst waiting for the line to be decided on. The transport was placed in the village of Troisvilles on the

> sunken road, one platoon of A Company was on my right and another to my right front, so that here were two tiers of fire. On the first shell coming over everyone got into their equipment, and I started the men in my trench enlarging it, as there was rather a squash for four of us. Shells began to come more frequently, but did little damage, mostly falling between my trenches and the farmhouse. Our guns replied. I could see infantry advancing the other side of the village in the far distance, and saw them caught by our guns badly. A few bullets began coming from our left through the maize, and one or two men of A Company were hit. One came very close to my head, and buried itself in the inside of the trench, so I heightened left cover as much as possible. The shelling died down and there was practically no rifle fire from the front, except a few snipers, who took a shot if anybody put their heads up. Did not fire as nothing to be seen, but front trenches fired occasionally. Directly our Gunners heard us firing at the village they started 'plunking' lyddite in front of and into the village. At first these shells went short and very nearly fell into the Royal Scots Fusiliers' front trench. The observing station was told about this, and they began registering a zone in front of the village , and into the nearest houses. I am quite certain that very little could have lived in that zone. It was rather interesting to watch the shells come over and speculate where they were going to pitch. They did little damage beyond knocking down a few houses, but it must have prevented anyone stopping these. I heard sounds of heavy firing in our right and left.

At 2.35 pm 3rd Division issued orders to break off the battle but such was the difficulty in communicating with the front line that not all of them would receive the order. Even the 1/Northumberland Fusiliers, who were in a better position than most to retire in some order, almost left a platoon on the battlefield. When the order was received at 9th Brigade Headquarters Major Stevens, the Brigade Major, was told to telephone the orders through to the battalions in the trenches but the line had been damaged and not repaired for many of the signallers had been taken away to form the scratch Divisional Reserve. Stevens called for his horse and rode off in the direction of the trenches attracting a great deal of enemy fire as he moved across the brow of the hill. He reached the Northumberland line about 4.19 pm and, riding up to Lieutenant Watkins's position, called out above the din of battle "I am afraid you must retire" then, as he turned to start down the slope to inform the trenches in front, fell mortally wounded.

> *St John.* At about 4.30 we got orders to vacate the position and fall back. As my company had been in reserve all day we were naturally ordered to cover the retirement of the remainder of the Battn., although as luck would have it we were the only Coy. who had suffered any casualties. However those which were not hit had had a very easy day and those who were hit were either buried or back in the ambulances as far as we knew. As soon as the rest of the Battn. had got away one half of my Coy. went back to another position and I remaining on to cover their retirement. The Germans advanced to within 1000 to 1200 yards of us and we blazed away at them but did not seem to do much damage as the enemy were in pretty extended order. When I saw that the other half Company were back in position we went quickly back, stopping on the road to examine and empty some ammunition boxes. When we had got back a bit Toppin signalled us to halt and came up to us and said Booth had been left behind in his trenches no one having told him to retire. I collected some men and went back again to help him out. As we got back however we found him coming away and we all retired together going into open order for about 500 to 600 yards across fields when we joined up with the other half company on a road and proceeded through a tiny village very knocked about with shell fire to where the Battn. was formed up. As soon as we had joined up the whole Battn. moved off in close order and we marched along behind a belt of trees till we were about another mile back when we again halted. Here we came upon other troops who told us unpleasant stories of defeat, which seemed to be more or less collaborated by the number of small bodies of straggling troops that kept passing us. As it seemed we were to wait for some time my Coy. was sent off to take up a protective position which we did. We had a good view of the country and could see the Germans all over and around the position which we had left while the whole countryside was well

> besprinkled with burning farms etc. Now and again a shell would burst in our neighbourhood but none very close to us. It was a heavy heart that I had in me during the time we lay there and to me the future looked very gloomy indeed, but still nothing happened and presently we were able to form up as rear guard to the Battn. and to continue our march.

The retirement was covered by the guns of 107th Battery who poured such a torrent of shells into the valley below that the enemy lost all inclination to advance up the hill. When the gunners had fired off all their ammunition, and with no means to remove the guns, the sergeant-major in charge removed the sights and he, and his men, joined the Northumberlands in their withdrawal.

> *Lieut. Watkins.* Had our dinners brought up in a dixie as they was no firing, but by the time it reached the section nothing was left except a greasy soup and some lumps of mutton fat. I could not face it, though had nothing to eat and only a cup of coffee at 8.30 a.m. The firing on the right and left had been getting nearer, and the enemy's shells bursting nearer the centre. I had seen men retiring on our right, but thought it was only an advanced line. About 4 o'clock the two guns in the open began firing off as hard as possible straight into the village. About 4.10 p.m. was very surprised to see our Brigade major ride up to my trench and say " I am afraid you must retire. " He rode on and told the trenches in front, and was shot in the groin on the way back. I dismounted guns and got A Company to let me have some men to help me carry the extra ammunition boxes. The other troops in front were retiring, so got hold of two ammunition boxes, a rifle, pick and shovel, and retired in the direction in which everybody was going. But I had no idea where to go to, nor had anyone else. I saw and talked to the sergeant-major in charge of the two guns in the open. He told me he had to abandon them, but as they had fired a large number of rounds and had also taken away the sights etc., they wouldn't be much use. I went back into the village, and collected the men together, but saw no signs of

my limber. I asked the Colonel of Royal Scots Fusiliers[38] in which direction we were retiring. He did not know. I found our companies reforming a little farther on, and saw the adjutant, who said the Battalion were going to reform further back. He told me he had seen the limber, and had sent it back to find me. Shortly afterwards it came up, and I put guns, etc., into it. I found the Battalion reforming in a field on the side of the road. I pulled to one side of the road and helped to bring the stragglers in from the road to the Battalion, who were then told to do rearguard. We marched back, and whilst doing so saw the " Heavies " limber up and move off. I believe that they had had no orders to retire until then. Whilst retiring from the trenches only heard one or two shots fired at us. If we had been fired on, confusion and casualties would have been great. Took up a position of rearguard supported by guns. As an engagement seemed imminent, decided to lighten rear limber, whose wheel had been nearly broken, by throwing away siege lamps, clinometers and dixes which we had collected, and some extra ammunition. Before I could get into position, we moved off and halted in the village of Audencourt, where we found some ambulances moving off, leaving surplus wounded in the houses. Had a drink and a bit of chocolate and filled the water bottles, and after a short halt moved on again. Stopped about 11 p.m. in a small village for about three hours. Told that another division was crossing our front. Trekked all night. Very Tired. Major _____ and self kept bumping into each other fast asleep, also had hallucinations, imagining the trees were large villages. My horse had gone off, and I had to walk.

St John. It now became a question of daylight. There was only about 1 hour to go before it was dark and if the Germans did not catch us before then there was a good chance of our getting away under cover of the night. It was an exciting hour. Progress was slow owing to the blocked roads and checks were frequent. We closed up our rearguard when we got to ------------ I don't know what protection we had in the

38 Lieut.-Col. Douglas Smith.

rear of us except of course the cavalry who were apparently in close touch with the enemy. Occasionally we saw little groups of mounted men on our flanks but could never make out whether they were friend or foe. As dusk began to fall a wet mist came down which served the double purpose of wetting us and hiding us from view. When the darkness became complete we were halted in a tiny village. At first we thought that it was just the ordinary halt due to a minor block on the road. As we stood in the dark not a sound was to be heard barring an occasional shuffle as some man shifted his equipment or the unique splash of the invariable and inexhaustible expectoration for which soldiers must surely be world famous.

As time went on and no advance was made we sat or lay down on the road and most men slept and snored uneasily. They were too tired and too scared to talk though this did not prevent one or two thoughtless idiots from striking a match to light his fag. This was invariably followed by the low murmur of a stream of suitable invective uttered by the offender's platoon or Coy. commander. It is an extraordinary thing but in spite of explanation of the cause of the order forbidding it, one would consistently find some men who would risk the safety and lives of the entire Army Corps by lighting a match and disclosing our very precarious position to the enemy rather that curb his craving for his precious woodbine. I could not sleep myself. I was tired enough but I was cold and a steady drizzling rain made slumber in the open impossible. I did not like to go away from the column to a cottage in case a move was made while I slept.

Casualties at Le Câteau:
Killed: ***'B' Company***: 9588 Pte Smith, 1706 Pte Fawkes.

Wounded: ***'A' Company***: 207 L/Cpl. Keeling, 3302 L/Cpl. Woodrow, 1623 Pte Tonkinson, 2510 Pte King,
'B' Company: 3196 Pte McGrath, 9645 Pte Robson, 922 L/Cpl. Marquis, 1636 Pte Tweedell.
'C' Company: 1573 Pte Groom, 9626 Pte Tweedy and 2374 Pte Middlebrook.

'D' Company: 9288 L/Cpl. Pickering, 9468 Pte Roberts, 1223 Pte Meadows.
2nd Lieut. Dorman Smith, Capt. Toppin and Lieut. Ovans.

During the late afternoon the exhausted troops of the 9th Infantry Brigade assembled at Clary from where they continued their retreat south-west to Beaurevoir. Although their battle casualties had been light many men were missing having become mixed up with other units in the precipitous retreat from the trench line, but during the evening, as they slowly proceeded along the congested roads, the men began to sort themselves out and battalions, such as the 1/Northumberlands, which were still under the firm grip of their officers and NCOs, gradually reformed.

With the onset of darkness, to add to their discomfort and misery, a soaking drizzle set in making the surface of the unpaved roads muddy and slippery but it had the consolation that it hid them from enemy patrols.

When they reached Beaurevoir they found streets blocked solid by the convergence of troops from the 3rd and 5th Divisions, all mixed up with a tangled mass of transport and guns. As the rearguard the 1/Northumberlands had to cover the town until it was clear of the mass of troops so they pulled back into the northern outskirts and, too exhausted to build defences, threw out a screen of outposts and sank to the soaking ground immediately falling asleep beneath the steady, cold drizzle. By 2 am the town was clear and they staggered after the 3rd Division along roads turned into river of liquid mud by the mass of men and transport ahead of them in the darkness.

The comparative ease by which II Corps disengaged and withdrew in the middle of a battle was due, in part, to those units which, for one reason or another, never received orders to retire. The heavy casualties suffered by the enemy during the 'mopping – up' of these scattered groups instilled a caution in the German infantry that delayed any plans von Kluck may have had for pursing II Corps closely after the battle. On the 3rd Division front the order to retire was not received by the 1/Gordon Highlanders, nor the company of the 1/Royal Scots on their right, or the two companies 2/Royal Irish Regiment on their left. By chance the positions held by these troops were best placed to prevent the enemy moving up the slope from Inchy in pursuit the 3rd Division and throughout the afternoon, and well into the evening, they held the enemy at bay. Unfortunately, when they finally withdrew at midnight, they lost their way in the darkness and stumbled into a large body of enemy infantry and forced to surrender.

On the left, where the line between Caudry and Hancourt collapsed, groups of infantry, ranging from sections to companies, were cut off in the confused fighting that marked the German penetration of the British defences. These troops fought on to the bitter end until their ammunition was exhausted or they were overwhelmed to be killed, or captured, depending upon the temper of their enemies. Around Harcourt and Ligny, the survivors of two companies of 2/Royal Dublin Fusiliers, two of the 1/King's Own Royal Lancaster Regiment and about two to three hundred men of the 1/Royal Warwickshire Regiment, all from the 4th Division, continued to fight on in their positions until 11 pm, seven hours after the withdrawal of the rest of their Division and over the next few days many of these men were to be killed or captured in numerous small firefights that flared up as they worked their way through the masses of the *First Army*. Only a small group of survivors eventually rejoined their battalions, including a young Lieutenant of the 1/Warwickshires called Bernard Montgomery.

Chapter 4

The Retreat Continues

27 August, Thursday

The night march from Beaurevoir to Hargicourt was one of the worst of the retreat. II Corps had been in action with little opportunity for the men to eat or sleep for four days and now, cold, hungry and exhausted, they stumbled and staggered in the wet darkness along the country roads of northern France pursued by a powerful enemy. Asleep on their feet they bumped into one another, or fell unseen at the roadside, to be woken up in the morning by German cavalry scouring the countryside for stragglers. Exhaustion brought hallucinations and strange sights.

> *St John:* Some time after midnight we again marched and made slow though fairly steady progress till an hour before daybreak when we were given an hours halt. This time I made no bones about it but lay down on the wet grass by the roadside and, rain or no rain, went right off to sleep. I had been nearly asleep all the time we were marching and had imagined all sorts of weird sights. All the time I thought there was a bright light about a mile in front of us and another about a mile behind. I was also quite certain that on each side of us was a broad sheet of water that followed the road all the way along. Beyond these waterways were more troops both mounted and dismounted.
>
> At daybreak we fell in again. I felt very stiff and tired and was surprised to see no water or other troops and as far as could be seen there was nowhere that could have furnished the bright light referred to. In the growing light the FIFTH[39],

39 It was common practice for officers to refer to regiments by their old number designations. In this case the FIFTH refers to the Northumberland Fusiliers' position of precedence in the list of Infantry of the Line (The 5th Foot)

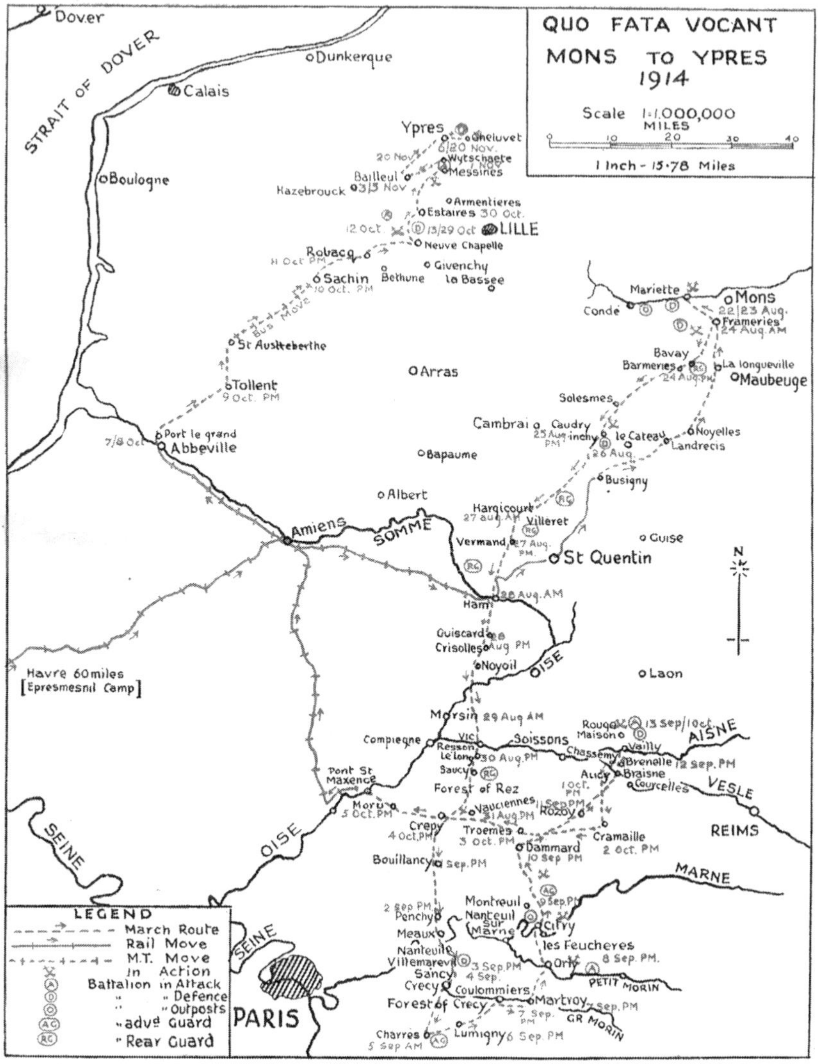

Battalion wanderings Aug.- Nov. 1914

bringing up the rear of the column, stumbled along through the paraphernalia of a retreating army All along the road we saw signs of hurried retreat, overturned motor vehicles, and wagons and dead horses were strewn by the roadside and, although supplies and equipment were scattered along the side of the road, nowhere among this debris was to be seen the rifles or ammunition carried by the exhausted infantry. Numbers of fed-up and exhausted men sat looking desolate

> across the banks of the road, no longer caring about the pursuing Germans. This was not to happen in the ranks of the FIFTH. March discipline was maintained by the unfailing efforts of the officers and N.C.O.s, urging and persuading their men on and when needs be, kicking them and pulling them up, to continue the march when they sank to the ground exhausted.
>
> The sight of these men by the roadside made our men wonder why they were foot slogging along instead of sitting down on a nice bank. They all of a sudden seemed to become exhausted and unable to keep up and for the next couple of days my life became a burden to me as I was all the time urging, persuading and even kicking men on. It was no good explaining to them that they had no choice but to go on or else fall into the hands of the Germans. They simply did not believe me. Another evil that we had to contend with was the kindness of the inhabitants of the villages through which we passed. They all did what they could for the men in the way of offering them fruit and the men used to have regular sort of free fights for it. This all tended to check the pace of the column which was stretching along the road for ten or twelve miles. Here again the mere issuing and reiterating of orders was of no avail and I was continually using physical force to get the men back into the ranks. I felt for the men too, for we had the misfortune to always march behind a badly disciplined regiment whose men appeared to be allowed to straggle to their hearts content. The sight of these men filling every village, wolfing everything to be got, while ours had to march along in proper formation must have been highly galling to our wild north country pitmen reservists who really, on the whole, behaved very well indeed.

At 9 am they reached the village of Villeret where a halt was called for the rest of the morning.

Immediately after the battle von Kluck seemed to have dismissed the BEF from his strategic thinking. He believed that II Corps was retreating north-west towards Calais where it would, in all probability, be picked up and taken back to England out of the way. On the other hand there were confused and conflicting reports from his cavalry patrols of scattered groups of British and French infantry stranded in the villages, and along the roads, over a wide area between Le Câteau and St Quentin. This did not unduly concern him for he took the evidence of the large number of prisoners, and a countryside littered with abandoned transport and equipment, to indicate that the British Army was a spent force retreating in disarray. But just to make sure, and 'hussle' them along, he sent out, at dawn on the 27th, strong fighting patrols of cavalry, supported by Jägers and horse artillery. In the late morning one of these patrols found the cavalry screen covering the retreat of the 3rd Division and as the cavalry were outnumbered they fell back on the 9th Infantry Brigade resting around Villeret. Exaggerated reports of the strength of the enemy had already filtered back to 3rd Divisional HQ who, fearing that they were the advance scouts of von Kluck's Army, ordered the Division to be roused from its rest and continue its retreat with all speed.

> *Lieut. Watkins.* About noon Germans reported advancing. Ordered to fall in and 9th Infantry Brigade to do rearguard. The farm where we were was very small and a good mark for artillery so the Commanding Officer took the Battalion out into a turnip field. I went with the limber, but the ground was very heavy, and horses could hardly pull limber. As we expected an action on this heavy ground decided to leave rear portion of limber with cracked wheel behind and put guns and ammunition boxes, etc., in front portion throwing out of the front kit to make room for the guns etc. Had to throw three rifles, some ammunition, packs and own great-coat. Saw in the far distant to north-west a large column of cavalry, which at first we thought were Germans, but afterwards were believed to be our own cavalry Division, or French, probably the latter. We retired about a mile with our cavalry patrols who had had a small scrap with German cavalry. We took up a position to cover the retirement of cavalry who came through us. Found the Germans were coming on our right flank but did not advance towards us, entrenching themselves with two guns and about 300 men (probably brought up by motor lorries) about 1,500 yards from us. We retired without firing, and got to Vermand about 7 p.m., where we were told we were to have four hours' rest.

St John. We plodded through a hot morning always within earshot of gunfire behind us and at mid-day were halted for two hours in a farmyard. This was with the idea of letting us cook and eat a meal but we had no rations to prepare. However we were glad of the rest and there was a fine well so we got a good drink and were able to wash a bit. We fell in at the appointed hour but told that we were to let the rest of the army through and again act as rearguard so we fell out again. Before the column had passed through shells began to burst around and about us, as rearguard we closed up and made a demonstration away from the road in conjunction with our Divisional cavalry, which had the desired effect and the shelling ceased. When the column had gone through the village we fell back and took up a commanding position about a mile behind and on the other side of the road. While lying here we saw some German artillery trot leisurely into the plain at the foot of our hill and, just as leisurely proceed to unlimber. They were too far away for any fire from us to touch them and we could not get close enough to them without exposing ourselves in the open. Here we longed for a gun as they did not take any trouble to get their horses under cover, but most of our very meagre artillery had been knocked out at Frameries and Le Câteau and the Divisional Commander[40] was not risking any of the precious remainder in a minor rearguard action. The German gunners lolled around for a time and, as no enemy soldiers presented themselves as a target, they fired incendiary shells into all the farms within range. Very fine farmsteads they were too, some of them being in fact quite small chateau and it made us furious to see them so wantonly burned. We hung on in this place for about an hour and a half and then carried on the retirement in open order. At one place I had to take up a position behind a wall which formed one of the boundaries of a large paddock in which were two old horses and an ancient cow. In order to facilitate a retreat if necessary I had the gate at the far corner opened. Shortly afterwards I noticed that this gate was shut and found on examining it that it was padlocked. I looked about and saw the farmer

40 Major-General Hubert Hamilton.

> walking away and called him to come and open it!. He came but refused to open it on account of the horses. However the sight of my revolver that I drew with the intention of blowing in the lock made him change his mind in a hurry and he unlocked it. To make it quite safe I got some men and we removed the gate altogether.
>
> We were not long in this position and when we had gone back another half mile or so we formed up on the road and marched along in close order until a mile or so further on we came upon the rest of the Battn. halted by the roadside. We waited here to let the cavalry occupy a ridge some distance away on our right. While waiting, the Colonel, who was on his horse behind the Battn. suddenly called out " Retire double ". The ensuing panic showed how jumpy everyone was. I myself thought for a moment that the enemy were on top of us. However we rushed to our men and got them in order again and I found out that the Colonel's horse while grazing by the roadside had shoved his nose or foot into a nest of hornets and the Colonel was afraid that the brutes would attack the men who were rather close to them. We saw a lot of these hornets but I did not hear of any casualties resulting from them.

In the last 24 hours the 3rd Division had retreated a further 30 miles and during this time the 1/Northumberlands had acted as the rearguard imposing a severe additional strain on already exhausted men[41]. There was also the question of supplies, or more accurately, the lack of them. Not knowing the precise line of the retreat the Army Service Corps were dumping rations at cross roads ahead of the troops

41 As rearguard they detached two Companies from the battalion to form a screen along both sides of the road protecting the retreating Divisional column, some fourteen miles long. In turn these two companies left parties of riflemen at every crossroads and hilltop guarding the flanks and rear, until the retreating column was out of sight. Then these isolated parties, starting with the furthest away, fell back by alternate and successive retirements to join the rest of the battalion, only to start the process all over again with the other two Companies. As a result of these manoeuvres the rearguards covered much more ground than the troops marching in the main column and had much less rest. After a few hours of this work the nerves of the officers and NCOs controlling the rearguard were stretched to the limit, with tempers very short, as they fought off the exhaustion that came from the continual effort needed to keep the rearguard parties awake and on the move.

so, as the battalions passed by, they could pick up what they required. This worked well for the troops at the head of the columns but by the time the rearguards reached these collection points the rations had vanished. The problem was more acute for the 3rd Division, whose re-supply column missed it on the road and they were without rations from the 25th to the afternoon of the 27th, when rations were issued at Vermand. It was worse still for the 1/Lincolns, They had replaced the 1/Northumberlands as rearguards on the afternoon of the 27th and came in too late to pick anything up at Vermand and did not catch up with their supplies until after 6.30 pm on the 28th. Some supplies could be bought from the farms and villages but the halts were never long enough for the men to cook the chickens, never mind the sheep, bought by the officers to feed them. Even in retreat discipline was enforced and free enterprise, in the form of looting or "scrounging" was forbidden and treated as a serious offence, even though anything left behind would be swept up and used to sustain the enemy who were rapidly outdistancing their own supply columns.

> *St John.* As soon as the mounted troops had covered the ridge we went on again and after a few miles march we passed through a line of outposts. The sight of the Scotsmen furnishing the outpost troops digging themselves in gladdened our hearts for it looked like a night in bed. This however was not to be. Our commissariat department had commandeered four or five sheep by the wayside and these were now killed and made a meal of them for the men with a very small ration of bread and biscuit. Having seen the men supplied we officers departed on a foraging expedition of our own. Several hundreds of officers seemed to be on the same track but dear wily old Toppin had as usual got the weather side of them and had found a nice little cottage where we were provided with an excellent meal of roast duck and omelette and some bottles of wine. Neither had he forgotten our past scarcity of provisions and when we rode away there was a bottle of cherry brandy in each holster while the weight of a couple of ducks slung on one side of his saddle was balanced on the other by a goose! After our meal we went back and lay down in the street for an hour or two and got some sleep.

Friday 28th August

St John. At mid-night again we fell in as ordered but it was an hour and a half before we got away from the town. During one of those weary halts when one did not know if one would go on the next minute or not there was nearly a panic owing to a gun or wagon team behind stampeding in a narrow street. At once the report flew up the column that the enemy's cavalry were charging us and it is significant of the state of our nerves that no one doubted the report for a moment. I was greatly relieved when we got out of the streets and into the open country where one had some chance if attacked. We marched till daybreak when we had an hours halt and I got a little more sleep. I had several times gone to sleep while marching and found myself in the ditch. I gave up trying to drive the men back to the ranks when they fell out, they knew what was in store for them as well as I did and I knew the agony they must be suffering from their feet many of them having raw heels and toes from the hard marching we had done. Not many gave in absolutely, some would fall out, but at the next halt would come limping in again. We felt a bit better after our halt. The pace to begin with had been killing. I don't know who was to blame for this but Gott Strafe him whoever he was. Soon after restarting we came to a paved roadway along which we painfully hobbled. I can't call it anything else. I don't suppose we were doing two miles an hour. I myself was suffering from an abscess on my toe that felt like hot knives at every step. Toppin lent me his horse now again, which relieved things a bit, but at last I could stand it no longer. As our doctor had been killed at Frameries I took over my own case and removed the offending abscess with my pocket knife and felt much relieved after doing so. We were told that our destination was Ham.

While waiting outside Ham the incident of the horse occurred. At Le Câteau or Frameries I forget which, the company cob had become a casualty but the Coy groom, with memories of South Africa Mounted Infantry service still fresh in his mind, had annexed the mount of a gunner trumpeter which he stated was without an owner and running loose. As we passed along a column of transport

> and artillery halted by the roadside Toppin had observed some sleepy gunner become suddenly wide awake and very interested in his mount. Toppin had at once crossed to the near side of the column and, dismounting had covered the harness and as much as possible of the horse with rugs and coats but it was no good. A short time after we halted a Major of the RFA strolled up and identified the animal and we had to hand it over. However the Major was very good about it and produced a much more comfortable cob which his trumpeter had annexed from a farm house and handed the animal with a plain saddle and bridle over to Toppin.
>
> There was big block on the road crossing the narrow bridge over the Somme and as we were likely to be held up for some time we were told off to prepare defence works. The lot of the Battalion was a cemetery, which we put in a state of defence. My Coy on this occasion being in reserve we decided to cook our goose. We also bought a ration of chickens and some rabbits for the men. Before we got the grub properly cooked however we were off again and our goose was wasted though luckily the men got their meal finished in time. I got a little food when we swapped half our goose with the Sergeants for a tin of bully, half a tin of jam and half a biscuit each. As soon as we were over the bridge it was blown up much to our relief as we had heard gun-fire in the distance behind us which sounded to be coming much closer as time went on.

The road to Noyon was practically straight and like most French roads it was lined with tall poplar trees but, rather than offer shade, the trees seemed to trap the heat and dust in a long tunnel and it was now that many men began to fall out due to exhaustion, or with feet so sore and blistered that they could no longer walk or even hobble along. Farm carts were commandeered to carry the most exhausted while others draped themselves over the guns or clung to the carriages and wagons to stagger along as best they could. It was becoming a rag-tail Army. Many battalions had discarded all equipment except rifle and ammunition and men had cut the uppers away from their boots, forming a sort of sandal, in an effort to relieve their blistered feet. Each day the sun shone hot and bright and men who had lost their caps stole, begged or borrowed hats and caps, both male and female, from the villages they passed through. When all else failed they covered their heads with giant leaves pulled from the growing crops in the fields along the side of the road and which, tied under their chin with a piece of string, gave them the appearance of a band of Chinese coolies.

The 9th Infantry Brigade reached Crisolles at 4 pm having covered over 60 miles in the last 48 and here they found their transport, complete with rations, so everyone had a good meal before settling down in the corner of a large field.

> *St John.* At Crisolles I was able to buy two pairs of socks and after a sumptuous repast Toppin and I turned into real and comfortable beds. I threw the old ones which were ------, but never mind what they were! Suffice to say that I threw them gladly out of a window and that they fell on to a soldier sleeping in the garden, who if rumour is truth, never recovered consciousness again.

29 August, Saturday

It was hoped that by putting the river Somme between II Corps and the enemy a day's rest would be possible so this Saturday started off as a rest day with the officers and men spending the morning trying to clean themselves and their weapons as best they could. As the transport had been sent southwards they were left to do their own cooking and, as the mid – day meal was being prepared, the sound of artillery indicated that the enemy had again came into contact with the cavalry screen. Orders were issued for the 3rd Division to pack up and continue the retreat while the 9th Brigade was ordered to hold the enemy off until the Division was across the river Oise.

When Captain St John and the Colonel arrived at the place where the 1/Northumberlands were to entrench they found that, in the haste and confusion, the 7th Infantry Brigade, who were to replace them as rearguard that evening, had already detailed some of their troops for rearguard duties and these were already entrenching. Not wishing to dampen their enthusiasm they quietly withdrew and the battalion settled down for an afternoon's rest until the evening when they fell back through the 7th Brigade, who by now had officially taken up their duties. They crossed the Oise at 10.30 pm.

> *St John.* Next day the Battn was detailed to furnish outposts and I was sent to guard a certain road. As it was rather

an important spot the Colonel came with me to see if the two platoons I had with me were enough. We attempted a short cut to the place and got into a spinney with thick undergrowth through the middle of which ran quite a deep, though not very wide, stream. We could not see any sign of the bridge and were prepared to wade, a performance I regarded with anything but delight, when my eye caught a depression in the undergrowth that looked like a track, which moreover led us to a small footbridge over which we crossed dry shod. We reconnoitred the position and decided what to do with it when I saw troops about half a mile out beyond us. We at once thought they were Germans but on bringing our glasses to bear upon them we saw they wore kilts, which reassured us. We found out they were a Company from another Brigade also sent out to furnish outposts at the same spot. We decided magnanimously to allow them to do the work and were just starting back when another Company from yet another Brigade appeared on the same errand approaching us in battle order under the impression that we were Germans. We left the two new comers to make up their own minds what to do and took our departure to join up with the Battn in a nice wood where I lay for the rest of the day in peace.

. At about 5 o'clock the outposts were attacked by some mounted Huns with a couple of Horse artillery guns. I do not think they were anything but a strong patrol for our fire drove them off with very little difficulty. At dusk we were told that the column had safely crossed the Oise at Noyon and that we were to follow on leaving the Lincolnshire Regt. to block the road after we had gone through. We marched away and at about midnight crossed the Oise, all the bridges being blown up as soon as we were over. We hoped we would get some rest then, but no, we plodded all through the night except for one long block on the road when the Colonel produced some soup squares and we got a small fire going. I got two delicious mouthfuls of hot soup that the keen night air made very acceptable.

GHQ had decided that the enemy's presence meant that von Kluck had regained contact and, wishing to put as much distance between themselves and the *First Army* ordered the B.E.F. to march from the Oise to the other side of the Aisne, a march that would take over twenty-four hours. Under a blazing sun the long lines of troops, transport, and artillery marched through some of the most attractive countryside in France, as yet untouched by war, but it is doubtful if the exhausted troops even noticed the ripe corn; the orchards groaning with fruit; or the attractive villages situated in lush valleys or clinging to the sides of the hills. Increasingly footsore more men dropped out to be picked up by the wagons, or continued to hobble along in the long line of stragglers trailing for several miles behind the main marching columns. At about 6 pm on the 30th the 9th Infantry Brigade crossed the Aisne at Vic-sur-Aisne and an hour later, having been marching with short breaks for almost twenty-four hours, the 1/Northumberlands found billets at Resson Le Long. These turned out to be the best they had ever seen.

30 August, Sunday

> *St John* We moved onto the village of Cuts where we were to cook breakfast. Very little time was allowed and I spent most of it urging the men to get to work and get fires going. We just managed to get them all a hot drink and a bite of food but it was a tiresome job getting them to take the trouble to use the opportunities given to them. An hour after Sun-up we were on the move again and marched along lanes and by roads till noon when we were given a long halt and to our joy provided with some rations while Toppin rode on and found a little shop where he got some potted meats and delicacies of that sort. While we were halted we were officially informed that the situation was considerable relieved and that the need for all the strenuous marching which we had experienced was gone and we should be able to take things easier in the future. This cheered us up a lot.
>
> After resting we again fell in and continued our march expecting every few minutes to reach our billets. Hour succeeded hour however and it was nearly 7 before we reached the Aisne at Vic-sur Aisne. As we crossed the bridge I asked a staff officer how far it was to our billets. " Just up the road and round the corner to the left " was his reply. We plodded on for about another two miles and found our billets were a lovely big Chateau with room for the entire Battn in

the large outhouses and we had visions of great comfort for the officers, lots of good food and wine too. Alas it was not to be. To our great wrath and indignation we were told that the arrangement for billets had been changed and that the Divisional staff had taken over our nice chateau. Apparently some staff officer motoring around had spotted the chateau and had obtained leave to appropriate it for the staff in place of the hotel in which they were quartered in the town. What was more galling to us was the fact that we could not take the hotel as it was out of our brigade area, but had to trudge on over another two miles to the top of a high hill which was the far extremity of our area When we got to the top of the hill we had to search for billets in the dark. Finally we found a small chateau that could take nearly all the Battn and which could provide a bed for each officer which was a joy. The owners were arranging it as a hospital and they gave us an excellent dinner with champagne and cigars galore.

31 August, Monday

St John. Next day we made a quiet and uneventful march only doing about 15 miles. The Brigade was finding the rearguard as usual but we were not called upon to do anything but march along. I began to have a weakness of my innards on this day but was not very seriously inconvenienced thereby though I did not feel as fit and well as I had felt so far. We passed through Villers Cottérêts where we were able to buy some bread and were billeted that night in a sugar factory at Vauciennes. Just before we were arriving at our billet we noticed a lot of men were suddenly overcome with the heat and fatigue. We also noticed that we had just passed an estaminet. I went up to one poor man who had fallen out and was lying by the roadside apparently in extremes with his cap over his face and on lifting his cap was met by a very bright and hopeful eye and a most healthy and hearty countenance, the property of one of the biggest scoundrels in the Battn. I said nothing to him but passed on knowing that Toppin with the provost party were waiting round the corner behind us with a view to raiding the estaminet when the Battn. had passed along to its billet. The raid was a most

> successful yielding some 20 or 30 exhausted ones including my bright-eyed corpse.

It was now possible to reduce the length of the daily marches and for the first time in five days the cooks could provide regular meals and for most nights the men billeted in cottages and farm buildings. Lost equipment was beginning to be replaced, but with the priority given to weapons, ammunition and other front line stores it would be well into autumn before many were re-equipped with greatcoats and other personal items lost during the retreat.

Chapter 5

The Battle of the Marne and the Advance to the Aisne

The General Situation

By the beginning of September five of the German Armies; the Crown Prince's *Fifth Army*; the Duke of Wurtemberg's *Fourth Army*; and von Hausen's *Third Army*; von Bülow's *Second Army* and von Kluck's *First Army* had forced the French back from the Frontier and by were driving them south-west towards a gap, just over a hundred miles wide, between Paris and the River Meuse where the German High Command had hopes of manoeuvring the French into a position where they would could become entrapped and encircled by the *First* and *Second* Armies.

Almost too late Joffre realised the enormity of the crises facing the French Armies and the immense problems associated with developing a solution. Not only did he have to find a way to stop the retreat and stabilise his front, but at the same time he needed to develop strength, if not numerical superiority, on his left flank to prevent envelopment by the *First* and *Second Armies.*

His response to the crises was to issue on 25th August his Second General Order informing the Army Commanders that: "further operations would be carried out with a view to forming a *mass of manoeuvre* on the left flank to carry out an offensive". To do this he proposed to create two new armies, the Sixth and Ninth, by bring together all the troops not actually needed to slow the enemy advance and these, together with the Fifth Army and BEF, would form his 'mass of manoeuvre' to be used to renew the Allied offensive against the Germans. To give himself time he ordered his commanders to 'arrest, or at least delay, the advance of the enemy by short and violent counterattacks'. This translated at the regimental level into a simple instruction 'Fight in Retreat', which they did with almost suicidal bravery.

The British almost miss the Battle

The most important element in this new strategy was to build up the Sixth Army, under the command of General Maunoury and it was partly to give Maunoury time that Joffre ordered Lanrezac to counterattack at Guise on the 29th August. Here Lanrezac held the *First Army* at St Quentin and drove the leading Divisions of the *Second Army* back across the river Oise but with the ever present danger of being outflanked he was forced to break off the action and continue his retreat on the 30th.

If the new Sixth Army was one of Joffre's successes in late August, then the BEF was almost one of his failures. Ever since Le Câteau the morale of the GHQ staff, and that of Sir John French in particular, was increasingly pessimistic about the chances of an Allied success. Sir John was acutely aware that he commanded most of the trained troops immediately available to Britain and his orders not to expose them to unnecessary danger made him almost paranoid about Joffre's plans in case his Army was drawn into some mad French scheme that would spell its end.

On the afternoon of 29th Joffre visited Sir John to discuss British cooperation in his plans but after an hour or so of fruitless discussion he got no clear commitment and left in a bad humour. Worst was to follow.

Soon after Joffre had departed Sir John French received an inaccurate report that Lanrezac had been defeated at Guise and was retreating across the Oise. Always ready to assume the worst as far as Lanrezac was concerned, Sir John immediately issued orders for his army to continue its retreat on the 30th. A little later when GHQ received an accurate account of Lanrezac's success Sir John refused to rescind this order, inflicting an unnecessary gruelling twenty-four hour march on his exhausted army and in the process breaking contact with the French Fifth Army.

It was clear that GHQ was loosing its nerve. On the 30th Sir John telegraphed Joffre informing him of his intention to retreat beyond Paris and to move his main base from Havre to St Nazaire and would therefore be unable to take part in his planned offensive. Presented with such an ultimatum Joffre could only reluctantly agree but stipulated that the BEF must retreat east of Paris so as not to interfere with the lines of communication of the Sixth Army. This would also ensure that the BEF continued to fill the gap between the French Fifth and Sixth Armies for a few days longer.

Rumours of Sir John's intentions spread to London where they disturbed the tranquillity of Lord Kitchener, who sent an urgent telegram requesting clarification. He was even more disturbed when he received the reply. Sir John stated that it was unsafe to keep the Army in the front line as the French around him were in continual retreat and this increased the risk of the BEF being attacked by a superior enemy. He also stated that the BEF had suffered very high casualties since arriving in France, (GHQ consistently overestimated the number of casualties), and proposed to pull his Army back behind the Seine to rest, refit and be reinforced before rejoining the battle. For good measure he stated bluntly that he had no confidence in the French High Command and doubted its ability to mount a major counter-stroke of the type proposed by Joffre.

Sir John's opinions, both in the strategy to be adopted in dealing with the German invasion, and his attitude to liaison with his French allies, were as equally unacceptable to Lord Kitchener as they were to General Joffre and in was agreed that pressure would have to be brought to bear on Sir John French to strengthen his resolve.

On the 31st Joffre renewed his appeal for cooperation; on the same day Sir John received a telegram from Kitchener expressing the Government's surprise at his decision to withdraw from the battlefield and urged him to reconsider and participate in the French plans; even the French President, through the British Ambassador, urged him to cooperate and 'fill the gap'. However Sir John was both adamant and stubborn and would do nothing until his Army had been refitted and reinforced.

This was too much for Kitchener who made immediate arrangements to met Sir John at the British Embassy in Paris where he set the tone of the meeting by turning up in his Field Marshall's uniform sending the unmistakable signal that he was not only Sir John's political "boss" but, as the most senior Officer in the Army, outranked him. When the discussion that followed became heated Kitchener suggested that they retire to another room and continue in private. No one knows what was said behind those closed doors but when they returned a very subdued Sir John French agreed to remain in the battle and cooperate with Joffre.

Von Kluck searches for a German Solution

While the Allies squabbled von Kluck, increasingly aware that time was running out and the German offensive was falling behind schedule drove his soldiers ever harder. He ordered them to sleep along the sides of the roads in their columns of Route each night rather than assembling by regiment to bivouac or go into billets. This gained him an extra 5-10 kilometres a day, but such measures only served to increase the strain on his men, many of whom had been marching and fighting since 4th August. Signs of exhaustion and lowered morale were commonplace and it would appear that they could only continue the daily schedule of punishing marches when fuelled by large amounts of alcohol and, as they passed through the French countryside, they ravaged it. A diary found on the body of a German officer killed on the Marne recorded;

> " *They drink to excess but this drunkenness keeps them going. Today after inspection the General was furious. He wanted to stop this general drunkenness but we managed to dissuade him from giving too severe orders. If we used too much severity the Army would not march. Abnormal stimulants are necessary to combat abnormal fatigue*".

By the end of August the German invaders also had a serious manpower crises. The *First, Second* and *Third* Armies had started the campaign with 17 Army Corps but by the 6th September this had been reduced to12, representing a decrease of 225,000 troops. In the last thirty-two days they had marched most days and fought major engagements with the Belgium, French and British armies resulting in higher than expected casualties. Now with every mile they advanced across Northern France they were losing fighting effectiveness. Reinforcements were urgently needed; not only to replace battle casualties and the sick, but the two Corps dispatched to the Eastern front to counter the unexpected Russian advance; the Corps left in Belgium to cover the Belgium Army holed up in Antwerp; the Brigade left to garrison Brussels; and the troops required to invest Maubeuge. Men were also required to garrison captured French towns and protect the roads and railways on their increasing vulnerable lines of communication. The list was endless and, as the crises approached, the German armies needed reinforcements desperately and as these were not available von Kluck offered a tactical solution.

In his view the major opposition left was the French Fifth Army which. although in retreat, had shown at Guise that it was still a force to be reckoned with. After this battle it had retreated in a south-westerly direction keeping in contact with the BEF and as these two armies approached Paris German air reconnaissance reported that the French/ British line did not extend as far west as had been expected and would pass north-east of the City, keeping well clear of it's outer defences.

Von Kluck seized upon this observation as an opportunity for a bold commander to bring the war to a swift conclusion for he immediately saw that if he swung his Army northwards towards Paris there was just sufficient room for him to squeeze between the city's outer defences and the French Fifth Army. He could then swing north-east to trap the French against the *Second Army* and create the opportunity to crush the other French Armies as in a vice.

Von Kluck was no fool and was well aware that such a move would expose his flank to the possibility of an attack by the Paris garrison and Maunoury's Sixth Army who were falling back on Paris but he assessed the threats to his army and concluded that the gamble would pay off if he moved quickly.

The final factor that confirmed von Kluck in his decision to change direction was a message from von Bülow at 6.30 pm on the 30th requesting his help to exploit the outcome of the Battle of Guise by turning his *First Army* south-east to assist in the annihilation of the French Fifth Army. To have his nominal superior, and professional rival, request that he moved his Army eastwards appeared to support his own analysis that a decisive victory could be achieved by sweeping north of Paris rather than south of the city. Leaving the *IVth Reserve Corps* to protect his flank against any ill judged attacks from the Paris garrison, he issued orders to change direction.

1 September, Tuesday

> *St John.* I spent that night in an empty garage on a heap of straw and early next morning we had to take up a position to cover the retirement of the Division which went right through us. We stuck on there for 8 or 10 hours and we heard heavy fighting going on to the west of us all the time but did not see much ourselves[42]. We had to get back through a big wood which was slow work and very alarming work too and it was not until about 9 that night that we reached our billets. I slept that night in a very dirty cottage and was feeling very seedy as I had so felt all day. The inhabitants had almost entirely deserted the village and we could get no food other than the rations we had with us.

42 Probably the attack on I Corps's rearguards at Villers Cottérêts.

2 September, Wednesday

St John. Next morning we made our usual early start and got off for a wonder very nearly at the hour named. As a rule we would be ready to march at 4 a.m. but not move till 6.0 but this morning we got away quite soon as we were leading the column. The result was that many of the men had not been able to fill their water bottles, as there was only one pump in the village. We did not march very far, for about 12 miles and halted in a village about a mile north of Meaux which we reached early in the afternoon. During this march we came upon a company, or what looked like a company, of Gordons all strung out as an advance guard. We asked them where the rest of their Battn was, and we were told that they were all that was left of an entire Battn. I felt rotten all that day and could hardly get along at all. The heat was intense and my complaint very troublesome. I at once secured a bed and turned in but as we had so much time the Colonel took the opportunity to tell off malefactors. As I was evidence against several culprits I had to turn out again and attend. We got a good dinner that night, a real five course one, but I was not feeling inclined for food at all.

3 September, Thursday

Once across the river Marne, the BEF moved slightly south-eastwards to avoid becoming mixed up with the outer perimeter of the Paris defences and in doing so regained contact with the French Fifth Army under its new commander General Franchet d'Esperey[43].

St John. Our Battn. told off to furnish day and night outposts. Putting these out took most of the rest of the day and I must have covered a good many miles visiting the various sentry groups. Our cavalry patrols came through with the information to the effect that the enemy had crossed the Marne and that we might expect to be exterminated at any moment and that they could not get in touch with the column on our right and also intimated that they had no intention of doing anything else but get behind us as soon as they could. The prospect was

43 Joffre removed Lanrezac as commander of the 5th Army on 3rd September.

> not alluring but I did not think it was as bad as the horsemen made it out to be. I sent a man or two on bicycles to find our right which they soon did and my own patrols saw nothing of any Germans. My wretched disease kept me awake nearly all night otherwise the night passed without incident.

During the retreat mistakes had often been made in distinguishing between 'B' and 'D' companies when verbal orders were issued and to prevent this happening in the future the Colonel renamed the companies W, X, Y and Z.

4 September, Friday

> *St John.* I got a dish of hot bacon and potatoes cooked in the field and lay down on a corn stook as soon as I could. At 10 p.m. we were aroused and, leaving our campfires burning we started our last trek south. All that night we marched steadily through sleeping towns, over rivers, through forests and vineyards all looking very ghostly in the moonlight. We covered about 28 miles and then halted in a village called Chatres about 15 miles S.E. of Paris. We were very crowded here for billeting space but Toppin found room for us in the priest's house where I got the priest's bed and turned in.

5 September, Saturday

At Chatres the battalion welcomed their first reinforcements in the shape of Lieutenant H. C. Stephen and a hundred men. Amid great excitement orders were issued stopping the retreat and directing next day's advance eastwards towards the enemy. Captain St John gave into his increasingly severe attacks of dysentery and reported sick. [44]

---

44 It is difficult to determine now many men were evacuated sick during the as the names of the sick were not recorded in the War Diaries, as are battle casualties. It had been estimated thatt during the retreat eacheach infantry brigade was evacuateding up to a 100hundred men a day through sickness or about 25twenty five men per battalion so a battalion could have could have lost up to a quarter of its fighting strength through sickness alone before the retreat was finished. IThere is no doubt that, in addition to blisters and other injuries to the feet inflicted by long marches in ill fitting boots, many men also suffered from the excessive heat leading to cases of heat stroke and stomach troubles by eating half ripe fruit and drinkingother produce when their rations failed. There was also poor quality drinking water obtained from streams, wells and even ditches, all polluted by the effluent from local farms and by an army with tens of thousands of horses and men to water every day.

> *St John.* I got a few hours fevered sleep filled with fearsome dreams of defeat and catastrophe and when I awoke I felt so bad that I went and found our doctor who told me that my temperature was nearly 104 and took me away to the field ambulance. Here I was doped and put to bed on a stretcher under a hay rick.

6 September, Sunday

The French counter-attack, known as the Battle of the Marne, took place along the whole western front, from the outskirts of Paris to Verdun. East of Paris Joffre had assembled a hammer blow of 41 Infantry Divisions and eight Cavalry Divisions to smash the *First and Second Armies*, whose combined strength was 23 Infantry Divisions and five cavalry Divisions. The offensive was planned to start on the 6th, but the day before Maunoury's Sixth Army had unexpectedly ran into the *IV Reserve Corps* protecting von Kluck's flank along the River Ourcq. At first taken by surprise the French recovered and by the end of the afternoon German resistance began to crumble. Maunoury renewed his attacks the next day and, sensing the danger to his right flank, von Kluck started to move the bulk of his Army westwards but in doing so created a gap of over thirty miles between himself and the *Second Army*. The BEF, protecting Maunoury's right flank, would advance into the gap and as a consequence not encounter any serious fighting until they reached the river Aisne.

> *St John.* Next morning I was put in a wagon with a bundle of straw to lie upon and told I should stop there till there was a chance of sending me down to the base hospital. I lay in the transport park which was about 5 miles south all day. Fortunately we were parked near our own wagons and I got my own kit and had a wash and shave (the first for a fortnight). While lying in the park a Taube flew over us and dropped three bombs but its aim was bad and no harm was done.

> *Lieut. Watkins.* Marched 6 a.m. and did advanced guard; arrived about one mile outside Lumigny, and remained there about two hours, expecting an engagement which never came. During this halt, we watered the horses and filled the men's water bottles. After two hours we were sent

back to billets in Lumigny. Battalion Headquarters was in a very small cottage, not yet deserted. Two companies were billeted in the school. Got the woman to stew rabbit and had quite a good dinner, with wine procured in the village. Also got some dubbin and tobacco, the former very much needed. It was decided that the front platoon of the leading company was the only one to fire at aeroplanes under the direct orders of the Colonel.

7 September, Monday

St John. That night we shifted north and after being jolted about all night I found I was back with my Battn. again. I asked if I could not rejoin them as I felt better but I was told not. I walked over to see them in the morning but felt so weak that I quite realised that the doctor was right. At about mid-day I was told that a motor convoy was just going to the railhead and so I said good-by and departed. I did not think that I should never again see so many good pals Toppin, Matthews, Beachamp Selby, Dick Gatehouse, Boyd were all dead before the week was out. My feelings at that moment were very mixed indeed. For one thing I hated to leave the regiment. I felt that we had had our worst time and that things were looking up a bit. I also felt rather a renegade to be going to the base. On the other hand I had undoubtedly had enough for the time being and I was moreover still very seedy. On the whole I must own that the feeling of relief at the prospect of a spell of rest and comfort in safety outweighed the regrets I felt on departing and it was by no means a heavy heart, which I carried to the motor transport convoy. I collected my belongings from the horsed wagon and found a place on a motor lorry. We were soon started off on our journey to the railhead. I have never experienced a dustier motor ride in my life. I sat in the front seat and there was no windscreen and we were about the twelfth lorry in the convoy of fourteen and going about 15 to 20 miles an hour on dusty roads. I was like a snow man when we finally reached the station. Here we learnt that a hospital train had just departed about a quarter of an hour before and there would not likely be another till next afternoon.

Other convoys came bringing each it's offering of sick and slightly wounded and we soon collected quite a party. They were a heterogeneous crowed and at first I seemed to be the only officer. I went up the station platform to try and find somewhere to lay out my bed for the night so as to get cover from the weather which looked like rain. It was then that I discovered several other officers. At least every available space was occupied by an officer; or his valise; so wandered out again. As luck would have it I came across an ordnance officer whom I knew. From him I learnt there was an empty ordnance train returning some time that night to Le Mans which was where the Rail Transport Officer had told me I was to be sent. I went and found the train and made friends with the officer commanding it and ensconced myself with my valise in a 1st Class carriage. As I had been told that the train was not going to start for 3 or 4 hours I got out and went in search of food.

I was met by a deputation of men from all sorts of Corps who seemed to like my face and who begged me to get them some food. I agreed to do what I could for them and ordering all but four to stay where they were I set out with them and again found my friend of the ordnance corps. He was no use in the way of providing me with food but showed me where food was, in another siding, and pointed out the supply office to me.

His refusal to supply us was curt but then he was somewhat young in years and full of importance, his rank being a 2nd Lieutenant. I was about to argue the point with him but spotted the arrival of a supply staff colonel to whom I hastened. He was most genial and said that the supply office would give me anything I wanted which was there to be given. I explained that my personal application to the Supply officer had not met with success and suggested that perhaps his written order would be necessary. " Not at all," he replied. " he is here to supply the fighting units with food when and where it is required and its issue is feasible". I again approached the young gentlemen and proffered my request to be supplied with food for myself and men and was again refused curtly so I commanded the lad to accompany me to the staff officer. This he objected to doing but fortunately the appearance on the scene of the staff officer saved me the trouble of placing him in arrest. His demure soon changed and after the harsh words of the Colonel he came out with me to the supply train and produced all the grub I wanted. I selected a side of bacon (best cut), enough bully to last two days and with bread, biscuits, jam, tea, sugar and a jar of rum we returned to my command who honoured me with a cheer. I got them to procure me water to wash in and cook me some bacon and tea which they did and when I was abluted and fed I went to sleep.

While St John was waiting at the railhead the battalion continued its leisurely advance towards the Grand Morin River. They billeted at Martroy where, outside the station, they picked up Lieutenant Platt with 97 other ranks as the 2nd reinforcement.

Lieut. Watkins. Chatres to Le Martroy, 18.6 miles.- Ordered to be ready to march at 7.30 am. Actually marched at 12.30 pm just as the men had decided to cook dinners, which had to be left. The road was very congested, as another division was on a road converging towards Colommiers. About nine o'clock German aeroplane came over, which was fired on, thought to be hit, but did not come down. The road at times was quite blocked with troops and ambulances. Went through Colommiers and saw evidences of Germans hurried retreat, in wagons left behind, many houses had been ransacked, places strewn with bottles and the telegraph wires all cut.

8 September, Tuesday

St John. We started our journey about 8 p.m. The soft cushions and gentle movement of the train was most soothing and I slept like a cartload of birds. When I awoke at 7 a.m. I found we were still in the environs of Paris. Some Red Cross ladies invaded my carriage and were most anxious to dress my wounds. I explained that I was not " blesse " but sick and did not need assistance so they procured me some hot coffee and a tin containing five acid drops and a packet of chocolate.

At the next stop I got out and found several of the other officers I had left at the railhead. These had joined my train at the last moment and had spent the night most uncomfortably in a closed truck without straw. I brought them along to the 1st class carriage and we proceeded on our journey once more. All day we bumped and shunted and stopped and bumped along again until about 6 in the evening we stopped just outside Le Mans. We thought our journey was over but we sat there for over two hours before we again moved and were finally brought to a standstill with a giant bump in Le Mans station itself.

I got hold of the RAMC people and after some delay and doubtful consultation was sent in an ambulance up to the hospital in the Bishop's Palace. At first they wanted to send me to a rest camp but to this I strongly objected. It was raining and dark and I was tired and cross and did not fancy finding my way to a wet camp alone. The hospital was no means the home from home that my imagination pictured it. This was no fault of the R.A.M.C. officials nor any one to do with it at all. They, poor things, owing to the rapidity of the German advance and the allied retreat had been obliged to leave their original hospital at Rouen and shift hurriedly south to Le Mans. I pictured myself abed with soft sheets and, joy of joys, a bath hot and if possible deep but at any rate hot and of sufficient size to be taken in a sitting posture. What I found was a good enough bed but with new hard canvas sheets and not only was there no bath but there was no bath at all and no hot water either. True they were putting in a bath as quickly as possible but as far as I was concerned I had to content myself with a bucket of cold water. I got over the sheet trouble by sleeping in my flea bag on top of the bed.

The objective for the 8th was to cross the Petit Morin and advance to the Marne and there establish a bridgehead. The Petit Morin is a small river that flows swiftly between steep wooded banks which makes it a suitable place for a rearguard action so it was no surprise when at dawn the Scots Greys, accompanied by a detachment of the Royal Horse Artillery, approached the bridge at Orly and spotted a strong force of Germans taking breakfast at Gibraltar, a small hamlet on the other side of the river. These they soon dispersed with shrapnel and in the belief that they had chased off the enemy rearguard cantered down to the bridge only to be driven back by a hail of artillery and machine gun fire from the enemy concealed in the woods on the northern bank. They called for support and the 8th Infantry Brigade was ordered forward to secure the crossing. As they had lost all their machine guns they were to be supported by Lieutenant Watkins and his section.

> *Lieut. Watkins.* Marched about 6.30 a.m. Comparatively cool. Heard rumour that the French had hammered the Germans at Monceaux. About 11.30 heard firing fairly close in front, and battalion was taken under cover of a wood, with one other regiment in support. Saw shells bursting on the road about 800 yards in front, and heard that a shell had killed some of the cyclists' section. The Germans were apparently on the other side of the River Petit Morin, and were shelling the road to prevent transport coming along. The shells bursting dead on the road showed usual German accuracy of range. Was called up to see General Shaw, and was told that M.G.'s were wanted badly to get at some German trenches, which could not by reached by guns. A gunner officer had come up to tell them so. Also that the 8th Brigade, who were attacking, had no M.G.'s left, and that the whole line was being hung up by three German maxims. So was told to report myself to Brigadier 8th Brigade.
>
> Guided by gunner officer, I took the M.G.'s round by a path clear of the road, passing some cavalry who could get no further. Found 8th Brigade staff near a small village and reported myself to Brigadier. I was told to go up to the firing line, and see what I could do. I left the limber and my horse in the village, and carried guns. Found the Scots Fusiliers going in single file along a ditch over some open ground which was being shelled by the Germans. I followed them up, and as we were going along the men must have been spotted by the German artillery, as we got a heavy salvo very close, but no casualties. I got into the slope of the valley, and on the road found some supports of the Royal Irish under cover. Found the major, commanding the companies in the firing line on each side of the road, at the edge of the wood with some men of the Middlesex. Saw a gun at the corner of

the road, which the gunners had brought up to try and shell the trenches in the valley. They had got caught by a maxim and had temporarily to abandon the gun.

The Petit Morin River is a small river with high hills on each side. The descent on each side is steep, and the hills are covered with woods and orchards. The main road zig-zags down on each side to the village of Orly. Another road runs parallel to the river, and is lined with poplars. On the east side of the village this road is hidden by small woods, the distance across the valley from top to top is about 2,000 yards. The woods of the southern slopes end about halfway down; on the northern slopes to the west of Orly, come nearly down to the road, and to the east of Orly end a quarter of the way down. The Germans had trenches all the way along the road with poplars, which afforded a good mark. There were also some forward trenches, which were very conspicuous and probably dummies. Some German guns and cavalry were reported to be in the village.

I selected a place for the M.G.'s on the edge of the wood in the firing line of the Royal Irish, and started firing at the trenches under the poplars. It may have been a coincidence, but the German rifle fire seemed to slacken considerably. I was pointed out positively three different places where German machine guns were supposed to be, and plastered these places with bullets, but it did not seem to have much effect, and we never actually located them. In order to get a bigger field of fire, shifted one M.G. about 50 yards from the other one through the wood. We had a good deal of rifle fire and machine gun over us, but I am quite certain they could not see us, and that they were only searching the edge of the wood. A shell nearly destroyed one gun whilst I was with the other one, but think it was only a chance shot. Could see with my glasses Germans moving towards village along the trench, the range being 900 yards, and put frequent bursts of fire at them. My supply of ammunition was well kept up. I had a sporting shot at a limber, which galloped up the road the other side of the valley at 1,350 yards, but did not stop it. Saw Germans trekking into the woods at 1,700 yards, and gave them some reverse fire, which, I think, frightened them, but cannot say if any other effect.

About 3.30 p.m. the Germans started to clear out of the trenches in twos and threes, and they were heavily fired on. About 4 p.m. they were mostly gone. During this period some regiments had been working through the wood on the right flank, and about 4.30 entered Orly. I called up the limber, and was told by our Brigade-Major, whom I met, to come on with the Royal Fusiliers. We went down into Orly and found a good many prisoners, some of them the M.G. detachments of the Garde Corps. I saw the trenches, where the Germans had been, and found one or two dead. The trench was continuous, and the Germans must have slipped away under cover. I met the battalion in the village, and we went to the top of the hill, where the guns were shelling the retiring Germans. We waited there a short time and then trekked about 2½ miles and billeted in the dark at 7 p.m. at the foundry at la Fucheres. The billets were very close, but managed to get butter, milk and wine for Headquarters. Found that we had fired about 3,500 rounds. Guns fired very well, but lost feed block and clearing plug. Had pickets out, but no disturbance, men slept with equipment on, and horses ready harnessed.

9 September, Wednesday

St John. Next morning I was examined by the Medical Officer who said that there was not very much the matter with me as far as he could see and that it was not worth my going down to the base at St. Nazaire.

The 3rd Division reached the Marne two days behind schedule. The Northumberlands were instructed to secure the crossing at Nanteuil but to proceed with caution, as the Brigade was unable to provide artillery support for their attack. In the darkness "W" and "Z", the assault companies, took up their positions in the woods along the top of the valley that overlooked the river. As soon as there was just sufficient light to see each platoon, in steady lines ten yards apart stepped out from the wood and onto the grassy slope and stared down into the abyss. Before them lay over 1000 yards of open slope, stretching to infinity in the pale dawn towards the river, they were without cover, and in full view of any enemy concealed on the northern bank.

They moved steadily down the hill, the only sound the tramp of boots on the damp grass and their own rasped breathing painfully aware that a single traversing machine gun could wipe them from the face of the earth but from the enemy there was nothing; no artillery; no machine guns. At the bottom of the hill the Companies separated, "W" moving on Nanteuil, and "Z" on Citry, a hamlet about half a mile to the southeast unable to believe that they were going to be allowed to reach their objectives unmolested. In the village even the bridge was intact and the excited inhabitants who crowded around them, told of exhausted columns of German infantry, cavalry and artillery passing rapidly through the village and across the river the previous day, not even stopping to loot the houses as they passed.

Once the battalion had crossed the river and passed over the top of the ridge on the northern bank the nature of the countryside changed. They now found themselves in a tangle of small roads and lanes that threaded through woods choked with a dense undergrowth of brambles, bracken and small bushes through which they pushed with difficulty. It was in these woods that Lieutenant Cogan's platoon came to grief. They were in a wood covering the flank of "Z" Company when they pushed out of the undergrowth onto a small rise leading to a clearing. Moving cautiously forward to reconnoitre, Cogan, using his field glasses, could just make out the spiked helmets of a well-concealed machine gun crew across the clearing and although invisible to the naked eye he called forward his best six shots and ordered them to fire at the base of a tree just behind the machine gun. Unfortunately the enemy must have laid their gun on their exact position for no sooner had they opened fire when the enemy retaliated with a single burst which wounded Lieutenant Cogan and all six men.

Casualties, 9th September:
Killed: ***'X' Company*** . 692 Pte Connor.
'Z' Company. 8811 Pte Cawthery, 963 Pte Lucker.

Wounded: ***'X' Company.*** 740 Pte Barron, 1170 Pte Chatfield, 925 Pte Lumerton, 703 Pte Morris.
'Z' Company. 1066 Pte Bestwick, 8707 Pte Lough, 1574 Pte Demain, 1606 Pte Wheeler, 1307 Pte Gandon, 1375 Pte Williams, 9310 L/C Udal
Lieut. C.T.S. Cogan.

10 September, Thursday

Progress was still unsatisfactory. The 5th Division was held up all day in desultory fighting around Montreuil, while further to the west the newly created III Corps[45] had only managed to get small detachments across the Marne. Plans for the BEF to make a vigorous advance on the 10th were thwarted when von Bülow, increasingly worried about the dangers of encirclement by the French, ordered the *First* and *Second Armies* to disengage and retreat behind the river Aisne.

This move took the British by surprise and, believing the enemy were now in full flight, resumed their leisurely pursuit. The 9th Infantry Brigade, for example, made little progress on the 10th. Harassed by irritating sniper fire from the woods the Brigade halted for the best part of the day while the Northumberlands were sent to remove the nuisance. The battalion entered on their task in the spirit of an afternoon shoot on a country estate. Deploying "W" and "X" Companies in line, with "Y" echeloned in the left rear and "Z" in reserve they 'beat' their way through the woods, shooting fixed volleys into the trees and undergrowth at regular intervals, driving the enemy snipers out in front of them. Their "bag" at the end of the day was twelve snipers, killed or captured, without any casualties to themselves.

In the late afternoon, resting at the side of the road after their 'shoot', they were curiously watching a column of enemy prisoners pass when someone shouted out some of their names. Surprised the guards stopped the column and one of the prisoners stepped forward. A few years previously the battalion had recruited a number of men from Nottingham and these were now back in the ranks, having been called up with the reserve and they immediately identified the prisoner as a very popular member of Nottingham town band and well-known drinking companion. He, before parting company loaded with gifts of tobacco, made it clear that he would rather be back on his bandstand than fighting from a trench on the Marne!

11 September, Friday

> *St John.* I stayed in the hospital at Le Mans for three days and then went out to the Chateau of Le Prince de L----- with whom I stayed ten days. I shall never forget the kindness of the Prince and his charming American Princess. We drove

45 Formed from the 4th Division and 19th Infantry Brigade.

out one wet and miserable afternoon and I had the most glamorous hot bath, with all the best imaginable etceteras in the way of bath salts and delicious soaps that go to the making of the modern luxurious bath. Then bed with my dinner brought up to me. I was still very short of sleep as the noise of the hospital made sleep very difficult and every night was awakened by the arrival of Convoys, while the hour of being called was never later than 5.0 a.m. However that night I made up for a good deal of overdue shuteye and awoke next morning feeling very much better. I must have looked very blooming for the Princess's maid, who came into see me, asked if I was wounded. When I told her no, only a sick officer, she remarked 'well you don't *look* so very sick anyway'.

I stayed at the Chateau for ten days. I felt much better but I was pretty weak and found that if I walked for more than three or four miles I got knocked up and the old complaint returned. I used to go into Le Mans every third day to see the Doctor who said it was no good sending me back to the Battn. until I could do a bit more without breaking down.

After ten days of the luxurious life of eating and drinking, shooting and motoring I said good-bye to my kindest of hosts and took what was called light duty in the garrison at Le Mans. At first my work consisted of looking after the discipline, pay and interior economy of some 1000 to 1500 cavalry men of every kind of Corps who were at the base for all sorts of reasons. Some were lost patrols, some were horse casualties (most were there on that account), some stragglers and a few criminals undergoing punishment. Some were sick and slightly wounded. They were a good lot and gave me no trouble but after I had them for a day or two they were swept from me to a camp some two miles away and I was given temporary command of the stragglers and casualties belonging to the Departmental Corps and the 19th Brigade.

While at Le Mans I came into contact with a very good example of the thoroughness with which the Germans had laid his plans, pointed out to me by a member of the French intelligence department. Evidently it was part of the German plans to come round the west of Paris and to exploit the valley of the Loire as they did in 1870. About six to eight months before war broke out a commercial traveller came to Le Mans and proceeded to flood every sort of little shop with a patent boot polish called the " Lion Noir ". This was planted on very advantageous terms to the middle men or retailers on condition that a sign showing a black roaring lion on a yellow background with a tin of boot polish between its pads was exhibited outside the shop. In addition to these signs were posters and larger signs on all the places where posters and advertisements were allowed. To the casual observer these signs appeared to be exactly alike only of different sizes but if you looked at them a little carefully you would notice that they were no means so exactly similar. In some the head would be looking one way in others the opposite way. Some had their tails going straight, some had a twist in them, the legs of the beast were different in some to those in others and so on. The object of all this was a code for directing a rapid raiding party to every sort of place such as the Bank, the Cathedral, the Barracks, etc. I used to amuse myself following up the various clues to see where I got.

I carried on with light duties for about a fortnight. It was tedious work and the hours 8.0 a.m. to 6.0 p.m. were long. Sometimes I would get a break in the monotony by being president of a court martial and once I got myself sent to St. Nazaire with two hundred scallywags who were not well enough to go back to the front within a fortnights time. I enjoyed my trip to St. Nazaire. It took me two days and nights to get there and back but it was a change in the dreary routine.

By now I was fit enough to go back and got my papers cleared by the Principle Medical Officer, but it was not until the 10th October that I got away. They were about to move the 3rd Div. from the Aisne to the North and were not taking drafts just prior to or during the move. For a week or more I waited ready to move at an hours notice or at any rate get away at that notice. For the last two nights of my stay I slept in a tent with my draft and one night at mid-night got orders to move on the following day at 6 a.m.

Chapter 6

The Battle of the Aisne

12th–14th September

The General Situation

During the night of the 12th/13th September, in a raging storm of heavy rain and high winds, the German *First* and *Second Armies* withdrew across the river Aisne, blew up the bridges, and started to fortify the heights above the river. For most of the last week the weather had been atrocious, making air reconnaissance impossible, and the Allies remained ignorant of the fifteen mile gap that existed between the two armies, or even that they had decided to stand and fight on the heights above the river.

Paradoxically von Bülow's order for the German armies to disengaged, issued on 10th September, resulted in the BEF coming into contact with more German troops although these were mostly the sick and stragglers unable to keep up with their units. This is not how it was seen at GHQ who were jubilant at the number of the enemy troops being captured and interpreted their lack of resistance as proof that the German armies were demoralised and in full retreat. Sir John French's operational orders reflected this optimism and were very ambitious considering the slow and leisurely progress his Army had made to date. I Corps were instructed to secure the crossings of the Aisne at Bourg and Pont Arcy; II Corps those at Vailly and III Corps the bridge at Bucy-Le-Long and be establish on high ground north of the river by evening.

The advance started at dawn in thick mist and heavy rain and went downhill from there. The thousands of men and vehicles travelling on the unpaved roads, along which the retreating enemy had fled only a few days before, turned them into rivers of mud which made any movement slow and difficult. By mid-afternoon the advance of I and II Corps had ground to a halt about two miles short of the river Aisne but the 4th

Division (III Corps) showed more aggression and continued to slosh along in the darkness allowing Brigadier-General Hunter-Weston to establish the 11th Infantry Brigade across the river at Venizel before midnight. The bad weather had also slowed the French advance and this gave the enemy an additional twenty-four hours on which to work on their fortifications. By the evening of the 14th Von Kluck's *III Corps* were securely entrenched along the northern edge of the Aisne valley, east of Soissons, prepared to repel any attempt by Maunoury to establish himself on the northern bank[46].

At the Vailly crossing the advance guard of the 3rd Division found the railway bridge across the river totally destroyed but only the central arch of the road bridge had been blown up and, to their surprise, a single plank, with a rope handrail, bridged the gap, probable left in position by the enemy in their haste to cross the river. Both banks of the river were under enemy shellfire but there was no sign of their infantry. At 1 pm General Hamilton[47] inspected the bridge and ordered the 8th Brigade to dribble men across the plank and by late afternoon they had established a bridgehead on the northern bank, about a mile north-west of Vailly. The 9th Infantry Brigade, including the 1/Northumberland Fusiliers, were to cross in darkness. When their turn came each battalion assembled close to the bridge and, guided by hooded lanterns, moved forward by sections, first across the intact portion of the bridge then, one by one, across the plank spanning the river. All was pitch dark except when an enemy shell burst close to the bridge throwing into sharp relief the macabre dance across the plank for each heavily laden soldier knew that a single false step, right or left, would mean a long fall through the darkness into the raging river below and certain death. By a miracle no one was lost and before dawn on 14th September the 9th Infantry Brigade had established a precarious foothold on the northern bank of the Aisne but they were without artillery or transport and, until the engineers could build a pontoon bridge across the river, all supplies, including ammunition, would have to be manhandled across that single plank.

46 This area of the Aisne valley would bleed the French army white. Joffre's offensives between December 1914 and September 1915, occupying only 43 days of actual battle, cost over 400,000 casualties compared with 362,000 casualties in 10 months fighting at Verdun. There would be another 182,000 casualties in Neville's failed offensive in 1917.

47 G.O.C. 3rd Division

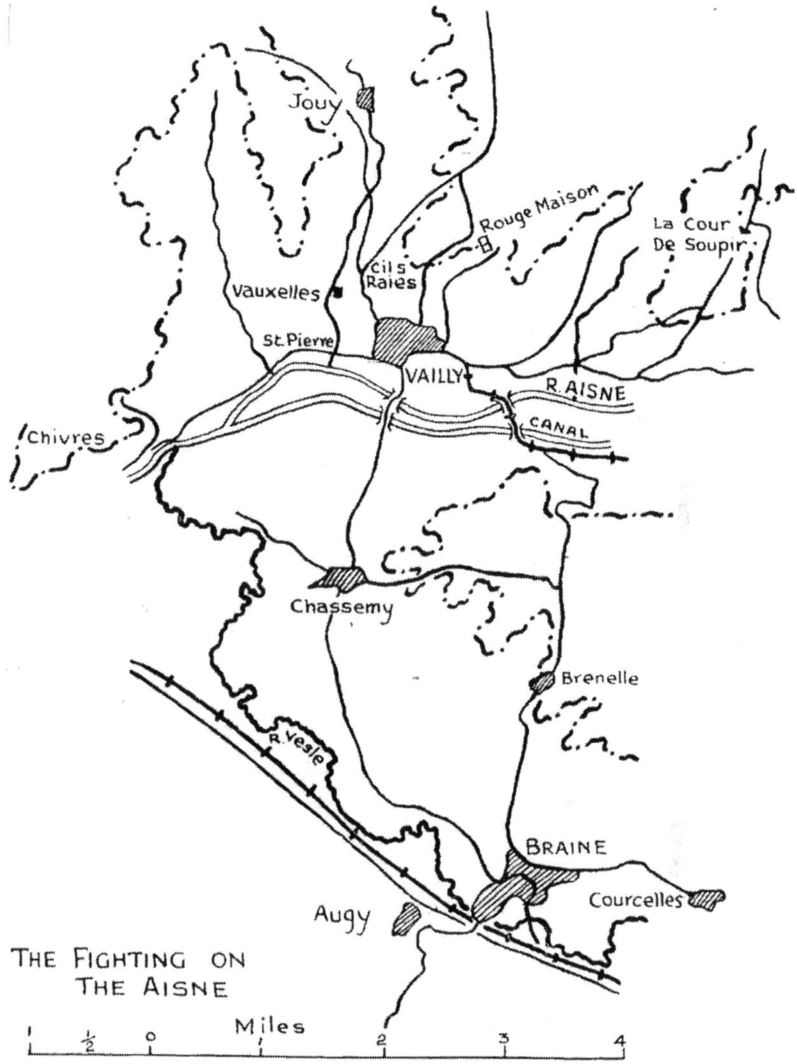

The Fighting on the Aisne.

14 September, Monday

The Battle of the Aisne

The British were to stay on the Aisne for just over a month but the Battle of the Aisne was, in reality, three days of intense fighting from the 13th-15th September during which the BEF succeeded in widening their precarious bridgeheads but failed to drive the enemy from the heights of the Chemin des Dames that ran above the river. After the

15th they were never strong enough to mount further attacks and the battlefield settled down into the stalemate of trench warfare in which the BEF was at a total disadvantage. Their enemy was entrenched on the higher ground and superior in all types of artillery, with an apparently unlimited supply of ammunition, which they used to pound the British positions day and night. Under this bombardment the British infantry crouched in their sodden trenches and primitive dugouts and hoped to survive, for not only did they lack the means to construct safer and better trenches, but also the experience and training on how to do so.

A British trench on the Aisne. It is very rudimentary lacking parapet, parados or traverses.

The 3rd Division's position was centred on a large farm, the Rouge Maison, about a mile northeast of Vailly and, as they had arrived after midnight, all they had managed to accomplish were some shallow foxholes that formed a rough firing line starting close to the farm and straggling for about a mile and a half across the valley. The 9th Infantry Brigade was close to the farm with the 8th Infantry Brigade strung out across the valley floor. As the bridgehead was too small to accommodate all three Brigades the 7th, which was in reserve, remained on the southern bank with the artillery, ready to provide support if needed.

Throughout the night the troops of the 9th Brigade had neither seen, nor heard, the enemy so before dawn patrols were sent out to find him. The 1/Lincolns established that the farm was unoccupied but soon found the enemy, present in great strength, occupying a trench about

300 yards further up the valley. The 4/Royal Fusiliers were ordered to occupy the farm and, as they moved forward, a sudden gust of wind thinned the heavy damp mist exposing another enemy trench half way up a the hillside on their right flank. One of the support companies immediately turned to face this new threat and sent out a patrol to investigate, but this was driven back by an outburst of rifle and machine gun fire as they approached the enemy's position. As the members of this patrol stumbled back down the hill the Germans infantry suddenly jumped out of their trench and charged after them forcing the whole company of the 4/Royal Fusiliers to take refuge in the farm buildings.

By now the enemy artillery had the range. Under cover of the bombardment fresh infantry attacks were made against the 4/Royal Fusiliers and the 1/Lincolns the latter, lying out on the wet ground, were soon in trouble as their rifle bolts kept getting clogged up with mud and grass. To relieve the situation the 1/Northumberlands were ordered to counterattack and, as they passed over the positions held by the 4/Royal Fusiliers and 1/Lincolns, were to pick them up and continue the attack up the valley to threaten the German artillery that was now shelling the pontoon bridge, preventing reinforcements and supplies from crossing the river.

As the 1/Northumberlands drew level with the 4/Royal Fusiliers, "Y" Company, taking advantage of a sudden reduction in enemy fire, charged across the brow of a small hill directly into a storm of fire from yet another enemy trench. This cut down the leading platoons, killing Captain Gatehouse and severely wounding Lieutenant Sutherland who remained conscious long enough to order the survivors to leave the wounded and take shelter in the farm. As part of the same attack Captain Toppin had taken "W" and "X" Companies up through the woods in an attempt to outflank the enemy trenches but they ran into a large body of the enemy and after fierce fighting at close quarters, in which Captain Toppin was killed, the survivors were driven out of the wood and back to their start position.

This abortive attack was quickly followed by a powerful enemy counter-attack that drove the garrison from the farm exposing the flank of the Lincolns. The German infantry quickly installed a machine gun in the farm buildings enfilading the Lincolns still lying out in the open and now in danger of being overrun. Two companies of the 1/Royal Scots Fusiliers were sent up in support but before they could reach the Lincolns they came under heavy fire and were forced back down the hill to take refuge in a small ravine at its base. Without support the Lincolns could not hold on and Colonel Smith ordered them to withdraw by platoons across a large muddy field full of huge sugar beets.

The whole of 9th Brigade's line now collapsed and the survivors of the 4/Royal Fusiliers and the 1/Northumberlands retreated down the hill to the neck of the valley where they dug in for a last stand, backs to the river and their right flank completely open with a two-mile gap between them and the nearest troops of the 2nd Division.

The 7th Infantry Brigade had been trying all morning to get across the river to give support but the enemy bombardment in and around the pontoon bridge was so intense that nothing could cross. In desperation they were ordered to use the plank bridge but unfortunately Colonel Smith of the Lincolns had decided that there was no suitable defensive positions left on the northern bank and had started to withdraw the Lincolns and Royal Scots Fusiliers across the plank, blocking it for most of the afternoon.

With no sign of the 7th Brigade, and running low in ammunition, it was an anxious afternoon for the men left at the foot of the valley but their luck held. The enemy infantry attacks petered out in the early afternoon and eventually the 7th Brigade got itself across the river but it had been a bad day for the 9th Infantry Brigade. They had lost over 600 officers and men killed, wounded or missing.

With the onset of darkness a small party, wearing red-cross armbands and carrying lanterns left the 1/Northumberlands position and walked up the hill to the place where "Y" company had come to grief. Here they were met by a German officer who, on discovering their business, regretfully informed them that he could not allow them to approach any closer to his positions but assured them that he already had men out looking for wounded and that any British found would be treated exactly the same as his own men. With salutes and polite 'good-nights' both parties then returned to their own trenches.

Casualties, Vailly:
Killed: Captain H.S. Toppin
'W' Company. 5625 C.S.M. Longden.
'X' Company. 493 Pte Brown, 201 Pte Earles, 8712 Pte Mather. 2128 Pte Leith.
'Y' Company. 6000 C.S.M. Luke 854 Pte McAulay.

Wounded: ***'W' Company***. 701 Pte Gardiner, 1420 Pte Atkins, 9205 Pte Ables, 680 Pte. Baines, 1585 Pte Barker, 9182 Pte Hoyle, 689 Pte

O'Brien, 9924 Pte Peper, 757 Pte Phillipson, 9543 Pte Armstrong, 1059 Pte Devereaux, 695 Pte Perry.
' X' Company. 9316 Pte Coates, 9857 Pte Wand, 195 Pte Grace, 1190 L/Sgt. Baldwin, 9274 Pte Martin, 9294 Pte Greenfield, 9764 Pte Mearns, 253 Pte Wilson, 5953 Pte Leatherly, 9655 Dmr. Moore.
'Y' Company. 9936 Pte Evans, 553 Pte McGreavy, 2107 Pte Moore, 9176 Pte Brand, 559 Pte Cluer, 636 Pte Patterson, 9285 Pte Buck, 8773 Pte Davidson, 3004 Pte Spiers, 8045 Pte Sweethove, 8701 Pte Himbrow, 3254 Pte Oates, 484 Pte Popplewell, 9352 Pte Percival, 7757 Pte Ryan, 9153 Pte Barlow, 1954 Pte Bennett. 145 Pte Clark, 468 Pte Gilchrist, 430 Pte Garrod, 8183 Pte Denton, 8514 Pte Carver, 292 Pte Alexander, 266 Pte Welch, 1033 Pte Ford, 1404 Pte Hill, 1312 Pte Youngs, 287 Pte Struther, 1575 Pte Thompson, 577 Pte Gibson, 997 Pte Morgan, 3714 Pte Doolan, 9351 Pte Cunningham, 8778 Pte Revell, 75 Pte Beanland, 3839 Pte Taylor, 290 Pte Walker, 8807 Pte Johnson, 3728 Pte Norman, 1162 Pte Sutcliffe, 9950 Pte Milway, 1017 Pte Edwards, 1138 Pte Groves, 9856 Pte Kealey.
'Z' Company. 8835 Pte Septon, 9522 Cpl. Woodhead, 9341 Pte Broguin, 431 Pte Hammond, 9960 Pte Tidy, 9505 Pte Higgins, 683 Pte Fairbairn, 691 Pte Wilson, 6943 Pte Coulton, 1639 Pte Bennett, 5709 Sgt. Brown, 340 Pte Clements, Cpl. Wadsworth.
Captain Forster, Lieut. H.L. Ovans, Lieut. G.O. Sloper.

Wounded and Missing: Captain R.F. Gatehouse[48], Lieut. H.O. Sutherland.

15 September, Tuesday

Having failed to capture the Chemin des Dames with the attacks on the 13th and 14th GHQ ordered the BEF to entrench on the positions they currently held while waiting for reinforcements of men and artillery. This day may also mark the first time that the troops of the Northumberland Fusiliers experienced the daily harassment by enemy artillery and with it that most debilitating feature of trench warfare, the daily 'wastage' from enemy high explosive shells. In their rudimentary trenches, hastily dug the day before, there was little protection, and among the casualties on this, their first day of trench warfare, were Captain Matthews, the last of the four company commanders who had embarked for France just a month before.

48 Killed in action.

Casualties, Vailly:
Killed: Captain J.H. Mattews.
'W' Company. 491 Pte Prater.

Wounded: ***'Z' Company.*** 631 Pte Dale, 2407 Pte Davis, 1618 Pte Cowleshaw.
Lieut. A.F. Geddes.

16 September, Wednesday
Trench life was a misery. The days and nights were wet and cold, and so far only a few men had been issued with greatcoats to replace those lost during the retreat. There was not even hot tea to drink for smoke arising from fires in the trenches immediately attracted the attention of enemy artillery.

In the evening Captain Hardman Jones, and 2nd. Lieutenant Tottie arrived for duty.

> *Lieut. Watkins*: Still in same place. The Germans must have got the range of our trenches because they were enfiladed with high explosives of which three burst right into Z Company's trenches causing a good many casualties. As soon as this was over the trenches were deepened and high traverses made, though very much work could not be done during the day. The Germans shelled the town all day and gave us a few " iron rations " at intervals. At dusk took M.G. into a trench on the right of our line and made the trench suitable. The sun had not been strong enough to dry our clothes properly and they were still pretty wet.
>
> Some tea had been made in the town, boiled in various kettles found in the houses, and been brought up to the troops, and the transport looked after Headquarters with some stew and tea. The Lincoln's, who were in support, were on the road we had originally come up on the morning of the 14th, and had got a good cover from shell fire by burrowing into the side of the road. But troops and transport could not move by day up this road (the only one into Vailly) as directly any movement was seen shells promptly began to come. Movement of troops and transport up the road could only take place at night. There was no water at all anywhere near the trenches and parties of men had to go into Vailly

to fill the water bottles, rations came over the bridge at Vailly by night and a ration party went down and brought up rations by hand. Slept in the trenches, very cold, a heavy dew, and very dark. Companies by night stretched a trip wire about 50 yards in front of trenches. This wire had been got in Vailly.

Casualties, Vailly:
Killed: ***'Z' Company.*** 4170 C.S.M. Wilkinson.

Wounded: ***'X' Company.*** 880 Pte Neal.
'Z' Company. 2336 Dmr. Dowtill, 338 L/C Clark, 3467 Pte Clements, 9146 Pte Kent, 9145 Pte Warner, 11239 L/Cpl. Hood,1097 Pte Bailey, 2592 L/Cpl. Sheridan, 8717 Pte Dalton, 9387 Pte Collins, 9234 Pte Clements.

17 September, Thursday
Sir John French realised that he did not have the resources to capture the Chemin des Dames ridge in the foreseeable future and his Operational Orders for this day instructed his troops that the line must be strongly fortified. With hindsight this marks the official notification of the beginning of trench warfare for the BEF.

Lieut. Watkins: Stood to arms at 4 am, and took the guns down at dawn. About 9 am set the men to dig a day pit out of sight behind the wood 50 yards to the rear. The men of the companies were, as much as possible, taken out of the front trenches and put in other trenches behind and only observation men left. It rained most of the morning. The Germans gave us our daily 'iron rations' and continually shelled the town and tried to destroy the canal bridge. They had many close shots at the latter, but never succeeded in hitting it. They also began shelling, if they saw any movement of troops on the road or anywhere else. The transport in the town did not have a pleasant time.

Matches were exceedingly scarce, but luckily I had a flint and tinder apparatus.

Lambert and a reinforcement of a 100 men were to arrive that evening, but did not come up. Had limber brought up to the quarry well under cover and only about 800 yards from my trenches. The quarry was the headquarters of the Royal Scots Fusiliers and the sappers. No cooking could be done behind the trenches. Another regiment had tried it and, as soon as smoke arose, they got badly shelled. The Brigade Staff got their house in Vailly shelled and had to move out of it.

Our own artillery had not been able to come across the river, as there were no good positions. If they were placed in the valley the sides of the hills were too steep for them to reach the Germans. However, as soon as the German guns were located they did good work from the other side of the river. Aeroplanes kept coming over, both German and out own, both I suppose, trying to locate trenches and guns. We could tell the shell from our own 'cow guns'[49] as their shells came over very high and with a peculiarly calm sound about them. We were continually annoyed by one German gun which seemed to our left front and not very far away, because the shell gave no indication or noise of its coming, as shells from a distance do. All that was heard was the burst. Slept in the trenches. Fine in the evening.

Casualties, Vailly
Wounded: *'Y' Company*. 2559 Cpl. Dawson, 1595 Pte Fairbairn

18 September, Friday

In the heavily wooded valley the Northumberland Fusiliers had established a small outpost in the corner of the wood about 300 yards in front of their trenches that gave a good view of the enemy trenches and with it an early warning of an attack. All went well for the first few days until, late in the afternoon of the 18th, a strong enemy patrol made a surprise attack killing Corporal Allen and driving the three survivors back to the main trench. The battalion immediately retaliated and after a sharp fight, retook the outpost and left a larger piquet of 20 men to defend it against further enemy interference.

Casualties, Vailly:
Killed: *'W' Company*. 9217 Cpl. Allen.

---

49 These were the obsolete 4.5 inch guns referred to as " cow guns" from the South African War where they were moved around by large teams of buffalo or oxen.

Wounded: *'W' Company*. 9841 Pte Stubbs
'Y' Company 1440 Cpl Ellison

19 September, Saturday

The enemy were not happy with this new arrangement. They made another strong attack which drove the piquet back into the wood but an immediate counter-attacked recaptured the post, which was now re-garrisoned with 50 men. The Colonel decided that this tit-for-tat fighting was not going to achieve anything and as an alternative built a small 'hide' manned by two men along the edge of the wood. This was protected by a patrol of fifty men spread out through the wood to prevent the enemy massing there for a surprise attack.

The enemy were obviously planning something. During the afternoon the shelling steadily increased until, at about 6 pm, their infantry launched an attack along the whole front held by the 9th Infantry Brigade, but it was half hearted and soon beaten off. A second, even weaker attack was made a little later and then, just before the light finally faded, the enemy bugles sounded the attack for the third time but this time the infantry refused to leave their trenches. Realising what was happening the British trenches broke into a pandemonium of loud clapping, jeers and 'cat calls' intermingles with shouted words of encouragement such as 'come on and fight' and 'show us what your made of" but in spite of all this encouragement the enemy infantry still refused to leave their trenches.

Casualties, Vailly:
Killed: *'W' Company*. 1837 Pte Brine.
***'Y' Company*.** 1500 Pte Vernon.
***'Z' Company*.** 1263 Pte Lundy.
Wounded: *'X' Company*. 574 Pte Berry, 828 Pte Thurgood.
***'Y' Company*.** 2642 Cpl. Lamb, 9778 Pte Harris. 9340 Pte Maughan,938 Pte Murray. 181 Pte Patterson. 929 Cpl. Kreley.
***'Z' Company*.** 1616 Pte Chattle, 1742 Pte O'Reilly, 1840 Pte Stewart, 437 Pte Jameson, 9506 Pte Elliot, 810 L/Sgt. Pawsey.

20 September, Sunday

During the night the enemy dug a new trench along the edge of the wood, less than 400 yards away and well within close rifle range. At first it looked as though this was to be used as the jumping off position for another attack but instead became the base for extensive sniper activity and the slightest exposure, or attempts to fire over the parapet as retaliation, drew immediate fire from several directions. During the morning the artillery made several attempts to demolish this trench but it was difficult to spot as it was skilfully constructed to take maximum advantage of the cover along the edge of the wood. Lieutenant-Colonel Anslie refused to concede the initiative to the enemy and, borrowing a company of the 1/Lincolns to act as his reserve, moved his whole battalion into the woods to sweep them clear and drive the enemy from the trench. Although the casualties among the other ranks were light for such a risky operation at three killed and five wounded the battalion suffered a further loss of experienced officers with Lieutenant Boyd killed, Captain Selby and Lieutenant Tottie mortally wounded and the medical officer wounded.

That evening the Battalion was informed that it was to be relieved.

Lieutenant Lambert with 103 other ranks joined, and Captain Gordon started his journey to France.

> *Captain Gordon.*[50]. Before war was declared I have been for 1½ years at the regimental Depot, Newcastle. On August 13th I took up the duties of Intelligence officer, North Eastern Coast Defences. During the precautionary period the office was at Newcastle but on the declaration of war, August 4th was moved to Tynemouth. Having been appointed a 3rd Grade General Staff Officer I saw very little chance of getting to the front. However on the night of September 19/20th I was on duty (Night) at the Office, and at midnight was rung up by the Adjutant, 3rd Northumberland Fusiliers and detailed to proceed at once.
>
> Application to the War Office was however necessary in consequence of my appointment. Receiving no reply to my enquiry, and with the sanction of Brigadier-General Baylay, I left Newcastle at 10 a.m. on the 20th and in company with P reported my arrival at Southampton on the same day at 9 p.m. Billeted at Dolphin Hotel with instructions to wait there

50 From an unsigned, typed manuscript, in the Regimental Archives Alnwick Castle, titled 'European War 1914.' This manuscript recounts the experiences of an Officer from Sept 20th 1914, until 2nd May 1915, by which time the diarist was an intelligence officer with the R.F.C. The account of the trench fighting on Oct 26th makes it clear that the author is Capt E.B. Gordon, Commander of 'Z' Coy. Mentioned in Dispatches Nov 20th 1914. Also in the archives at Alnwick are Gordon's diaries from the Boer War.

till further orders. Quite prepared even now to receive orders from the war office to return to my appointment at once.

Casualties, Vailly:
Killed: Lieut. E.F Boyd
'W' Company. 1460 Pte Drewry, 9096 Pte Marsden.
'Y' Company. 3729 Pte Burkin.

Severely Wounded: Capt. Selby, Lieut. Tottie, Lieut. Fisher (R.A.M.C.)

Wounded: *'W' Company.* 952 Pte Osborne, 9347 Pte Brown, 365 Pte Moffitt, 9482 Pte Parsons.
'Y' Company. 530 Pte Gill.

21 September, Monday

Lieut. Watkins. Stood to arms as usual. Got orders we were to be relieved by the 16th Brigade. Fired about 50 rounds into the right of the wood to check snipers, which was fairly effective. Were relieved during the day and at dusk by The Buffs. Battalion was collected under the hill at about 7.15, ready to start down to the town, when Germans began shelling and firing. We stopped to see if we could render any assistance, but none was required. The firing on our side was heavy, but on the German's side, from the sound of the bullets coming over, there were only a few snipers. It must have been a case of jumpiness.

From 6 to 7 p.m. the Germans shelled the town heavily, and with one shot nearly destroyed the bridge. We marched down to the town, to the bridge, where we found waggons dumping rations, and also the remaining battalions of the 16th Brigade crossing. From the bridge to the edge of the woods there was about 800 yards of open ground, continually shelled by the Germans, to prevent people coming down it, and several dead horses were lying about. As many of them had been dead for some days the smell was almost unbearable. It was one of the nights on which the Germans, luckily for us, did not shell the bridge. Marching through Braine, we reached Courcelles at about 11.30 p.m.

> Troops billeted with remainder of the Brigade in the village, billets very close.

The 21st marked the end of the battalion's first experience of trench warfare. For the last eight days they had lived in their narrow cramped trenches surviving enemy attacks and the continuous shelling. Expecting further enemy attacks at anytime they had worked incessantly to improve their trenches but, without adequate supplies of suitable building materials and other ' trench stores', it was hardly possible to make them bomb proof, or even safe from near misses by heavy artillery. Many men were still without replacement greatcoats and, as dugouts were practically unknown at this period, they had suffered severely from the bitterly cold and wet weather.

The casualties in the battalion had been relatively light at 22 killed and 136 wounded, and these had been replaced by regular drafts of reinforcements. However these casualties included some of the most experienced and valuable soldiers in the battalion. All four Company-Sergeant Majors and four Captains and two Subalterns had been killed and one Captain and six Subalterns wounded, some fatally. With Captain St John still sick, the total officer casualties to date were six Captains and eight Subalterns and only one Captain and three Subalterns had arrived as reinforcements.

Casualties, Vailly:
Died of Wounds: Capt. B.H. Selby.

Wounded: *'Y' Company.* 972 Pte Webster.

As Captain Gordon had not been recalled to his duties in Newcastle he continued to make his preparations to join the battalion in France.

> *Capt. Gordon:* Up at 8 a.m. and make arrangements to get Hilda and the Bowers to come down and see us before sailing. They all turn up during the morning and we do some final shopping. At about 1 p.m. receive orders to report at Embarkation Office at once. Drive down in Bowers car with P and say au revoir to her at the dock gates. Embark in the S.S. Minneapolis. There are no feeding arrangements on board and we all draw six days rations. Move out into the stream at 4.45 p.m. and await Admiralty orders as to our

destination. Believed Harve or St. Nazaire – probably the former as it is believed the base is being returned there, appears to depend upon the result of the battle on the Aisne. I make pals with Capt. Kentish R.I. Fusiliers who is a friend of the embarkation officer and in consequence I find myself in a state cabin. All to myself with every luxury – including a writing table. At 10 p.m. we are still at anchor in Southampton Water and I am off for a hot bath – it may be the last for some days or even weeks.

22 September, Tuesday.
The battalion had four days at rest at Courcelles, with the almost forgotten luxury of hot cooked meals and a place where they could sleep undisturbed by enemy shelling or alarms.

Casualties, Vailly:
Died of Wounds: Lieut. E.F. Tottie.

Capt. Gordon; 9.30 p.m. Still at anchor in Southampton water. We managed to get a boat to bring off daily papers and some provisions to supplement our rations. Naval seaplanes from Calshot flying around all day.

23 September, Wednesday
The only event of note during their four days at Coucelles was the arrival of Lieutenant The Hon. D Mitford and Lieutenant C. Leather with 162 other ranks as reinforcements.

Capt. Gordon: Waken at 3 a.m. by the engine-room telegraph wires and get up to find we are starting. At 7 a.m. we drop our pilot and by breakfast (8.30), the Isle of Wight has disappeared. We are bound for St. Nazaire, about 24 hours. Three other transports also en route but we soon out distance them. About 1 p.m. we are stopped by a French Cruiser, which is busy searching a small sailing vessel. After about 10 minutes we proceed all rather disappointed not to see the sailing ship sent to the bottom instead of being allowed to go. No other incidents. Extraordinary few vessels in what is usually a crowded thoroughfare. A perfect day. Our mess, having made friends with the mammon of unrighteousness (cook and chief steward), we now live like fighting cocks on curries, bully beef and rice, eggs etc.

24 September, Thursday

Capt. Gordon: 10 a.m. We drop our anchor outside St. Nazaire having missed the tide. An uneventful voyage – calm and very pleasant. 5 p.m. Weigh anchor and proceed into harbour – very narrow and very shallow but a very pretty little harbour and town. It is 8 p.m. before we are tied up alongside a coal jetty. Order, counter-order and disorder – eventually we are ordered off the ship with our kits by 9 p.m. when transport is promised to take the kits to the Casino where we are to billet. No transport arrives and I carry my 35 lbs. to the Casino – arriving about midnight very tired and very dirty. Ordered to report at base Depot 7.30 a.m. tomorrow.

25 September, Friday

Capt. Gordon. Reach Base Office 7.30 a.m. – no staff. Get breakfast at a Cafe and return to office at 8 a.m. Sent off to report to O.C. Base Details at Camp Villez Martin – about 2 miles. After a long wait get sent back to Casino to await orders. Find Coles and 93 men at the camp. Also came across Col. Shanahan R.A.M.C. at base Depot and have a long talk with him over S. Africa days. Messing and sleeping at Casino – floor very hard, no orders and no war news but plenty of "shaves".

My French improves rapidly and I am quite a success at the end of a French telephone. Many wounded here on their way home and meet many men from the front with intensely interesting news of earlier fighting. Russian "shave" very strong tonight!

26 September, Saturday

The battalion left Courcelles at 5.15 am to march back to Vailly and the trenches. With the fighting along the Aisne dying down following the stabilization of the front line it was possible to hold the trenches with less men so 'W' and 'X' Companies were detached, under the command of Major Yatman, to act as reserve to the 16th Brigade stationed about three miles away.

> *Capt. Gordon*: Chaos – ordered to leave Casino and go to Base Camp. Do so, and get orders then to go and find billets for ourselves in the town. Do so at a very dirty hotel, been there about 1 hour when we are ordered to go to Base camp again. Eventually settled in here in tents – no orders to proceed. This is a vile dusty spot.

September 30, Wednesday
The battalion is told that they are to be relieved tomorrow and, although they do not yet know it, this was the end of their fighting on the Aisne.

> *Capt. Gordon.*: Walked down to Base Commandant's office this morning to find out what prospects there are for getting up to the front. Apparently very slight. 6 p.m. orders to " stand by " to be ready to move at any moment. This affects all details of 3rd Division, some of which do move.

Chapter 6

Flanders Again

The British Move to the North

By early October the French trench line stretched northwards from Soissons for almost 150 miles to the industrial city of Lens making the British position on the Aisne something of an anomaly. There was no obvious necessity to keep the highly trained troops of the BEF squashed between two French armies, occupied in what were essentially garrison duties when this job could be equally well carried out by reserve, or second line troops, of which the French had many. Also situated as they were to the west of Paris, the BEF had long lines of communication that stretched back to the Channel ports and cut across the lines of communication of the French armies fighting in the north. This led to frustrations and delays in delivering supplies to both British and French Armies, an undesirable situation between allies especially after the recent recriminations about Sir John French's commitment to supporting the French.

Taking these, and other factors into consideration, Sir John wrote to Joffre on September 29th suggesting that the BEF be transferred to Flanders, taking up its original position on the left of the French line. Here they would be much closer to their supply bases and more easily absorb the significant reinforcements already arriving in northern France such as the 7th and 8th Infantry Divisions; the 3rd Cavalry Division, and the two Indian Infantry Divisions and a Cavalry Division due to arrive in late October. These would create a powerful British striking force of ten Infantry Divisions and four Cavalry Divisions with which to assist the French in operations against the German flank. Joffre replied on 1st October agreeing to the move and laying down the disposition of the British troops in relation to the French already in the area.

October 2, Friday

These troops movements delayed Captain Gordon's transfer 'up country'.

> *Capt. Gordon.* Still " stand by ". Walk into St. Nazaire in the morning and enjoy a hot bath. Stroll along the beach in the afternoon. The hundreds of soldiers bathing remind me of the bathing ghats at Bluares. The sight is also enjoyed by the French Ladies at close range[51].

October 4, Sunday

> *Capt. Gordon.* No orders. St. John turned up – I have a bath and lunch with him. Just as I am getting into bed I get a message from Ovans. On board the hospital ship " Asturias ", go down and find on board Evans, Douglas, Forster and Sloper.[52] Very cheery greeting.

October 5, Monday

> *Capt. Gordon:* On board the Asturias this morning to see our wounded again. I spent about 2 hours there talking to Bim Evans, wounded in the arm and chest, Douglas Forster wounded in the leg and Sloper and Ovans both wounded in the legs. Delighted to see Evans again. All very pleased with themselves, and pleased to be on their way home. The Asturias sailed at 3 p.m. Learn from Bim that his wife has had an operation for cancer but is going on well. Our " stand by " orders are cancelled and we are told that no more officers for 1st or 3rd Divisions are to be sent up till further orders. Large batches of officers arrive almost every day. Rumour the Captains are to be sent home for K's army.

October 6, Tuesday

> *Capt. Gordon.* 37 today – no letters – no orders no news.

---

51 Most of the troops would have been frolicking in the nude.

52 Capt. Forster and Lieuts Ovans and Sloper were wounded at Vailly 14th Sept.

October 7, Wednesday

Capt. Gordon. Orders at last, 2.30 a.m. Camp Sergeant major comes with orders to entrain at 8.20 a.m. Train leaves St. Nazaire 8.45 a.m., about 140 Officers and a few cavalry details. Our destination is " railhead ".The Base is being removed from St. Nazaire to Boulogne, a great blow to the local populace who must be reaping a golden harvest, charges exorbitant, bread 7d a loaf. Paid 5d for a Times of October 3rd. Travel through some beautiful country on the Paris-Orleans Railway through the valley of the Loire. French railways appear to me to be almost prehistoric !. 8 p.m. Dine at Le Mans.

October 8, Thursday

Capt. Gordon: Many happy returns of the day to my wife. Bless her. Spent a fairly comfortable night in the train – awakening to find ourselves at Versailles and at 8.30 a.m. arrive at Villeneuve St. George's. Wait here till 3 p.m. and then proceed in same train for Abbeville. Very slow progress it is now 7 p.m. and we have done about 7 miles. Destined to another night in the train. Even at this stage of the war our reception by the French people everywhere extraordinary, they give us fruit, wine, bread, soap etc. all along the route. Find the H.A.C. and the London Scottish (TA) on the L of C. 9 p.m. We are back in Paris again at the Gare du Nord

October 9, Friday

Capt. Gordon: Hot coffee at Amiens at 6.30 a.m. Arrive Abbeville 10 a.m.. Spend the day there, nice old fashioned town with old cathedral (1664). Sir John French here today. Very busy scenes here – many French and English troops and about 50 of the new motor ambulances. On again at 10 p.m.

The Strategy in Flanders

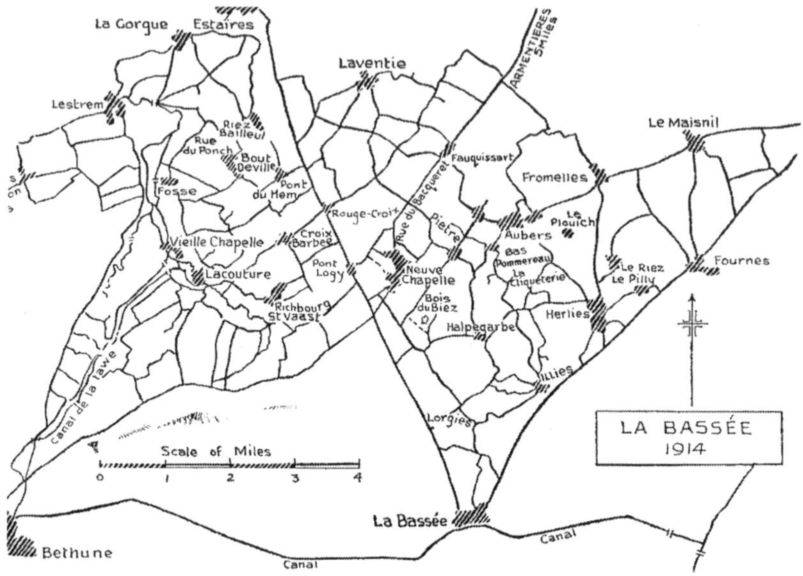

The Battle of Le Bassée.

By the 9th October II Corps had completed its move to Abbeville, but its area of operations was at Béthune, about fifty miles to the northeast, where they were to take up a position on the left (north) of the French Tenth Army, occupying the line of the La Bassée canal from Aire to Béthune.

At a conference on 10th October Sir John French and General Foch agreed that the combined French and British armies should attack eastwards with the intention of turning the flank of the German *Sixth Army*. Participation in this French offensive would involve all of the BEF; Haig's I Corps and the 7th Division would advance along the Ypres – Menin road to secure the important rail and road junctions at Menin and threaten to outflank the Germans beyond Lille; III Corps would protect the flanks of both I and II Corps by advancing up the valley of the river Lys and II Corps would advance between La Bassée and Éstaires to come around to the north of Lille to protect that important industrial city from falling into enemy hands and at the same time cut the lines of communication to the enemy who were holding up the advance of the French Tenth Army on the line La Bassée – Lens – Vimy.

II Corps had a gruelling march to be in position by the 11th October. They started early in the morning of the 9th and marched until late afternoon when they rested. Starting again at midnight they marched throughout the night to rendezvous with a fleet of buses that transported them a further 21 miles, then a final march towards La Bassée although during this stage of their journey the nature of the countryside did not commend itself to either officers or men. Once again they found themselves operating in a sprawling industrial area of smoking factories, brick kilns, mines and spoil heaps situated along railways and canals. Outside the industrial areas the land was flat, featureless and very heavy and wet, drained by numerous ditches that fed into broad deep dykes in which a heavily laden soldier could quickly drown. Plank bridges, designed to take light farm traffic, crossed the larger dykes whereas wet, slippery, single planks without handrails were used on the smaller dykes and ditches that seemed to line every field and lane.

From the military point of view the countryside was almost impossible for an attacking force. The flat featureless land provided few places where artillery could be safely sited and was practically devoid of cover although it was heavily populated with single cottages and farm buildings that could be converted into strong points by a determined enemy

The only notable feature was a low ridge, fifty to seventy feet high, and several miles long which split towards the west into two shallow spurs. Near the top of the eastern spur was the village of Aubers, and on the western the village of Illes. The troops who possessed this ridge would dominate the whole countryside.

October 10, Saturday

Capt. Gordon. Detrain at Hesdin at 8 a.m. and go by motor ambulance to Pernes, discover that 9th Infantry Brigade is on the march for Sachin, return there in the motor and find the Regiment just marching into billets. All very well, take over command of D (or Z) Double Company.

October 11, Sunday

Capt. Gordon. March at 7.35 a.m. after a comfortable night in billets. French cavalry are heavily engaged about 15-20 miles on our left – heavy gun fire audible all day. Road strewn with refugees from Lille and district, many have lost

> everything. All very cheerful and much amused at the English soldiers. Their hospitality is wonderful, they shower bread, fruit etc. upon us all along the road. Billet for the night at Robecq in a comfortable farm house. Seldom see our valises and have to live on what we carry on our backs. Men usually sleep comfortably in barns etc. with plenty of straw and the inhabitants are usually delighted to billet officers and give us of their best.

October 12, Monday

> *Capt. Gordon.* Marched at 6.30 a.m. the Brigade being in reserve to II Corps. As I write our guns are in action about 3 miles ahead of us in the vicinity of Vieille Chapelle. Immediately on our right one of our aeroplanes has just been rigorously shelled without any harm to it – it was a pretty sight. 2.30 p.m. Reach Vielle Chapelle – desultory gun and rifle fire, Church tower burning. Remain here till 4.30 p.m. during which we come in for a little shell fire. About turn and march to near Paradis to billets. Company on outpost. Have seen much of French troops today, mostly cavalry – they appear fine troops but their kit is unsuitable, blue and red. The Cuirassiers are fighting in their breast plates and brass helmets. 7th and 8th Brigades were quite smartly engaged today and had some casualties. Three villages are burning along our front, including two churches. Saw the enemy fire over 40 shells at one of our aeroplanes without effect.

II Corps' offensive started on a cold, wet morning with the countryside wreathed in a thick damp mist; the harbinger of many such mornings to come. The 5th Division, astride the canal, were to secure La Bassée, which the French believed was only lightly held by the enemy and the 3rd Division, north of the canal, were to sweep westwards and secure bridgeheads across the canalised river Lawe to reach the La Bassée – Éstaires road. To their surprise both Divisions ran into strong resistance almost as soon as they started. The enemy had converted La Bassée, and its surrounding industrial area, into a fortress and the 5th Brigade lost heavily trying to find a weak spot in the defences, while the advance of the 3rd Division was contested at every hamlet and dyke by strong rearguards of enemy cavalry and Jägers[53]. Never strong enough to stop the British advance they retreated when pressed but, for whatever reason, they seemed determined to slow the 3rd Division as much as possible.

October 13, Tuesday

> *St John.* We got entrained by 7.0. There were several officers of a Special Reserve Battn. going up with a big draft of their regiment and I had a few men of various 3rd Division units. There was also a charming gunner major with his horses and groom. I soon got my men into the train and took possession of the best of the two 1st class compartments allotted to the officers where I was joined by the major and a young man who informed us that he had been appointed as adjutant of the train. This did not interest me particularly until he invited two of his friends in with him. When I pointed out to him that as adjutant it was his job to see that the train was *properly* filled and that five officers in the carriage in which Major---------- and I were was one more than the allowance. He was somewhat nonplussed by this but seeing that I meant what I said he went in search of his magic Major to support him. This simplified matters as we threw his kit out after him and this saved the arguing that would have ensued to decide who was to go. When his Major arrived Major--------- pointed out the facts of the case to him and there the matter ended. We bumped along all that day and at about 6.0 p.m. we bumped our way into a siding at Rouen. We sat in our carriage there for two hours expecting to be moved or receive some sort of order. As none were forthcoming some of us went in search of information climbing over all sorts of obstacles and wondering all the time whether the train would be moved on while we were away. We eventually found the R.S.O. who did not know who we were, where we came from, nor to where or when we were to go. He took steps however to telegraph and find out and at about midnight we were informed that we would not move before

53 Jägers were specialised infantry travelling by bicycle or lorry who accompanied the German cavalry adding greatly to their firepower. In WW 2 this role was taken by the Panzer Grenadier regiments who accompanied the armoured divisions.

> 5 a.m. I cadged some hot coffee from the red cross sisters at the station ambulance and then bethought me of trying to find Edmond. This I managed to do and he came down and had half an hours chat with me, and about 2 a.m. I went back to the train and slept there until 7 a.m. when I awoke to find we were still at the same old place.

As Captain St John's train slowly made its way across northern France his battalion was becoming involved in some heavy fighting.

With the 5th Division held up in front of La Bassée the 3rd Division was ordered to secure the La Bassée-Éstaires road and then swing behind La Bassée to cut off the enemy's supply lines and force him to withdraw.

At first they made good progress despite being constantly harassed by enemy snipers and machine guns and having to cross fields so sodden with rain that with each step they sank ankle deep but in the late morning they were brought to a halt by intense enemy fire from the hamlet of Croix Barbee. While everybody waited for the situation to be resolved and tried to shelter from both the pouring rain, and the German machine guns, the enemy infantry made a sudden attack that almost overran the Gordon Highlanders[54] and threatened the left hand flank of the 8th Infantry Brigade. To retrieve the situation the Northumberland Fusiliers were sent forward only to find the situation in the front line utterly chaotic. In the thick mist and pouring rain they found it impossible to establish the exact position of the Gordon Highlanders, never mind the enemy, and as they moved around they came under fire from all sides, much of it coming from British troops in the vicinity. Unable to make any progress they selected the best defensive position they could find and dug in for their own safety. While this was going on the adjutant, Captain Herbert, crawled forward to see what was happening but was hit and severely wounded. Seeing him fall two stretcher bearers rushed out, but no sooner had they placed him on a stretcher when they were raked by machine gun fire that wounded the stretcher bearers and Captain Herbert for a second time. With everybody in the vicinity, British and German, firing wildly all three had to lie out in the open until after dark when they were safely brought in.[55]

---

54 With the capture of most of the battalion at Le Câteau these were raw, inexperienced replacements mainly made up of elderly reservists.

55 Capt Herbert rejoined the battalion in France in March 1915.

II Corps could ill afford to loose the 987 dead, wounded and missing suffered in a day's action in which they failed to make any significant impact upon the enemy positions, or secure the La Bassée road.

Casualties at Pont du Hem:[56]
Killed: 1 Sgt. Griffin, 3603 Pte Herrett, 8559 CQMS Orton, 3323 Pte James, Pte Johnson, 8665 Pte Batten.

Died of Wounds:709 Pte McCall, 8289 Pte Brunt.

Wounded: 1530 Sgt. Smith, 89 L/C Hart, 1105 Drv Wray, 312 Pte Ward, 668 Pte Hills, 1373 L/C Shelley. 2044 Pte Clark. 2372 Pte Clarke. 373 Pte Willis, 9865 Drv. Strickland, 2371 Cpl Saxby, 3334 Cpl Gillott. 9910 Cpl Brown. 1442 Cpl Potter, 421 Cpl Glew, 1142 Pte Jones 2422 Pte Morton, 2107 Pte Scott, 2543 Pte Coatesworth. Capt. & Adjt. W.N. Herbert.

October 14, Wednesday
The enemy seemed determined to hold the line of the La Bassée-Éstaires road and air reconnaissance reported the build up of large enemy forces around Lille. In an attempt to break the deadlock around Croix Barbee the Northumberland Fusiliers were ordered to attack the hamlet of Bout Delville in conjunction with French cavalry but, as they moved forward, the 'fog of war' descended to complement the heavy mist that shrouded the countryside. They were first told that the Gordon Highlanders had been heavily attacked again and forced to withdraw, so they must do the same. No sooner was this confirmed as untrue when they were informed that the French could not possible be ready before 1.30 pm, so with no orders, and unprotected flanks, they withdrew back to their positions around Croix Barbee to wait developments. The attack eventually took place in the early afternoon and by 4.30 the Northumberland Fusiliers were in possession of the Bout Delville. Elsewhere the attack was not so successful. The French had failed to take their objective and the 8th Infantry Brigade had failed three times to drive the enemy from Croix Barbee, but the capture of Bout Delville had given the 3rd Division a lever with which they could prise open the German defences.

---

56 With the wounding of Captain Herbert casualties are no longer listed by their Companies in the War Diary.

Captain Gordon: Advance early towards Bout Deville and on report of Gordons retiring on our right we returned and took up our original line. Forward again almost at once and eventually occupied line `under shell fire in the open and had three men wounded. Wet night and slept in the open. General Hamilton killed[57].

Casualties at Pont du Hem:
Killed: 981 Pte Whoolley, 2709 Sgt. Rowe, 162 Sgt. Raison, 1634 Pte Henderson.

Wounded: 157 Pte Maclaren, 9606 Pte Graham, 830 Pte Wiffen, 457 Pte Sanders, 9899 L/C Humphries, 1537 L/C Shaw, 9739 Cpl. Bicknell, 358 Pte Hunt, 65 Pte Bottom, 514 Cpl Banks, 804 Pte Parker, 222 Pte Waller, 1143 Pte Rogan, 1207 Pte Kirby, 8832 Pte Walker, 3718 Pte Burton, 177 Pte Coxon, 818 Pte Doles, 9813 Pte Prendergast, 17 Pte Sharratt, 3607 Pte Hedson, 1015 Sgt Davison, 2264 Sgt James, 9876 Cpl Godfrey, 200 Cpl Lowe, 2351 L/Cpl Warren, 620 L/Cpl Jones, 725 Pte Nichol, 1916 Pte Biggs, 1769 Pte Foy, 1588 Pte Eley, 1600 Pte Gatehouse, 9307 Pte Melville.

Missing: 363 Pte Scott.

October 15, Thursday
Following a forty-five minute artillery bombardment the 8th Infantry Brigade renewed its attack on Croix Barbee and instead of advancing across the fields, which proved so disastrous the day before, they now crawled along the bottoms of ditches and got round Croix Barbee and almost reached the La Bassée-Éstaires road before being brought to a halt by heavy enemy machine gun fire from the houses lining the road. The 2nd Battalion, Royal Scots were told that the road must be taken before dark and as they assembled for the attack, sheltered by a tall hedge, someone suddenly shouted an order and to the horror of the rest of the battalion "A" and "B" Companies ran towards the road. Within minutes, and to everyone's surprise, they were astride the La Bassée road and there was no sign of the enemy.

---

57 Major-General Hamilton, Commander of the 3rd Division, was killed while reconnoitring the enemy's position in front of the 2nd Battalion Royal Scots.

The Northumberland Fusiliers were in action all day. In the morning they assisted the French in their eventual capture of the hamlet of Riez Bailleul. At 2.15 pm, in support of the 8th Infantry Brigade's attack, they advanced, with the Royal Fusiliers and the Gordons, to the La Bassée-Éstaires road and captured the hamlet of Pont du Helm. Unable to move down the road due to heavy enemy machine gun fire from Croix Barbee they then swept eastwards towards Neuve Chapelle and established a defensive line along the Neuve Chapelle-Lavantie road for the night. This appeared to thrown the enemy off-guard for they started to retreat in some panic discarding equipment, rifles, ammunition, and dozens of bicycles. Around midnight, they eventually withdrew from Croix Barbee and at last, after three days heavy fighting, the 3rd Division controlled the La Bassée-Éstaires road.

It had cost the Northumberland Fusiliers 101 officers and men, killed, wounded and missing.

> *St John.* Rolled into Bethune at about 9 to the accompaniment of artillery fire not so far away. I found Stourbridge on duty at the station and we got a motor to take our valises to the transport park. He told me that the Colonel and Hubert were both gone and that on the previous day General Hamilton had been killed. We were ordered to proceed by march route to join our Brigade who were in reserve.
>
> We set off feeling very stiff and tired after our long journey and as we were in reserve we did not hurry. We got to Divisional H.Q. at noon and rested there for two hours to cook and eat our dinner. We then set off and reached Brigade H.Q. at ----------- at about 4.30 p.m. Here I learned that although the Brigade was in reserve my Regiment had been lent to another Brigade for a day or two and was at -------------- After a cup of tea with Barret who was acting as A.D.C. to General Shaw I set off with five of our men to find the Battalion. I found troops of the 9th Brigade, but no one I met could tell me where I was, where Brigade headquarters were, or where my regiment was. I set off to look and found myself under shell-fire and fell in with an intelligent man who was standing outside Brigade H.Q. and didn't know it! However I thought I would see what was inside the house which looked surrounded with bicycles and orderlies and found the Brigade Major who directed me to my own

battalion H.Q. Started off to find them in the dark, having been told to branch off the road when I reached a group of unpleasantly dead horses lying by the roadside. Here I ran into the quartermaster with the supply convoy and joined him, but when we arrived at H.Q. we found that they had moved on somewhere else. At last, about 9.00 weary and worn we found them.

Was sent off to my own Company which I found under the command of Mitford, with several utterly strange officers doing outpost duty, including my old friend Charles Nunnerly who had left the Regiment some eight years previously. I went round the sentries but would not take over command proper until daylight.

Capt Gordon. Advanced about 6.30 a.m. and lay in a ditch about 400 yards from Pont du Hem till about 2 p.m. Guns bombarded Pont du Hem and locality all day till 2.30 when we advanced with 7th Royal Fusiliers on out left to attack the main road through Pont du Hem . Captured a few houses and then were held up till guns had blown down houses loopholed by the enemy. Captured road about 7 p.m. enemy retiring N.W. leaving rifles ammunition and cycles, one of which I annexed for my orderly. Billeted at a big farm. The Germans ransack every house and take anything of value, drink all they can find and leave the place filthy.

Casualties, Pont du Hem:
Killed: 9721 CSM Miller, 1302 Sgt Whitman, 1439 Pte Peden, 383 Pte Charlton, 9877 Pte Hogan, 1150 Pte Mann.

Wounded: 510 Pte Dixon, 9902 Pte Pickering, 1587 Pte Basviga, 1040 Pte Cole, 1130 Cpl Smith, 325 Pte Ansley, 9462 Pte Gladwin, 8843 Pte Gorman, 9675 Pte Leers, 9625 Pte Rodgers, 1140 Pte Baldry. 424 Pte Jenkins, 3531 Pte Clark, 1174 Pte Wills, 565 Pte Sharples, 639 Pte Robins, 1297 Pte Stour, 1387 Pte Boyd, 1329 Pte Carter, 9515 L/ Cpl Baines, 8733 Pte Douglas, 1240 Sgt Darcy, 9611 Pte Forrest, 664 Pte Murray, 9134 Pte Watson, 9767 Pte Crossland, 9844 Pte Sadler.

Missing: 1180 Pte Mattews, 2515 Pte Connell.

October 16, Wednesday

St John. With the advent of daylight came breakfast and a look around the country. Apparently there had been quite a good scarp on the previous day and the Germans had left without bothering to collect their *Lajes and Pentes* for there were quite a lot of useful articles in the shape of war material lying around, including a number of bicycles which were appropriated. After breakfast we waited about for some time and eventually moved on the Battalion being broken up for various odd jobs as we were in Brigade reserve that day. My Company was employed up to 4 a.m. in blocking roads on the flank of the advance, which was a dull procedure. Later on the afternoon our advance troops got into touch with the enemy and for an hour or two there was a lot of noise and much banging of guns but we were not called upon to do anything except sit in a ditch. At about 5.0 we went into the little village of Fauquissart where we remained until 7.0 when I got orders to put out outposts. It took me a considerable time to go over the ground and to choose the positions, particularly as it was all done in the dark and I had only a hazy notion of where the enemy were and no idea of their strength or the probabilities of attack. However I got them out and the men fed by midnight and then I got some food myself and dossed down for an hour or two before going round the sentries again.

Capt Gordon: Marched at 7.15 a.m. Company advanced guard to the battalion as far as Fauquissart. At 12.30 the brigade deployed to attack Aubers where the enemy were entrenched and holding loopholed houses. My company then echeloned on the right flank of the 7th Fusiliers[58] – came under shrapnel fire in the open, 3 men hit. Dug ourselves in opposite Aubers but at 6.45 p.m. orders to return to billets at Fauquissart. Billeted in the School, last used by Germans for a hospital.

58 The Royal Fusiliers (City of London Regiment) (7th Foot).

During the night the 8th Infantry Brigade, which had been in front during the last three days[59] was withdrawn to the reserve and replaced by the 9th who, after their success in capturing the La Bassée-Éstaires road, were ordered to continue their movement southeast and occupy the small towns of Aubers and Illies on the Aubers ridge. For this purpose the 9th Infantry Brigade were split into two columns; the 4/ Royal Fusiliers and Northumberland Fusiliers in one; the Lincolns and Royal Scots Fusiliers in the other. Their advance started off as usual in thick fog but it was soon halted when they were informed that the French cavalry, who were to guard their left flank, would not be ready until after midday. Following a brief meeting of the senior British officers it was agreed that, as there was no sign of the enemy, the Brigade would continue its advance without the cavalry. However this meant that each battalion had to detach patrols that would be responsible for guarding the open flank and, as the heavy mist did not lift all day, keeping in contact with the flank guards slowed their rate of advance so it was late afternoon before they were on top of the ridge. They quickly established that the enemy was occupying Aubers, but with the fog becoming denser with the onset of early darkness they decided to delay their attack until morning.

Casualties, 16th October:
Wounded: 9850 Pte Murphy, 9138 Pte Sheppard, 1008 Pte Payne, 418 Pte Lee, 9247 Pte Jones.

Missing: 6033 Pte Sutherland.

October 17, Thursday
This would turn out to be the most successful day for the 9th Infantry Brigade in the whole campaign. The Royal Fusiliers, with the Northumberlands in support, attacked Aubers but the enemy had withdrawn during the night and they entered the village unopposed. Captain St John took his men to occupy the high ground north of the village but came under heavy fire from the village of Fromelles and, as they moved down the hill to remove this nuisance, the firing became so intense that they were forced to dig in about 500 yards short of the village. It was obvious that the enemy were holding Fromelles in strength. The task of taking Fromelles was given to the French who, at

59 Their casualties were 32 officers and 601 other ranks killed, wounded and missing.

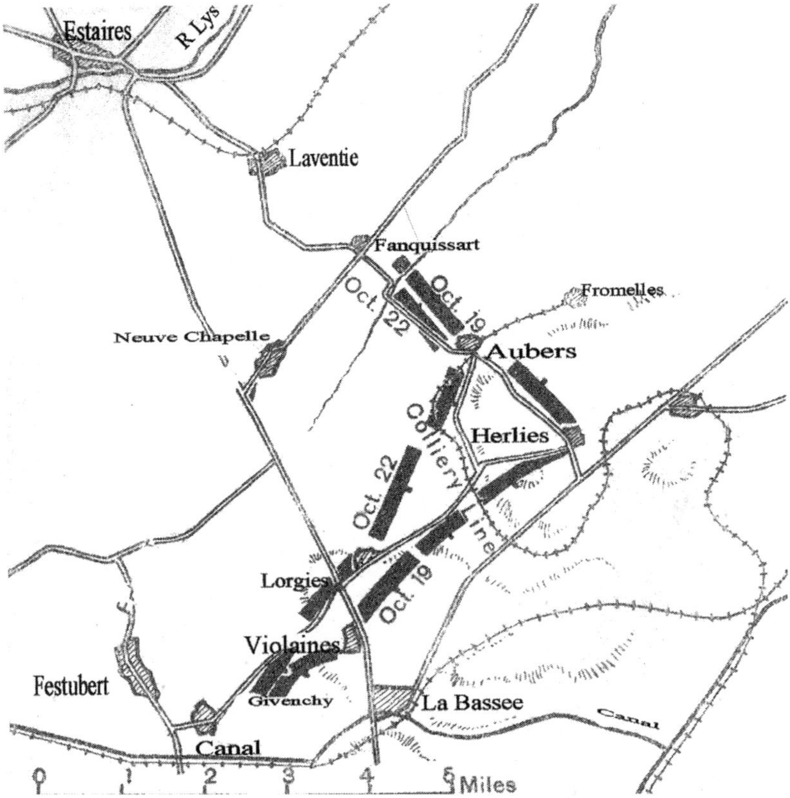

The attack on Aubers Ridge.

about 12.40 pm, opened their attack with a heavy bombardment that drove the enemy into the fields to be shot down by the Northumberland Fusiliers. The French infantry then attacked. Some rushed around the village to cut off the fleeing enemy and, seeing troops in a strange uniform dug in on the side of the hill, deployed to attack but fortunately Captain St John had command of sufficient French to convince the sceptical French officers that they were British.

With Fromelles cleared the next village was Herlies which, after some hard fighting, was captured in a daring bayonet charge by the Lincolns just as darkness was falling.

With these victories came unwelcome discoveries. So far they had been fighting enemy cavalry supported by Jäger units, and it was a very disturbing to find among the enemy dead and wounded at Herlies first-line combat infantry belonging to the *56th Regiment, 14th Division, VII Corps* whose presence in Flanders was totally unexpected. Although not yet apparent to II Corps, these dead German soldiers were the vanguard of an overwhelming force of two enemy Corps (*VII* and *XIII*) assembling around Lille to crush the British.

> *St John.* At dawn I went round the posts again and found that in the most important one all the men were asleep. The sentries and N.C.O. I put back for court-martial knowing of course that it meant certain death for them. It was a most disagreeable duty I had yet performed. What was the final outcome I do not know for I was knocked out before there was a chance of trying them though a summary of my evidence and that of my sergeant-major who was killed soon afterwards was duly taken.[60] We got our breakfasts just in time for at a very early hour we were told to advance to cover the left of the Brigade who were advancing on the town of Aubers. I spread the Company out into a convenient as possible formation and proceeded slowly and cautiously to the foot of the ridge on which Aubers stands.
>
> Here I called a halt until I was quite sure the ridge was clear and could get an idea of the ground on the far side of it. I also collected a few " bits " of the Company that had gone astray in their endeavours to avoid barbed wire fencing. We were at the foot of the ridge, which was I suppose about 50 feet in height, and to the north of Aubers in between that town and the village of Fromelles. I got half of the Company together and put them under cover and was going on to the top of the ridge when I was unexpectedly fired on from the direction of Fromelles. As I had been told that the French had cleared this village and that there was no one in it excepting perhaps a few wounded Germans I did not think much of this fire to begin with. However it became more intense and as it was very persistent I decided to swing round the rear half Company and advance towards Fromelles with the idea of finding out what the bother was about. As we advanced the fire became heavier and more accurate but I could not see anything to fire at in return. When we were within 500 yards of the outskirts of the village, I halted and we made ourselves snug while I sent back a signal for supports. We

---

60 In "Shot at Dawn" Putkowski and Sykes do not list any member of the Northumberland Fusiliers shot for this offence in 1914/15.

had eight or nine casualties and I could not see a sign of the Germans. The field we were in was ploughed and it was easy to entrench ourselves sufficiently against rifle fire and so far we had not encountered any shell-fire. I waited here for an hour or two for the supports but no one came and eventually I got a message to say I was to stay where I was as the French were going to clear the village.

The next order I got was to go back myself to interview Yatman. I did not like the idea of this too well but there was nothing for it but to go and go back. I went back and thanks to the bad marksmanship of the Huns who fired at me I got back in safety.

I had expected to be given some important order with the regard to the carrying out of a further advance but I found it was only to be asked what steps I had taken to evacuate my wounded !!!. It must have been quite obvious that such a thing was not possible until Fromelles was cleared or it became dark. I felt furious at having been called upon to risk my life to answer such an absurd question and showed pretty plainly what I thought about it. I went back to my Company and shortly after my return there the French began to clear the village.

If you can imagine the village to be in the middle of a square of which my Company formed one side and the French advance on an adjacent side you will see that I was in a position to see a very pretty sight and I settled down to enjoy myself. In the middle of the village was a church with a spire and on this the French Artillery began to range. Two or three rounds were enough to burst shrapnel quite close to the spire and then the rear business began. The French infantry were about 500 yards away from the village and between them and the village the 75's placed one and then a succession of curtains of shrapnel fire which steadily advanced right through the village and which spread across it. Germans came tumbling out of the trenches in front of us and running back, at least some ran back, others remained where they fell. We pumped rifle fire into them too and they got a very hot time of it. I believe there were about 3000 of them in the village and they lost nearly a 1000 in killed and wounded before the French had finished with them. When the fire from the 75's had ceased the French Infantry advanced and some came over to where I was and I thought they were going to " coupe me gorge " but I was able to reassure them we were English before any accident of that sort occurred. We stood up and I was able to collect my wounded and bury my dead. (total casualties 4 killed and 7 wounded). When I had completed this job we rejoined the Battalion, which I found in the market place at Aubers. We stayed there till it was dark (about 2 hours) and then marched to billets for which we were grateful.

Aubers was the first town I had been in after Germans had inhabited it for a short time. The whole place was strewn with bits of furniture (mattresses, chairs, wardrobes, etc.) and the filth was indescribable. Outside the church was a crucifix with a figure of Christ upon it and there were piles of broken and empty bottles and more filth while the crucifix was stained with what looked like wine. It was altogether a revolting site and showed but too plainly the type of animal we were dealing with.

Casualties, Pont du Hem:
Killed: 1273 L/Sgt. Howard, 708 Pte Morris, 9112 Pte Cave.

Wounded: 419 L/Cpl Sadler, 3767 Pte Kennedy, 8843 Pte May, 9675 Pte McMahon,
703 Pte Chaplin, 976 Pte Addams, 3298 L/Cpl King, 1402 Pte Ramsey.

October 18, Friday

St John. Next morning after a good sound sleep and a nice hot breakfast we marched off to the sound of enemy guns in the near distance. We went about two or three miles to a village called Herlies. As we approached the village we found several dead Scotchmen lying in the road and as we reached the outskirts we were greeted with a heavy shell fire, which luckily was a bit over and all the shell burst 30 to 50 yards beyond us. Had the range been accurate we should have got it badly as we were marching in columns of fours across the front at the time. We took up a position in rear of the village in reserve and there we sat all day doing nothing. All this time we had been under the impression that the Army was doing something in the way of a victorious advance and rather wondered why we were checked now. As the day wore on it became evident that quite a considerable battle was going on in front of us though we still thought that it was the German rear guard putting up a stiff resistance to our advance. As dusk began to fall we were told that the regiment, on the right of the Brigade were going to take at the point of the bayonet a road which the Germans were holding, and that we were to support their advance. Whether or not they ever got near their objective I don't know but the attack had failed before we could get near the place and so we returned to the shelter of a slag heap just in the village.

By this time it was dark and it was evident that we had raised a hornet's nest. The village was becoming an inferno of bursting shell and we clung very tight to our slag heap. The noise of battle and the light from the shells bursting in the dark gave the scene a very Dantesque impression. Just by the slag heap were two solitary fir trees and as each shell burst these were vividly outlined and the crash of the shrapnel bullets on the far side of the heap and on the roofs of the houses was like the noise of a sudden crack across a sheet of ice. My Company was soon the only one left at the heap all the others having gone off to support some point or other.

My orders were to keep in touch with the 7th (Royal Fusiliers) and support them if necessary, but I was not called upon to do so. At about 9.0 I went forward and was shown a line along which my Company were to be entrenched. For some reason or another a different Company was to begin digging the trenches under my orders and my Company were to relieve them after two hours. I gave the officer concerned careful instructions about the type of trench I wanted dug and their position and returned to my own Company who I got issued with all the spare ammunition I could raise which gave every man an extra 150 to 200 rounds. I also got water bottles filled and at the appointed hour marched down to our position. By this time the battle had died down and the silence was interrupted by spasmodic bursts of rifle fire though a search light was being played on our lines and the place was occasionally interrupted with flares and star shells.

When I got down to our lines I found the other people had started to dig quite the wrong type of trench and one which was no use against shell fire and which we had to fill in again so that some precious hours had been wasted. Fortunately as they had been digging for someone else's benefit they had not killed themselves by hard work so that the damage was less than it might have been. I got my own men to work as soon as I could but I could not induce some of them to put any go into their digging. I tried to impress upon them that their lives depended upon their efforts but they did not believe me and only worked when I, or one of my subordinates drove them.

As we could not be driving every one at once it began to get light before I was satisfied with the work done. I took care to give the lazy ones their own bit of trench to live in and as dawn was breaking we all got under cover and stood to arms.

Casualties, Herlies:
Killed: 1418 Pte Harbourne.

Wounded: 8720 Pte Grimes, 3613 Pte Jayne, 3522 Pte Pullan, 9625 Pte Walsh, 1632 Pte Hannan, 9629 Pte Kinghorn, 1585 Pte Smith, 1627 Pte Charlesworth.

October 19, Saturday

The 3rd Division was running into trouble. Their line jutted out in a sharp salient around Herlies and the increasing intensity of the enemy's artillery was making movement impossible. There was also a large concentration of enemy infantry around the hamlet of Le Pilly, about 800 yards in front, and the heavy sniping from that direction was adding to the general danger and discomfort of the men in the trenches. It was decided that the enemy at Le Pilly posed a particular threat and were removed by the 2/Royal Irish Regiment in a daring dawn attack.

The enemy reacted violently to this success and throughout the day tried to retake the hamlet with a series of powerful counter-attacks well supported by artillery but the Irish held on, although by evening they had lost over 200 men. Just before dawn on the Sunday morning the Germans renewed their attack and, after a heavy bombardment, battalions from the *16th* and *57th Regiments (14th Division)* assaulted the village.

The fighting lasted until 3 pm when the Irish, practically out of ammunition, and almost all the survivors wounded, negotiated their surrender. The battalion had been destroyed; 17 officers and 571 other ranks were either dead or prisoners, a loss keenly felt in the other battalions of the 9th Infantry Brigade who remembered how much the battalion had risked to rescue them from the Mons salient less than two months before. Only 30 of the Royal Irish managed to escape back to the British lines the following night.

The regiments of the *14th Division* were obviously spoiling for a fight for while their comrades dealt with the Irish at Le Pilly others attacked the trenches held by "W" and "Z" companies Northumberland Fusiliers. Within minutes the situation was so critical that reinforcements had to be rushed forward in the form of Captain Carey, 4/Royal Fusiliers and his company but, as they advanced over the open ground, they were swept by enemy artillery and machine gun fire and only a few survivors reached the Northumberland's trenches.

> *St John.* No sooner had daylight fairly broken than we realised that we were fairly in for it. Shells came all around us and over us, and before us. We all lay very low but the poor devils who had not dug deep when they had their chance had a bad time of it. One complete section of trench was wiped out and every man in it killed while a good many were wounded. All of them got well frightened and we were thankful when they turned their attention elsewhere. They made no infantry attack where my company were but I could watch them deploying for attack on our left. I managed to get a message to this effect back to the gunners who put a few shrapnel among them and I was able to see a lot of them lying where they fell. We lay there all day and at night I had no difficulty in inducing the men to work hard improving our position as far as it was possible with the tools we had at our disposal.

Casualties, Herlies:
Killed: 130 Pte Doyle, 483 Pte Cole.

Wounded: 257 Pte Bowman, 70 L/Cpl Annison. 466 Pte Taylor, 1983 Pte Trevor, 1941 Pte Cooper, 1509 Pte Wilkie, 2190 Pte Harrison, 363

Pte Scott, 717 Pte McDonald, 1453 Pte Cremer, 940 Pte Osborn, 9978 Cpl Moore, 1051 Pte Wunkling, 2423 Pte Gardner, 909 Pte Green, 5358 Pte Marlan, 916 Pte Chesser, 1118 Pte Hassett, 946 Pte Wheatley, 2088 Pte Hall, 9280 A/Sgt Vandepeer, 1376 Cpl Crockford, 3218 Pte Hunt, 505 Pte McDonald, 9949 Sgt Wodehouse, 256 Pte Hogg, 335 Pte Shannon, 3071 Pte Stone, 569 L/Cpl Hodsell, 947 Pte Bradley.
Lieut. Waddelove.

By the night of the 19th/20th October the troops of the II Corps were totally worn out. Since the 12th the weather had been appalling with heavy mists and rain every day. The battalions in the front line were kept awake day and night by enemy probing attacks and false alarums and so exhausted were they fell asleep over their rifles, sometimes even during an attack.

Even when they were supposed to be resting, in reserve, they were often woken in the middle of the night to turn out on a report of some German attack or another. By the 19th the situation was so critical that General Smith-Dorrien asked Sir John French for assistance and the 19th Infantry Brigade was sent from G.H.Q. Reserve to Fromelles to support the right of the 3rd Division. Unfortunately, due to the rapidly deteriorating situation facing the 7th Division and I Corps around Ypres, this valuable support was withdrawn on the 22nd, just as II Corps was to face its severest test.

20 October, Sunday

> *St John.* Next day and the day after were spent in much the same way. We had a very open field of fire in front of us, which was the reason I imagine of our immunity from attack. The troops in our right and left were being pretty heavily pressed all the time but except for being occasionally subject to spells of shell fire from an uncomfortably oblique angle on our left we were not threatened and our days were really almost dull. On the night of the 20th there were several attacks on our flanks but again no one troubled us. We used the darkness to fill up with water, provisions and ammunition and to generally repair and improve our trenches. On the night of the 21st I received orders that all tools and extra ammunition were to be handed over to the transport and that we were to retire to a new position about

a mile behind in order to straighten our line with the French, who had left us occupying a dangerous salient.

Capt Gordon: A hard day – incessant shelling and repeated infantry attacks which we drove off with great loss to enemy. Herlies a 'hell on earth'. Practically every house destroyed – had 3 down about my head. Church ruined. My company suffers heavily but does well and is congratulated by C.O.

Casualties, Herlies:
Killed: 8717 Pte Cole, 442 Pte Cooper. 9516 L/Cpl Kay, 404 Pte Jacques, 9940 Pte Craske, 9882 Cpl Collins.
Lieut Van Neck

Died of wounds: 9978 Cpl Moore, 947 Pte Baudley,

Wounded: 9165 Pte Popple, 5218 Cpl Stott, 3580 Pte Jones, 2185 Pte West, 1396 L/Cpl Axtell, 1540 Pte Shingler, 747 Pte Dixon, 178 Pte Burnett, 2196 Pte McDonald, 9116 Pte Gatherole, 9117 Pte Adcock, 2759 Cpl Bennett, 9335 Pte Phillips, 1356 Pte Girdlestone, 9135 Pte Randall, 351 Pte Chillingsworth, 1421 Pte Ward, 1280 Pte Leatham, 9230 Cpl Vose, 1665 Cpl Lane, 786 L/Cpl Hunt, 9728 Pte Bird, 9197 Pte Russell, 537 Pte Parker, 9975 Pte Allerton, 9467 Pte Royce, 9163 Cpl Gill, 532 Pte Pentlow, 289 Pte Dodds, 9771 Pte Large, 9106 Pte May, 9717 Pte Horner, 9980 Pte Armstrong, 1289 Pte Leal, 8847 Pte Cairns.
Lieut R.T. Vashell, Lieut Buckle, Lieut Bresswell Hobbs.

Missing: 9227 Pte Turnbull, 9908 Pte Barber, 2035 Pte Farrow, 9494 Pte Sparks, 264 Pte Hamilton.

October 21, Monday

Casualties, Herlies:
Died of wounds: 1289 Pte Leal (w 20/10/14).

Wounded: 8866 Pte Craine, 9678 Pte Donnelly.

For the night of the 20th/21st October II Corps held a line that stretched from the canal bridge, three quarters of a mile upstream from

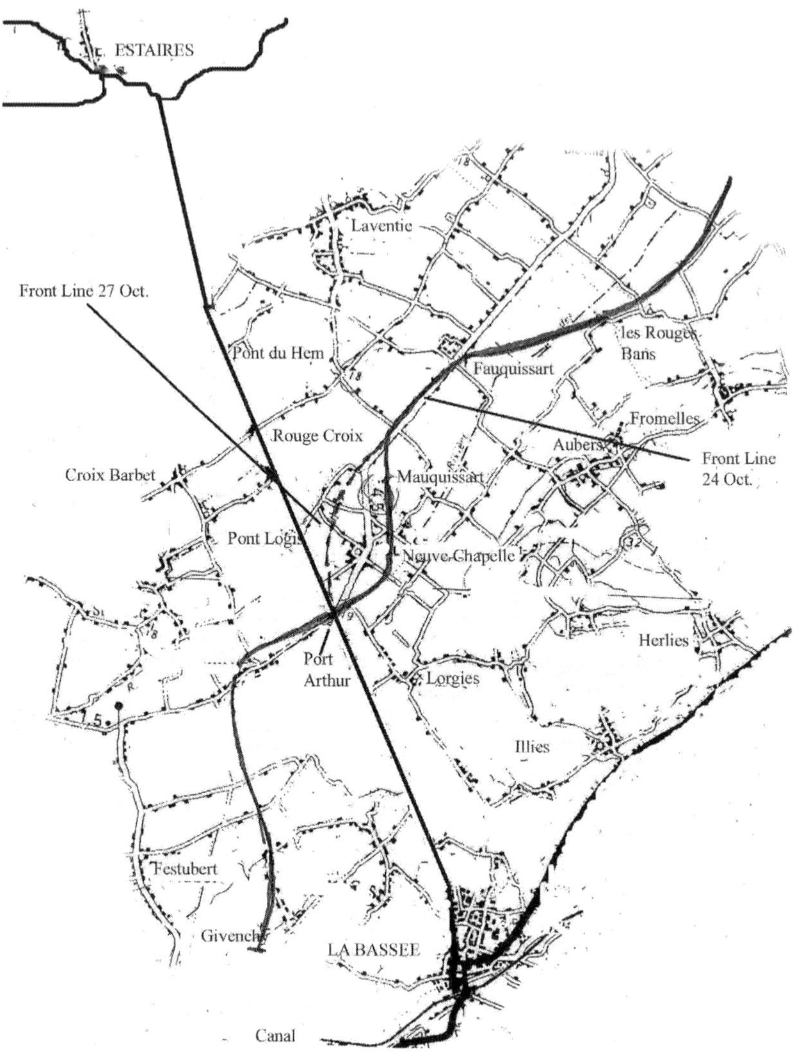

II Corps line around Neuve Chapelle.

Givenchy, through Violaines, passing the western outskirts of Herlies and stopping between Grand Riez and Fromelles; the 19th Infantry Brigade held Fromelles, and a mixed force of French cavalry, artillery and cyclists roamed the roads and lanes between Fromelles and le Mansil.

Chapter 8

The Battle for Neuve Chapelle

When Sir John French recalled the 19th Infantry Brigade to the fighting around Ypres the 3rd Division was left with insufficient men to hold their positions on Aubers Ridge leaving General Smith – Dorrien little choice but to pull back to a shorter line running eastwards from the village of Neuve Chapelle to the hamlet of Fauquissart. This move would give II Corps, for the first time in the campaign, an almost continuous defence line. Along the southern portion of this line, around Le Bassée, the 5th Division had suffered as much as the 3rd and a consequence of their high casualties, and general exhaustion of the troops, the French Tenth Army had agreed to move north of the Le Bassée canal to relieve the 5th Division in its trenches as far as the village of Festubert.

Starting from here the 5th Division, occupying rifle pits, field drainage ditches, and isolated strong points formed some sort of defence line as far as the western outskirts of Neuve Chapelle where it now joined with the 3rd Division. The 7th Infantry Brigade had taken up positions in and around Neuve Chapelle while on their left the 9th Infantry Brigade continued the line to the hamlet of Petre. From here it was carried by the 8th Infantry Brigade, occupying a line of shallow trenches and breastworks running through the sodden fields, approximately 200 yards in front of the Neuve Chapelle – Fauquissart road (now D171) to Fauquissart.[61] Beyond them was a gap of several thousand yards, patrolled intermittently by Conneau's French Cavalry Corps, before the trenches of the III Corps around Bois- Grenier

61 Although referred to as trenches the water table was so high that a 'trench' more than two feet deep soon filled with water. Throughout the winter of 1914/15 neither the British or German defences formed a continuous line and consisted of short shallow ditches protected by breastworks made of sandbags, supplemented with strong points and fortified barns and houses. The breastworks on the British side were about 6 feet high and 3-4 feet thick, hardly thick enough to stop a bullet.

were reached. General Smith-Dorrien hoped that this new line would be stronger than the one he currently held on Aubers Ridge but the trenches, which had been hastily dug with local labour were shallow, and lacked dugouts or any other form of protection from enemy artillery.

The withdrawal of the 3rd Division from Aubers Ridge to the Neuve Chapelle position was to be spread over two nights.

October 22, Tuesday

> *St John.* The Companies carried out the retirement from the left. My Coy, being the right hand flank Coy of the Battalion was not to move till the Battalion had all moved, and was in its turn supported by the Lincolnshire Regiment who were on our right. The whole movement being timed to be completed about an hour before dawn began to break. The enemy that night was very persistent with their night attacks, particularly on our left, and it was partly on this account that the regiment on the extreme left was late in starting. Other reasons also contributed to delay, and the consequence was that half an hour before daylight we had not budged. Major __________ of the Lincolnshire Regiment came up to me very excitedly and asked why we were not gone, and said that his Regiment had to wait for me before they could go. Of course I could give him no information but could only tell him that I could not go till Booth's Company had gone and that he was apparently hung up in his turn by the other Regiment.
>
> Major __________ then suggested that I should go on my own account and not wait to be scuppered by daylight. To which I replied he could do as he liked about it, but I was going to see my other Company off first and that if any scuppering was to be done the more of us there were to resist it the worse for the Huns. At the same time I did not like the delay at all. I got the men out of their trenches and lined up along the road all ready to move and then went and bustled Booth, who I found just preparing to shift having heard that other people were falling in. I got him started and he went through my Company and we fell in behind and so bustled along at a fine pace just as dawn was breaking.
>
> We did not get far before I found the road blocked by the Lincolnshire Regiment who apparently were not waiting

to be scuppered, so I turned off and made my way across country to the Battalion rendezvous, which we reached in safety. As a matter of fact the Germans never saw us go and did not wake up for a couple of hours after we had departed when they wasted about three hours heavy shelling the trenches we had vacated before finally launched an attack on them which suffered heavily from our gunfire.

I now looked forward to a rest in nice billets and was told that this was to be our position. In those days the trench warfare in vogue was a very different affair to the trench warfare of the present day (a year later). We had no reserves, and only an apology of a support. There was one Battalion in each Division that was occasionally taken from the trenches, and called a Divisional reserve while it was supposed to be taking a rest. The result of this was that we had only one line of trenches, which were more or less hastily contrived affairs, undrained and without dugouts. We had tried to make dugouts once, but being unable to procure any material for supporting the roofs they usually fell in the first time a shell bumped anywhere near them and buried the occupants. The habit was therefore discontinued by order of Divisional H.Q. Ones tour of duty in the trenches was not a comfortable period though personally I preferred it to our periods of so called rest.

We marched along to billets where we got breakfast, (hot), and a mail or two and we were just settling down after our meal and wash when we received orders to fall in at once and we were sent off to support the 8th Brigade who were in trouble at a place some three miles away. When we got there we found that their pressure had been relieved and we were not wanted for the moment. We stuck there in a wood for the rest of the day and at nightfall returned to our billets, which we found had in the meantime been taken by some sappers. We trudged away again and at last got into some very inferior billets in empty cottages that had no conveniences for cooking the nice hot dinner for which we yearned.

Here we were allowed to stay for three hours and at midnight or thereabouts we were again paraded and two Companies of which mine was one went off to dig some trenches under the guidance of an R. E officer somewhere in the rear. I got to the place all right and eventually found the R. E officer who took me around the trenches and explained to me how beautifully planned they were. This took him so long that by the time he was finished it was time to fall in again and join the rest of the battalion leaving a host of civilians, mostly refugees, to dig the trenches. I collected the Battalion tools, which I had laid out for instant use and also those of Brigade H.Q. By some unfortunate choice the Brigade tools got mixed up with ours so we got our tools cart quite full of picks and shovels and had to put some on the G. S wagons which came up with the Battalion.

Casualties, Herlies:
Missing: 2214 Pte Rose, 543 Pte Hope.

Wednesday 23 October
Unsure of what was happening the Germans restricted their daylight activity to shelling the empty British positions but at dusk they regained contact and, during the night, by a combination of patrolling and probing attacks, established the position, and extent, of the new British line, as well as its weaknesses. There were two, the junction of the 5th and 3rd Divisions in front of Neuve Chapelle where the 7th Infantry Brigade's trenches jutted out from the village in a shallow salient and the gap between the II and III Corps at the end of 8th Infantry Brigade's trenches at Fauquissart.

The 23rd October also saw the arrival of the Jullunder Brigade and the 30th Sikh Pioneers, the vanguard of the Lahore Division, and among the first Indian troops to go into action on the Western Front.

Sir John French's intention was to use the Indian Corps to relieve the exhausted II Corps but for the moment the Jullunder Brigade was to be used to relieve Conneau's cavalry and extend the British line from Fauquissart to Rouge Bons, bringing Smith – Dorrien's trenches closer to those of the III Corps.

St John. We reached our new billets at Rue de Bacquerot at dawn and my Company was told off to a very nice farmhouse where we got plenty of food and water to wash in. We spent quite a pleasant morning with mails and a general clean up but after lunch we were sent out to dig some trenches to be occupied in case of shell fire coming upon us. We were hardly out of the house before a " crump " landed right in the middle of the farm buildings. We stayed out till dark and then returned to our farm for the night.

Casualties, Herlies:
Died of Wounds: 3576 Pte Kennedt, 9117 Pte Adcock.

Wounded: 589 Pte Bianchi, 9773 Pte Bennett, 1928 Pte Parsons, 1503 Pte Robson, 289 Pte Dodds, 513 Pte Porter.

October 24, Thursday

The enemy's first attempt to break the British line was a dawn attack, beaten off with heavy loss and driving home the lesson that the open farmland in front of Neuve Chapelle was a death trap for infantry moving across it in daylight. The remainder of the day was relatively quiet except for some shelling, which increased in volume as the light faded in the early afternoon and, under cover of the shelling, the enemy began a series of small probing attacks all along the 3rd Division's line from Neuve Chapelle to Rouge Bons. As soon as darkness fell these were relaced by a major attack against the 2/Royal Scots and 1/ Gordons, holding the left flank of the 8th Infantry Brigade's line.

The Royal Scots repulsed the attacks on their positions but the 1/Gordon Highlanders, the last battalion on the 8th Brigade's line, could not. As the last battalion in line they were in contact with the 2/Royal Scots to their right, but were separated by a gap of about 400 yards from the 15th Sikhs on their left. It appears that the 1/ Gordons hunkered down in their trenches with no plans to patrol this gap, or put out listening patrols. They had not even bothered to collect the wire from the surrounding fields to protect their front[62].

62 As we have noted they had only recently been reconstituted following their disaster at Le Câteau in August and mainly consisted of inexperienced officers and men who had recently arrived in France. The Gordons were not the only Battalion to have few fully trained officers and men still in their ranks. II Corps had now been fighting in Flanders for thirteen days and had suffered heavy losses, particularly among experienced officers and N.C.O.s., which coming after the losses at Mons, Le Câteau and on the Aisne was beginning to have an impact on the fighting efficiency of most battalions. Reinforcements were being used up at a prodigious rate and experienced troops were at a premium. Most reinforcements arriving in France now consisted of the most out of date men in the Reserve or from the Special Reserve and young soldiers barely out of their training.

The enemy must have had some knowledge of these deficiencies for in the darkness about three hundred of them silently crawled up to the Gordon's trenches and, with a loud cheer, jumped up and rushed the position with the bayonet. They drove the 1/Gordons back onto the main Neuve-Chapelle- Armentières road (D171) and hearing the commotion in the dark the 2/Royal Scots sent out a small patrol who reported back that the enemy were in the Gordon's trenches. The 2/Royal Scots immediately swung two Companies round to guard their exposed flank and sent out a stronger patrol to determine exactly what was happening. As this patrol approached Fauquissart it came across groups of Germans and Gordons milling around in the darkness fighting one another, sometimes with fists, all trying to take each other prisoner! The Royal Scots tried to sort out the mess but, as they were not strong enough to retake the lost trenches, withdrew back to their own positions taking with them all the Gordons they had managed to round up.

A message was sent to 9th Brigade Headquarters requesting support to retake the trenches and the Northumberland Fusiliers, in reserve, were roused from their billets. Fortunately they were not required and after several hours of confused fighting the enemy were driven back to their own trenches and once again, as the trenches were cleared of the German dead and wounded, the British were surprised at the number of different regiments represented among the casualties. Most were from the *16th, 53rd, 56th* and *57th Infantry Regiments* of the *14th Division, VII Corps* with a sprinkling from the *119th* and *125th Infantry Regiments* of the *26th Division, XIII Corps,* an indication of the size of the enemy forces arrayed in front of them.

> *St John.* We spent the morning, and most of the afternoon, in our funk holes but the Huns were apparently too busy to pay us much attention. I had a busy morning fixing up arrears of clerical work and organisation. Interior economy, though important, does not get much attention during the kind of warfare that was being waged during those early months. In the middle of the afternoon we got orders to fall in and proceed to Rouge Croix where I took over billets in an abandoned Caberet.
>
> It was dark when I took over but we got in somehow and I found a bed for master to lie upon. We also managed to get some fuel for a dilapidated stove and got some hot soup. I

had just lain down on the bed when I was " wanted " at HQ I got up and stumbled into the rain and down to HQ, which was nearly half a mile away. Here I was asked some minor question or another, which did not apply to me, nor was I able to answer it. I got back to billets again and got turned in. Once more I was aroused and told I was wanted. I got half way to HQ when I met someone who told me to bring the Company along too. I went back and got them fallen in and marched them down to HQ. Here we stood fast for at least an hour when we were allowed to lie down in the wet grass by the roadside. The rain had stopped but there was a suspicion of frost and it was very cold.

Casualties, Herlies:
Killed: 1029 L/Cpl. Oxford, 1968 Pte Waters.

Wounded: 1503 Pte Robson, Pte Nicholls (RAMC), 9861 Pte Robinson. Lieut. W. Platt. D.S.O.

Sunday 25 October:

St John. We stayed by HQ till dawn, and then were ordered to dig ourselves in after which we were given a hot meal. The reason for this pleasant nights work was that the Germans had attacked the trench line and the Gordon Highlanders had broken and we were being held in readiness to support the counter attack if the Germans were not removed by other means. Fortunately they were so removed and we were left in peace for a few hours.

Somewhere about noon we were again fallen in and it was evident that excitement of some sort or another was going on. As soon as we had collected our men and fallen in I, with the other Company commanders, was sent for and we were told that the Germans had got through the Brigade on our right and we were to make a counter attack in conjunction with the Royal Fusiliers. We were to attack on the east of the Estaires – La Bassée road. My company was to lead the attack and I got it out in the required order and directed the platoon and section commanders. My instructions were hurried and rather muddled, but I was told to do with them and not waste time, so I set off feeling anything but satisfied.

We had not gone far when we came into contact with the 7th [63] who seemed to be doing our job. I reported this and received an order to halt and closed up the Company on the road, as we were now to attack up the west side of the road. This reversion now made us the rear Company and I was ordered to be in Battalion reserve. The delay caused by the change enabled me to make arrangements for the safety and welfare of my overcoat. I had been wearing it when we fell in and I had been precipitously ordered to discard it. There was some sort of order, which I personally had not seen, forbidding the wearing of great coats under certain conditions. As my coat straps were naturally on my saddle I had no option but to deposit my coat in a ditch with but a faint hope of seeing it again, and looked forward to a heavy cold in the near future.

We had progressed about one third of a mile with our new attack when we heard that the 7th had done the work required and that we were to return to the Rouge Croix. We did so and stopped there until dark. Here we saw a goodly number of German prisoners going back. I talked to one lot who looked very tired. They had an officer with them who was really quite polite. There was also a boy of about 15 to whom I offered a biscuit. He refused with scorn but one of the men took it and eat it with avidity. The boy showed a marvellous spirit, and an apparently inexhaustible capacity for hate. To my surprise I could not feel anything but pity for them although even in those days one had heard of the atrocities that have since been made public.

The Royal Fusiliers lost 12 officers in their attack so that it seemed a bit of luck for us that things were muddled as they had been. So bad was the confusion on this occasion that the Army Corps Commander came down to investigate this with the result that the Divisional Commander who had succeeded Hubert Hamilton was advised that he was looking seedy and had better try a change of air in England[64].

63 He is referring to the 7th Foot. The Royal Fusiliers. (City of London Regiment).

64 This was Maj.-Gen. C. J. Mackenzie who assumed command of the 3rd Division on the 15th October and was replaced by Maj.-Gen. F. D. V. Wing on the 29th.

As soon as it was dark we returned to our billets but I did not get much rest. It was the same thing time after time. I was routed out to go and answer silly question at Headquarters. At last I got an urgent summons and we were told that we were to relieve the Lincolnshire Regiment in the trenches and were given careful instructions as to how we were to get there and how the relief was to be carried out.

Capt Gordon: Stood to arms most of last night. Gordon Highlanders having left their trenches – they were re-taken with little opposition by 7th R. Fusiliers and the Middlesex Regt. We get mail nearly every day – the troops are extraordinary well fed. Fresh bacon, bully beef, bread or biscuit, tea and sugar, tobacco and matches. Every mail brings countless presents for the men. 11.15 a.m. battalion deploys to support Royal Irish who had been driven out of their trenches. Retire again to Divisional Reserve on learning that trenches are recaptured. The 3rd (Lahore) Division is now operating on our left – saw some of them today, 47th Sikhs. At 7.30 p.m. we get orders to take over Lincoln trenches 3 p.m. Beastly wet night. Back to our old billet.

The fighting during the last week had further depleted the ranks of II Corps and the survivors were now so exhausted that General Smith-Dorrien was no longer confident that he could hold the line. On the 25th he met with Sir John French and asked for more troops but with the battles raging around Ypres coming to a climax there were none to spare. The best that could be done was to authorise an increase in II Corps 18 pdr. gun expenditure from 30 to 60 rounds a day, and strengthen II Corps reserves in case of an enemy breakthrough. A cavalry brigade, an infantry battalion and a battery of field artillery, all "resting" from the Ypres fighting were moved to Vielle Chappelle, 3 miles behind II Corps line. The French also assisted. General Conneau moved his cavalry Corps back behind the 3rd Division and in the Le Bassée sector General Maud'huy, commander of the French Tenth Army, agreed to take over more of the 5th Division line, allowing some British troops to be withdrawn for short periods of rest.

To fill the depleted ranks of the fighting battalions the flow of reinforcements from the British base areas was speeded up. A thousand men arrived during the night of the 25th and another thousand on the 27th, which raised the strength of the average battalion to about 700. The majority of these reinforcements consisted of reservists that lacked proper training but in the circumstances this didn't really matter for all they were required to do was man the trenches and fire their rifles if the enemy attacked.

Over the next few days the brunt of the fighting at Neuve Chapelle would be predominately borne by six under strength British battalions; the 4/Middlesex; 4/Royal Fusiliers; 1/Northumberland Fusiliers; 1/Lincolns; 1/Wiltshires and the 2/Royal Irish Rifles, about 4000 men against an enemy that brought to the battle a powerful striking force of six infantry regiments[65], two Jäger battalions, and the combined artillery of two divisions. The enemy's initial attacks on the 27th were to evolve into a four-day battle for control of the village that was to leave both sides exhausted and the Germans with losses of over 5,000 for little gain.

Monday 26 October

The Battle for the Village

During the night of the 25th /26th the Northumberland Fusiliers relieved the Lincolns in their trenches north-east of the village.

At dawn on the 26th, undercover of a thick mist, the German infantry launched their first attacks at the junction of the 5th Division with the French Tenth Army around Givenchy. These attacks continued all day, but were feints, aimed at keeping

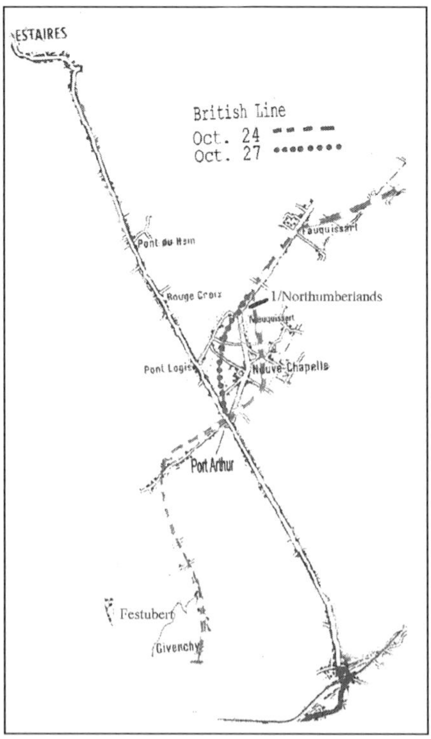

Neuve Chapelle. The dotted line represents the trench line after the German capture of the village.

65 A German regiment consisted of 3 battalions and a machine gun company of six guns and one spare gun. At full strength a battalion consisted of 26 officers and officials and 1,050 other ranks. Six infantry regiments would be about 18,000 men.

the 5th Division occupied so it could not reinforce the troops around Neuve Chapelle where the main attack was to be made.

Throughout the morning the troops defending Neuve Chapelle had been confined to their trenches by sniper and machines gun fire but at about 3 pm the Germans opened up with a heavy bombardment, so accurate in places that it drove the infantry from their trenches to take cover by lying out in the relative safety of the open fields. The 1/Northumberlands, positioned just outside the village, were protected from the worst of this bombardment by a bend in the trench line but the 4/Royal Fusiliers, on their right, were not so fortunate. They suffered so severely from the bombardment that they were driven from their trenches by the attack of the first wave of German infantry. This exposed the trenches of Captain Gordon's company, and a section of field guns that had been situated in front of the Northumberland's trenches, to assault by the German infantry and to protect his flank, and provide covering fire to the remaining gunners, Captain Gordon had his men deepen a ditch that ran at right angles from his trenches to some farm buildings on the Neuve Chapelle road.

When the enemy renewed their attack shells exploding on the gun platform disabling the last gun firing and killed or wounded the

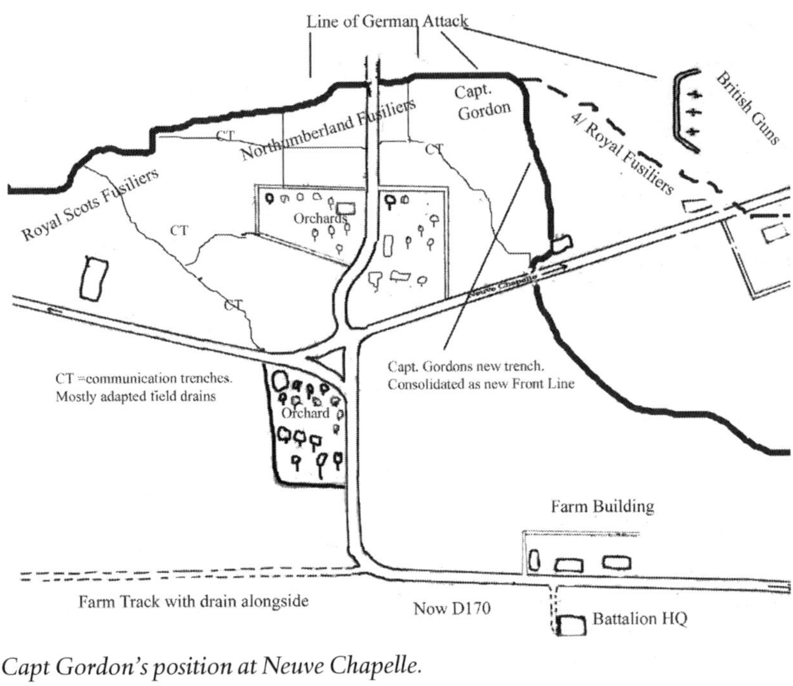

Capt Gordon's position at Neuve Chapelle.

remaining gunners. Seizing the opportunity a group of German infantry jumped out of their trench and dashed towards the gun position and to stop them Lieutenant Nunnery leapt up onto his parapet and, shouting at his men to follow him, ran across the field in a wild bayonet charge only to be shot down about 10 yards from the gun platform. Seeing this happen Captain Gordon shouted at the men to return and, as they ran back, they opened a clear field of fire to the abandoned guns giving the Company marksmen the opportunity to decimate the enemy infantry who were aimlessly milling around the guns and their limbers.

About 30 minutes later another party of German infantry dashed for the guns and this time it was Captain Gordon who attempted to head them off with a bayonet charge but only five men followed him from the trench and they, along with the enemy, became entangled in a broken down barbed wire fence along the edge of the field. Separated by only a few yards neither group could move forwards and after a few moments of wild shouting and firing at close range both sides seemed to realise how precarious and ridiculous was their position and withdrew back to their own trenches. Captain Gordon had three of his five men killed and a bullet through his cap.

At dusk the Germans infantry made a third attempt to destroy the abandoned guns. This included a very brave soldier who carried a bale of burning straw onto the gun platform and, before he was shot down, managed to stuff the bale under one of the wagons. Seeing that this fire could spread to the other wagons and set off any unused ammunition Corporal Fisk asked Captain Gordon's permission to dash across and put it out. Running the gauntlet of both friendly and enemy fire Fisk dashed across and extinguished most of the burning bale by tearing it out from under the wagon and, to everyone's relief, returned safely to his trench.[66]

While the Northumberland Fusiliers fought their private battle things were not going well in front of the village. The 7th Infantry Brigade, having lost heavily in the bombardment, was not strong enough to withstand the repeated infantry attacks and in the late afternoon the enemy drove a wedge between the 5th and 3rd Divisions and a large party of their infantry rushed triumphantly through the village. They were met on the other side by the 7th Infantry Brigade reserve, a very under strength company of the Wiltshire Regiment, less than 60 strong, who, in a ferocious counter-attack, drove them back

66 Corporal Fisk was awarded the DCM. He was killed in action two weeks later.

among the burning houses but were not strong enough to recapture the village.

At 6 pm a stronger counter-attack, mounted by the 1/Lincolns, the survivors of both the 2/Royal Irish Rifles and the 4/Royal Fusiliers, supported by 300 French cyclists, fought for several hours in the winter darkness, illuminated by the glare of the burning houses, to clear the village of the enemy, except for a triangle of large stone houses on its northern outskirts.

Darkness also brought added danger to Captain Gordon. The enemy finally succeeded in taking the gun emplacement and were now less than 60 yards away from his trenches with a clear line of sight directly into the backs of his men manning the front trench. To provide some form of protection he worked his men throughout night constructing a parapet along the rear edge of his trenches and the enemy, believing that the noise of the digging meant that Gordon's men were fully occupied, attempted to overrun them with a surprise attack, but were cut down in the darkness by riflemen firing from both the front and back of the trenches.

Relief for Captain Gordon's Company, who had been fighting practically non-stop for over twelve hours, finally came in the pre-dawn with a counter-attack re-establishing the 4/Royal Fusiliers in their trenches.

> *Capt Gordon.* Relieve Lincolns 3 a.m. Very dark and unpleasant spot, trenches being continually sniped. During the morning lost my subaltern 2nd Lieutenant Laws, promoted from Sergeant a few days ago – very good man and a great loss. Capt. Barnsley – 20th Fusiliers[67] attached to my company and joins. Have lost four officers in my trenches today (Laws, Nunnerly, Barnsley and Leather). The hardest day I have ever experienced – my Company's losses; 10 killed, 11 wounded and 40 missing many of the latter I fear are killed and wounded

Captain St John had a much quieter time.

> *St John.* At midnight we fell in and walked down to our rendezvous at Croix Rouge. I formed up my Company

67 The Lancashire Fusiliers.

as advanced guard along the road to Rue du Bacquerot as according to orders. When the whole battalion was fallen in I was told that we were to go via Pontfage so I counter marched my advance guard and formed them up along the La Bassée road.

We got started off at last and reached our sector about 3 a.m. Here we went into the farm where the Lincoln battalion Headquarters was and were shown our trenches on a map and I was given a guide to take me down to mine. It was a wet night and our route lay over ploughed fields and ditches, the latter being crossed by slippery single planks. I got to the trenches and found the officer in occupation feverishly awaiting my arrival and dreadfully afraid that I would not relieve him before daylight. I took a hurried look around and remarked that the trenches were not very complete. Was told by the officer that they had only been in them for three days (which I knew), and that his men had been too tired !!! to work them, although they had not been very much harried.

I went back to the rendezvous to find that my Company had been moved by some silly ass, who had not left word to where they had gone. I spent half an hour looking for them in the dark and at last found them mostly asleep in a ditch. As there was not room for all of them in the trench I left half a platoon behind with battalion H.Q. and took the rest by slow, slippery and at times sticky stages, to my trenches where I found the officer and men of the Lincolns nearly frantic with anxiety. However I got him and his men away on time and my own into their places but the margin was not very large one. We barely had time to settle down before we were standing to arms to greet the dawn.

Casualties at Neuve Chapelle:
Killed: 9545 Pte Devereux, 9880 Pte McCartney, 81 Pte Griffin, 1576 Pte Melville, 431 Pte Hoden, 58 Pte Drake, 221 Pte Gable, 887 Pte Seldon, 381 Pte Taylor, 9954 Pte Whithy.

Wounded: 355 Pte Benwell, 9636 Pte Purdy, 1022 Pte Hodgiman, 8233 Pte Coates, 9747 Pte Crutch, 9321 Pte Jennings, 9851 Pte Blacker, 9315 Pte Mc Dermott, 6932 Sgt. Clarke, 972 Pte Jull, 110

Pte Doyle, 1458 Pte Large, 9343 Harwood, 730 Pte Rose, 6943 Pte McQuade, 9173 Pte Slater, 1370 Pte Weaver, 146 Pte Sanders, 1444 Pte Lewis, 2392 Pte White, 90 Cpl Hampson.

Missing: 983 Cpl Rush, 9187 Pte Brearley, 8711 Pte Cutten, 1492 Pte Duck, 9563 Pte Johnson, 219 Pte Loughman, 7828 Sgt. White, 570 Pte Turner, 1990 Pte Rhead, 3771 Pte Willoughby, 7916 Pte Padget, 9547 Sgt. Thirknell, 579 Pte Brimskey, 9851 Pte Blacker, 919 Pte Bridgeman, 268 Pte Cass, 9232 Pte Dutson, 369 Pte Greaves, 1042 Pte Hills, 9646 Pte Ingram, 1565 Pte Jackson, 184 Pte Johnson, 8706 Pte Minfin, 9324 Pte McMann, 1792 Pte Office, 1350 Pte Plowman, 1637 Pte Potter, 3579 Pte Rawson, 1805 Pte Scorer, 467 Pte Sharratt, 3671 Pte Thompson, 9497 Pte Thomas.

Tuesday 27 October

The fighting around Neuve Chapelle was consuming the battalions of the 3rd Division at a prodigious rate. Even with a regular supply of reinforcements two days of intense fighting had reduced most battalions to 300-500 men, barely sufficient to hold the line and the 27th was to see two foolhardy actions that were to add substantially to their casualties.

The enemy had not been idle during the hours of darkness. Machine guns and snipers were placed in the houses and farm buildings that populated the lanes and fields around the village and their inter-locking fields of fire made any movement by formed bodies of troops in, and around, the village almost impossible. In addition the triangle of houses at the top of the village was converted into a veritable fortress by lining the inside walls with layers of sandbags through which were tunnelled sniper and machine gun positions. Nevertheless a decision was made to clear the enemy from the houses.

The first attack went in just after dawn and failed disastrously and one searches in vain why, after this attack, the local commanders continued to throw infantry at the buildings throughout the rest of the day. At this early stage of the war the British had no HE shell for its field guns and therefore could not demolish these strong points by artillery fire; nor were the infantry equipped with hand grenades so even if some of them did survive long enough to reach the walls of the houses they had no way of attacking the garrison other than trying to break into the building. By the time the attacks were called off in the early afternoon the 3rd Division had added substantially to their casualties, used up most of their local reserves, and achieved nothing other than boost the morale and self-confidence of the enemy.

The second foolhardy action started with a failed attempt by the survivors of the 2/Royal Irish Rifles to recapture the trenches they had lost the day before. The enemy, sensing how weak they were, counter-attacked and drove them back through the village in an encounter battle that cost the Royal Irish a further 54 men killed, wounded or prisoner. At the same time the enemy were mustering behind the Bois du Biez, a large wood about a mile southeast of Neuve Chapelle, in preparation for an attack of their own which fell on the 1/Wiltshires and the few remaining survivors of the 2/Royal Irish Rifles. They, with unbelievable gallantry, prevented the enemy taking the village and managed to hold out until late afternoon when their situation was eased by a vigorous flank attack by the 9th Bhopal that drove the enemy back to the Bois du Beiz. The 1/Wiltshires had lost 8 officers and three hundred men and at roll call mustered less than 300, including the transport, reserves and a hundred reinforcements that had arrived during the night that had not yet been involved in the fighting. The 2/Royal Irish Rifles mustered less than 200, including sixty reinforcements that arrived during the afternoon.

From an examination of the enemy prisoners it was established that eight different regiments, or 24 battalions from the *VII, XIII* and *XIV Corps* had been involved in the fighting, supported by combat engineers, a battalion of heavy howitzers and a trench mortar battalion

The enemy had now penetrated the British line twice in two days and it was clear that the 3rd Division had insufficient men to defend Neuve Chapelle and during the night the village was abandoned to the enemy and a new, shorter, defence line constructed in the fields between the village and the La Bassée –Éstaires road.

> *St John.* As soon as it was light I had a good look around and came to the conclusion that there were no Germans nearer to us than 800 to 1000 yards. I located our flank trenches and made a minute inspection of my own with a view to telling off working parties to improve them. I then breakfasted with a welcome tot of rum and posted look-out men and then decreed a general doss till noon. I had planned to begin work on improving the cover after the men had dinner at midday but here I counted without my host who, on this occasion, was represented by the enemy who spent almost the entire

afternoon throwing shells at us. It began with the usual appearance of a Taube, which hovered over us and dropped a string of glittering balls. One got to dread the Taube as a field mouse must dread the hawk. Only the Taube does not swoop and pounce (from choice that is to say) but instead drops its strings of glass balls on which the German gunners range. Fortunately on this occasion either the Taube was not correctly over us or the range takers were inaccurate, with the result that most of the shells went over us but they gave us a heavy bombardment and we suffered some casualties. It also prevented us from doing much useful work.

When darkness fell the shelling ceased and we started in. I put out two listening patrols calling for volunteers for this work, which in those days was somewhat of a novelty in soldiering. I could not get a single man to volunteer so ordered a man from each platoon to report to me at once and these I handed over in pairs to two N.C.O.s and drove them out over the parapet. They went out in fear and trembling although in reality there were just as safe as they would have been outside the parados over which they went backwards and forwards without any hesitation whatever.

I always had trouble with listening guards. The men were all undoubtedly jumpy and hated the job and were always continuously coming in to report imaginary advances by the Germans. I gave orders that they were not to come in until they actually saw men advancing but they imagined then that they saw them and I had to go out and show them it was only their imagination. The only use I had for them was in the first night when they reported that digging was going on about 200 yards to our front.

The Germans were very active all night and attacked on both our flanks but they did not touch us although we were kept standing to arms for most of the night which was well illuminated by star shell and searchlights. As far as possible we went on working but as I feared an attack I kept the men at their posts for a long time. I would not allow them to fire their rifles aimlessly as other men did. I found out by not doing so we were not fired at in return, a fact of which I made use of on succeeding nights to improve our trenches.

Capt. Gordon. At 4 a.m. my company being relieved in trench by Y Company returned to Regimental reserve, men dog tired but cheery – they are splendid. I often hate them in peace, but I love them all tonight. Battalion Headquarters move back about ½ mile to clear shelled area. Spend day in reserve while Brigade Reserve assisted by 47th Sikhs attack to regain lost trenches. Some heavy fighting results in some progress at nightfall. Our 3 companies in the firing line suffer some casualties from snipers. These snipers are usually concealed in trees or the roofs of houses and are very difficult to discover. One of our patrols this morning shot a sniper in plain clothes – he tried to surrender.

Casualties at Neuve Chapelle:
Killed: 4298 A/Sgt. Beaumont, 1133 Pte Askew, 738 Pte Darby, 16 Pte Newcombe, 226 Pte Paine 9821 Pte O'Leary, 2536, Sgt. Panter, 9879 Pte Monger, 9223 Pte Neep, 832 Pte Scarfe, 9713 Pte Percival, 927 Pte Broderick, 9611 Pte Marshall, 2171 Pte Dunbar, 8033 Pte Hebbron, 3063 Sgt. Lee, 628 Pte Nesbit, 1154 Pte Lewis, 971 Pte Hicks.Capt. E Lambert, Capt. Barnsley, 2/Lieut. Coles, Lieut. Leather 2/Lieut. Nunelly 2/Lieut. A Laws.

Wounded: 419 L/Cpl Hayes, Pte Pritchard, Pte Buckland, Pte Wakefield, Pte Rutherford, 255 Pte Edwards, 28 Pte Walker, 805 Cpl. Livingstone, 1542 Cpl Green, 9377 Pte Bell, 1660 Pte Patterson, 9756 Pte Ball, 9582 Pte Wensley, 477 Pte Brown, 9583 Pte White Pte Schofield, 8431 Pte Travers, 686 Pte Kilby, Pte Connellery, 2210 Pte Moat, 9318 Pte Carruthers, 752 Drvr. Hutchinson.

Wednesday 28th October
Having just abandoned the village the decision was made somewhere along the line of command to regain control of Neuve Chapelle in a joint action involving the troops of three nationalities; French Chasseurs and Cyclists from Conneau's Corps; the 2nd Battalion Royal Scots; the 47th Sikhs, 9th Bhopal and the 20th and 21st Companies Sappers and Miners from the Lahore Division. This attack was a shambles.

There was no proper coordination between the troops of different nationalities; the Royal Scots and 9th Bhopal were so heavily shelled when forming up for the attack that they were pinned to the ground and could not move. The French did not even make it to the battlefield.

The only redeeming feature was that four Companies of the Indian Army, two from the 47th Sikhs and the two Field Companies of the Sappers and Miners[68] exhibited outstanding bravery and were the only troops to penetrate into the village where they were to fight on throughout the day completely unsupported. When they came to withdraw in the late afternoon only 68 out of 289 Sikhs returned, and less than half the Sappers.

> *St John.* When daylight came we found the enemy entrenched 300 to 400 yards away from us, a most unpleasant surprise for me. However at first their trenches were not so good and on both that morning and that morning after I bagged two Huns in the early hours making a total of four to my own (or rather my Sergeant-Major's) rifle.

> *Capt. Gordon.* Situation remains much the same. Fresh troops attack supported by a large force of French Artillery and make some progress. French artillery is in position immediately in rear of my reserve trenches. This lets us in for heavy shell fire, enemy replying and I have more men hit.

Casualties at Neuve Chapelle:
Killed: 2535 Sgt. Vale, 9337 Pte Nugent, 1219 Pte Fleet, 9399 Pte Murray.

Wounded: Cpl Moss, Cpl Waddel, L/Cpl Hogg, L/Cpl Knowles, 61 Pte Baker, 746 Pte Whitelaw, 902 Pte Swabey, 8710 Pte McVittie.

Missing. 8617 Pte Marsden.

Thursday 29th October
After the attack by the Indian troops Neuve Chapelle became strangely quiet and at dawn a patrol that penetrated into the village found it deserted, except for the dead and wounded of both sides scattered everywhere. Unfortunately the enemy had not gone away and any

68 Sir John French abhorred the idea of using highly skilled sappers and engineers as storm troopers. He eventually issued orders forbidding the practice, as these men were too valuable to lose doing a job that belonged to the infantry.

attempt by the British to re-occupy the ruins was quickly terminated by the enemy who sniped and shelled anyone moving close to the village.

> *St John.* We were in the trenches till the night of October 29th, a total of four days and five nights during which we had a pretty lively time of it. In the first place we were heavily sniped all the time and we lost a lot of men that way. I myself had a narrow shave. I went up to look at the head cover of a traverse which was reported as being dangerous and no sooner had I stuck my head up than I got a bullet through the wrap I wore round my neck. It made a furrow in my beard but otherwise did no damage.
>
> The trenches were still bad and moving along them was a difficult matter and occasionally necessitated treading on dead men as to throw the body over the parados only drew fire. Thinking of this now and writing it down may appear to be merely bravado on my part but I mention it to show what impressed me greatly at the time how little one feared death in any form, or thought of it when one was always face to face with it. One knew one was certain to get a bullet in course of time and that it might come along during the next few minutes.
>
> During those days we were not blessed with fine weather a lot of rain fell and the trenches became very sodden though it remained fairly warm. My officers then consisted of Everard Lamb (2nd. Captain) and two boys from the O.T.C., one of whom was called Thompson and I cannot remember the name of the other. My pal Nunnerley was transferred to Gordon's Company after Herlies and was killed during Gordon's fight at Neuve Chapelle.

Casualties at Neuve Chapelle:
Killed: 9638 Pte Tait.

Friday 30th October
During the nights of the 29th and 30th October, the Lahore and Meerut Divisions of the Indian Corps replaced II Corps in the Le Bassée sector. The Northumberland Fusilier's trenches were taken over by the 2nd Gurkha Rifles.

St John. On Thursday the 29th I got orders that we were to be relieved at 4 a.m. and go into billets. I went down to Headquarters to report and meet the officer who was to take over about midnight. On the way down I was pretty heavily fired upon by some unknown man who seemed to follow me up though he never hit me. I found Headquarters, which had been moved since I last saw them, and took over my orders for relief and the officer who was to relieve me. He was in the Indian Army and we were being relieved by a Battalion of Gurkhas. I got him and his orderly down to the trenches in safety and en route selected a good spot on the road for my Company to assemble when they left. As we got in the Huns began a night attack which lasted all the time I was showing the other man around. It then slackened for a bit and he got away but they kept pretty hard at it all night. At about 4 our relief came along headed by the Englishman who was followed by a cloud of little boys. The Ghurka is only about four foot nothing in his socks and on this occasion as I was to learn afterwards his small stature combined with bad staff work was his undoing for no sooner had we left than the Germans attacked and the poor little men being too small to see over the parapet were scuppered and 400 of them killed. We were not warned till too late that we were to be relieved by Gurkhas or told to build up a firing platform for them. This incident is a good one to what a danger a staff officer is who neglects the smallest detail[69].

The orders I gave for carrying out the relief were as follows. The Gurkhas were to line up behind the Parados while our men were to go out under their NCOs and proceed along a certain hedge, through a gate into a grass field, up behind another hedgerow, through another gap, and through the cover of a turnip field onto the road at a point where it was banked up and to form up behind the embankment and wait for me. All went well as far as I could see and I got the Gurkhas into their trenches without any delay. Just as I started out a heavy attack on our right began to develop but only high shots were coming my way. These did not bother me and I made my way to the rendezvous to

69 In severe fighting on the night of the 2/3 November the 2nd Ghurkha rifles were driven from their trenches suffering 44 killed and 99 wounded or missing.

find no one there. I asked some gunners who were serving a howitzer in the turnip field if they had seen my men but they reported not. So back I went again and found them all lying flat in the turnip field lower down, having taken cover when the shots began to come over. I kicked them out of it and onto the road where I formed them up and told them what I thought of them. That done we went on to Headquarters. Other Companies who had experienced some difficulty in getting away joined up with us when we all proceeded down the road to Rough Coix, which we reached as daylight appeared. We went onto Vielle-Chapelle and got into billets there and had breakfast.

We had been fighting continuously now since the 13th October and were all absolutely tired out and we hoped for our long promised rest. We stopped all that day at Vielle-Chapelle as the General who was to take over our sector had not arrived and also things were not going too well with the Indians who had relieved us. At about 3.0 p.m. we fell in and eventually marched through Éstaires to our billets outside the town where we were told that we were to have a weeks rest and to refit. I had billets in a nice farmhouse where the inmates insisted on turning out of their beds and sitting up all night to allow the officers beds to sleep in. I turned into a soft bed with snow white sheets and was soon as asleep only to be woken up somewhere about 10 p.m. with orders to the effect that the Battalion would rendezvous at the crossroads at 5.45 a.m.

The news rather disturbed my nights sleep as I had reached that state of weariness when sleep will not come easily.

Chapter 9
Ypres

General Situation

The Anglo-French offensive to outflank the Germans in northern France, between Lens and Lille, was going nowhere. The French Tenth Army had failed to displace the Germans from Vimy Ridge and the British II Corps and III Corps, positioned along the valley of the river Lys, were hanging on precariously to their water-logged trenches. North of them, between Armentieres and the Channel coast the situation was equally dire. Against the coast the remnants of the Belgium army held onto a narrow strip of their country and only remained safe from destruction by allowing the sea to reclaim the flat land in front of their trenches. To the south French and British infantry hung grimly onto a shrinking salient around the Belgium city of Ypres, a salient being remorsesly squeezed by the over-powering might of the German *Sixth* and *Fourth Armies.*

A much-depleted Cavalry Corps occupied the strategically important Messines Ridge in the southern part of the salient and troopers of the Composite Household Cavalry Regiment, about 450 rifles, with little artillery support, held the section of the ridge in front of the village of Wytschaete. They had been under desultory attack for several days but on the morning of 30th October they were attacked by three battalions from *Army Group Fabeck*[70] well supported by artillery and infantry odds of 12:1 in the enemy's favour.

Throughout the 30th there was heavy fighting for the ridge and by the morning of the 31st the cavalrymen were reduced to desperately holding onto Wytschaete. They were in urgent need of reinforcements

70 This was a new assault army, made up of fresh divisions, and well supported by artillery, which was brought up by the German High Command to break through the Allied line south of Ypres.

and the closest uncommitted troops were the 9th Infantry Brigade, just withdrawn to rest and refit after almost three weeks non-stop fighting around Neuve Chapelle. The Northumberland Fusiliers, reduced to about 350 men, and the Lincolns, about 800 strong, were to have less

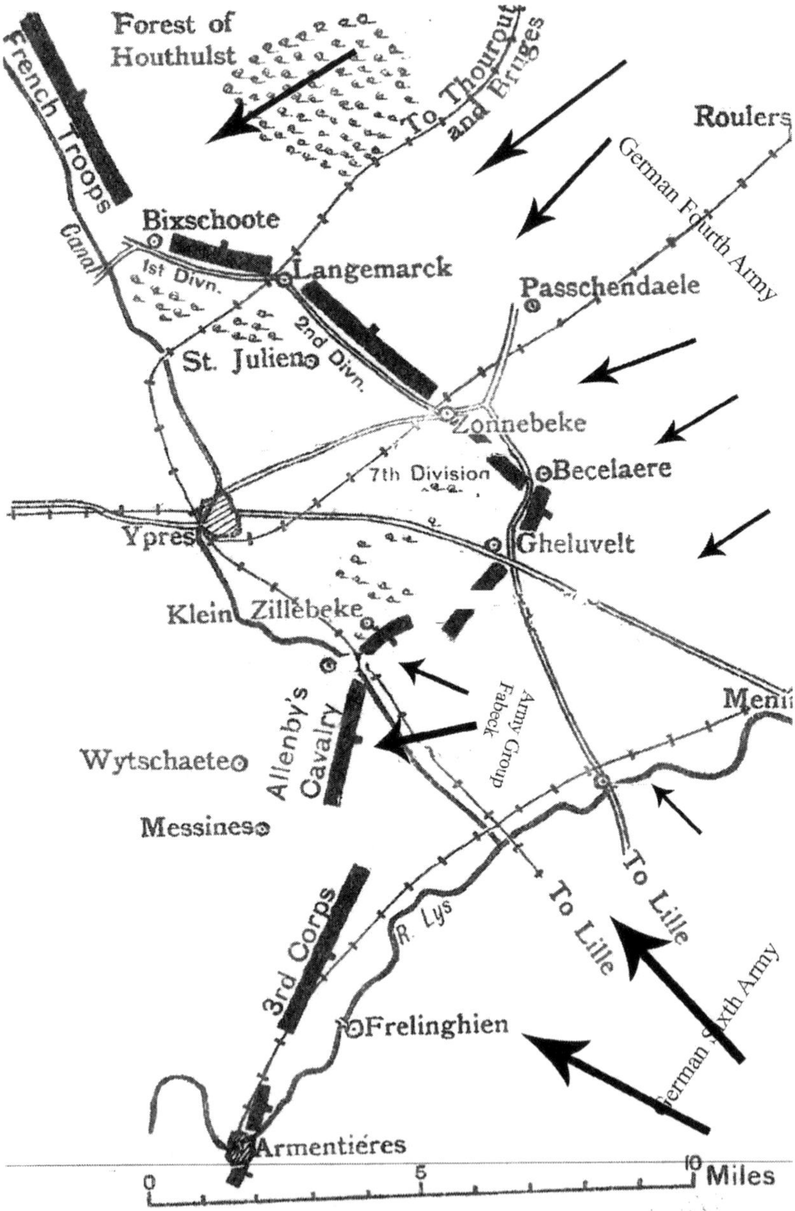

Situation around Ypres Oct. 23

than 24 hours rest before they were roused from their billets to march northwards towards the fighting raging around Ypres[71].

Saturday 31 October

St John. We turned out about 4.30 and got breakfast. I also got a bit of a wash in a bucket. I found the men quite cheerful being under the impression that they were going further back as our billets were wanted for someone else. I did not disabuse their minds and got them to the rendezvous in good time, everyone else was late as the hour for starting had been put forward at the last moment. I ascertained that we were going for a fifteen mile march to support the Cavalry Brigade who were holding the line south of Ypres and who were being hard pressed. We pressed on and got to a place called Neuve Eglise where my Company was told off to dig trenches which was bad luck on them as they were the only Company that had not been given any rest at Neuve Chapelle. However they were wonderfully cheerful and we had some new blood too in the shape of reinforcements who had joined us when we came out of the trenches. They had arrived under Bob Fletcher and Robin Williams, neither who lived to see a week of fighting. After we had been digging for about three hours they gave up the idea of entrenching there and we sat on the roadside till dark when we went into billets at Kemmel with orders to be prepared to turn out at a moment notice. I was very careful to carry out this order and saw that every N.C.O. knew exactly where his men were to fall in. It required some care as the billets were in a mill and the men had to climb down staircases and ladders out of lofts. My care bore fruit for as usual we were the first Company ready and were ready some time before the others that should preceded us according to the order of march. The result was I got a damning for waiting for the other Companies and we were sent into the forefront of the battle out of our turn; but that is another story.

71 This combined force, of the two battalions, was commanded by their Brigadier, Brigadier-General F. C. Shaw.

Sunday 1 November

On the Messines ridge, at about 1 am, the German infantry launched their final attack and after a fierce battle captured the village of Wytschaete at about 2.45 am.

Soon after the German attack started, at about 1.30 am, Brigadier-General Shaw received verbal orders from Major-General H Gough, GOC 2nd Cavalry Division, to march his infantry immediately to Wytschaete and support his cavalry. Battalion orders for 1st September, issued before they went into billets, had detailed Captain St John's company as the reserve company for the following day, and that should have kept them out of action, but St John had been too efficient in ensuring that his men could get out of the mill quickly and his company was the first to assemble outside battalion HQ. With the crises at Wytschaete developing rapidly he was ordered to take his men, and those of other company forming up, to the rendezvous point on the road between Kemmel and Wytschaete.

The 1/Lincolns were ahead of them and arrived first to find utter confusion. Wytschaete had apparently just fallen and there was panic and uncertainty everywhere. For the 1/Lincolns every senior cavalry officer they met gave them conflicting orders, while none could give a clear picture of the enemy's disposition or appear to have any plan, or instructions, other than the village and ridge must be recaptured immediately.

Eventually some sort of plan was cobbled together in which the 1/Lincolns would begin the counter-attack by advancing down the right hand-side of the Kemmel – Wytschaete road, supported by the 1/Northumberlands on their left. However co-ordination of the infantry seemed to be beyond the capabilities of the cavalry officers on the spot for when Captain St John and his men arrived they found that the Lincolns had already moved off. This made it difficult for them to catch up in time to support the attack but a passing cavalry officer offered a solution by suggesting that they could save time by taking a shortcut across the fields as this would cut off a large bend in the road. For good measure he added that as far as he knew there were no fences or ditches in the fields.

Meanwhile the 1/Lincolns had made good progress along the road and were approaching the outskirts of Wytschaete when they come under heavy artillery fire. They quickly deployed in the fields on the right hand side of the road intending to develop their attack from that direction but as they moved forward they ran into heavy rifle and machine gun fire from enemy infantry positioned along the rim of a tram-way cutting that ran across the front of the village. They made several attempts to get forward but each time were beaten back by the intensity of fire from the enemy who appeared to be in a jubilant mood shouting and singing while the Lincolns lay out in the field at the foot of the embankment. With the enemy artillery fire increasing in intensity the survivors of the Lincolns withdrew back down the road and took shelter behind some cottages just as Captain St John and his men came up[72].

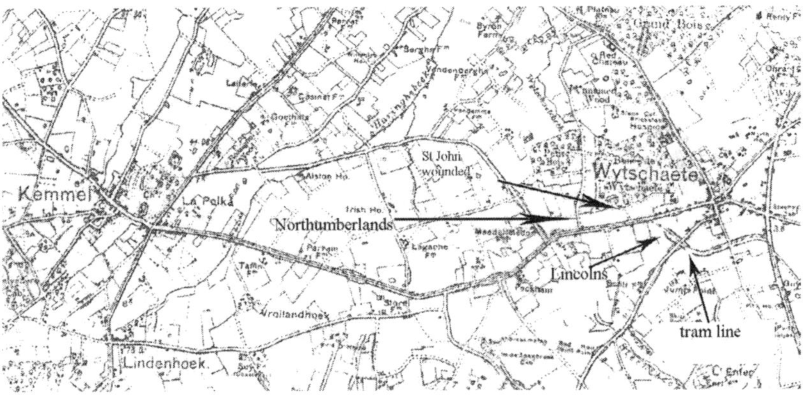

The counterattack on Wytschaete.

> *St John.* We marched off and halted again at some point on the Kemmel-Wytschaete road. Here was a limber on fire and every now and again a cartridge would blow up. The sky was lit all round by fires and there was a noise of continual musketry intermingled with the deeper note of field guns.
>
> I dosed for about half an hour with my body in a wet ditch and my head pillowed on a turnip. Turnips were bad material for making pillows and I woke feeling cold, stiff and rather a head on me to be told to go to the head of the Battalion at once. I went and was ordered to take my Company and Bob Fletcher's and support the Lincolnshire Regiment in their attack on Wytschaete. I could get no information about the strength of the enemy or the exact position of the Lincolns. All I was told was that the latter were on the right of the road

72 The line of this cutting can still be identified by the double line of trees that run diagonally along the hill on the right hand side of the Kemmel – Wytschaete road, almost directly opposite the British military cemetery.

and had started an hour before, that the country between me and the village was open, which was a lie as it was very enclosed chiefly with barbed wire, that we would come under artillery fire almost at once and that I was to hurry up and do what I could to support the attack.

I decided that the best thing to do was to pretend to develop a strong attack on the left or north side of the road and with this object in view we set off in lines of platoons across country in the dark. We soon got hung up on barbed wire and I found that only one of the four cutters, which were considered a sufficient issue to a Company of infantry by the General Staff was left, the three others having been borne by men who became causalities of some kind or another. I also had my own private pair and so we got along somehow but it took until dawn to get within 1000 yards of the village.

Here I called a halt and went to find Fletcher. Him I found digging a hole in the ground and murmuring something about it being his baptism of fire. I told him to keep close to the road so that I could find him if I wanted and went off to the left again to push my Company on into a wood which ran apparently right up to the village and round to the north of it. I found a young subaltern of the Life Guards in the wood with a few men and suggested he should push on and clear the wood if he could do so. He said he wanted his breakfast and did not know much how to soldier off a horse but would do his best. I also detailed a platoon to assist him and went on to find the two platoons in the firing line.

I had sent Everard Lamb up in charge of these two platoons in the dark as both of them were commanded by young inexperienced men and I had been afraid that they would loose touch with everyone in the dark. I now intended to send Lamb back to the support and to direct the platoons where to go and what to do and then to rejoin him. As a matter of fact I never found him and never saw him again as he was killed that day. We had lived together for a fortnight and I had come to be very fond of him. When I got up near the village I found one platoon digging themselves in about 100 yards away from the village. I walked out of the wood and up to them and told the sergeant in charge to push on as there was heavy firing going on our right where were the Lincolnshire Regiment. I then walked back to the wood to try and get hold of Lamb but no one knew where he had got to. I then came back to the edge of the wood and found that the other platoon had advanced about 20 yards and were lying down and digging head cover. I walked out to them and found everyone very jumpy and fed up with things generally and particularly the absence of breakfast. I told them to lie where they were till I found out where everyone was and then to go to the village when I whistled them to do so.

I next went to the road to try and get hold of Fletcher and to find out how things were going. I found Roderick with a few men and some wounded behind a cottage at the edge of the road one of the wounded had a broken thigh and was kicking up such an almighty shindy so I tried to get hold of a stretcher from the Lincolns across the road. Apparently the road was commanded by machine guns in the village and no one could cross it. I tried to find out where Fletcher was but no one knew. The Lincolns reported by shouting that they were having a bad time of it. I waited there for a few minutes hoping that Fletcher would come along so we could settle on some sort of combined action. While there someone reported that firing was coming from the wood. I asked Roderick to send a man over to find out what it was but he did not jump at the idea and as it was my Company who were supposed to be going through the wood I said I would go myself and return again to find Fletcher. I also could not make out where my other platoon had got to and this I was anxious to know.

I had just come across the plough field which was about 200 yards wide and had not been alarmed by any close bullets so I walked quickly out from behind the cover of the cottage and proceed towards the wood. I had not gone very far when I became the centre of attraction of a hot fire which must, I think come from a machine gun. I started to run to the wood at once and the ground all around me was spattered up like the surface of a puddle in a rain storm. I got another 30 to 40 yards when I felt as if I suddenly hit my right arm against a hard obstacle in the dark. It was a very hard and very sharp blow and left a numb sort of tingling sensation in my arm quite different from the stinging of the blows of one or two pebbles, which had been knocked onto my legs by the shots on the ground which had hurt me quite as much. I ran on but the wood looked a long way off and the shock of the wound had scared me a bit and I felt rather dizzy and out of breath (I was running with a coat and all my equipment on) so I decided I would do a die and selecting a comfortable place as I could I wheeled round in the most approved Coton Woodville fashion[73] and fell on my face. This had the desired effect for a minute of two as the firing stopped. I gave them time to turn their attention elsewhere and proceeded to get myself more comfortable with a view to examining the damage to my arm and of tying it up. I must have wiggled too much however for again a hot fire opened up on me. I lay for a few seconds wondering where it would get me, the bullets splashing mud all around me.

Suddenly I felt as if someone had gently drawn something rather hot along my shoulder and round my throat. This could not have been a bullet as it appeared to me to take quite an appreciable time to get from my left shoulder to the right side of my throat. I think must have been the blood flowing. Certainly as soon as it reached my throat I began to cough blood through my mouth and nose and felt as if i was choking and everything looked a sort of blue colour. I thought I was done for and wondered how my family would take the news and whether I would know how they took it. I felt aggrieved and angry at the though of leaving this jolly old world for to me it had always been a jolly place and it seemed hard lines having to leave without seeing Roger and Madge again. However I prayed to God to hurry the matter up as I was getting very uncomfortable.

How long all this took I do not know but one moment I thought I was gone and the next it seemed to me I felt as if I was away up in the high Alps somewhere breathing breath after breath of invigorating air. This must have been caused by the cessation of the bleeding which enabled me to breath not only through the nose and mouth but also through both wounds in my neck.

---

73 R. Coton Woodville (1856-1927) was a famous painter and illustrator portraying the nobler military virtues to glorify Imperial grandeur and sacrifice.

The field where Tudor was wounded taken from the CWC cemetery. The road is left of the wall and Wytschaete wood on the right. The cross is the 16th Irish Division Memorial commemorating their capture of the village in 1917. (Photo taken July 2002)

I lay there for I suppose about five hours. It was very cold and the ground was wet and I remember heavy fits of shivering either from cold or funk or both. I could not see what was going on in the way of fighting but once they searched over the field I was in with shrapnel. It was a narrow sort of field bounded on one side by the wood and on the other by the road and the width of the curtain presumably fired by four guns seemed to my eyes to cover the field most effectively. I watched two salvoes burst in front of me and then I thought I would surely get my quietus but the third effort went over me and all was well once again.

I could not use my right arm at all but I could wave my legs about in the air and also could manipulate my walking stick with my left hand. When I had been there an hour or two I saw some gunners at the edge of the wood. I waved both stick and legs at them and they stopped and conferred about me but would not risk coming into the open to see what I wanted. My heart sank as I saw them go away. Help eventually reached me through one of my own Sergeants who came along. He gave me water and then went off for stretcher bearers who arrived with a doctor about half an hour later. My but was I glad to see them !!. They cut off all

> my equipment and got me onto the stretcher and carried my to the dressing station which was about two miles away as far as I could judge. From the lurid language of the stretcher bearers it might have been ten miles and I might have been a ton of coals they were carrying.
>
> However I got there and my wounds were dressed with iodine which hurt horribly and I was given some more morphine which had no effect on me and I was put into an ambulance which I think belonged to an Indian contingent and taken joltingly to Kemmel where I was laid in a chapel and had more iodine applied. I lay there until about 5.00 p.m. when I was removed in a motor ambulance to Bailleul. It was an appalling journey for me. There were four slightly wounded Tommies in the ambulance which was closed up and all the Tommies smoked woodbines all the time and our way lay over a much damaged Route Pave. Every jolt gave me " gyp " and I was nearly suffocated and unable to speak. Every time I tried to speak the air blew out of my wounds instead of going through my larynx. By the time I reached the hospital in Bailleul I was pretty nearly done. I must have seemed hopeless for they did not take the trouble to transfer me from the stretcher to a bed and I spent a sleepless night.[74] I found one of my subalterns there with a broken wrist.

With all their officer casualties the survivors of the Northumberland Fusiliers streamed back down the road until stopped and rounded up by Captain Gordon. That was the end of their fighting for the day and the survivors returned to their billets in Mt. Kemmel to spend the remainder of the day in reserve.

Casualties

There are no accurate records of casualties for this abortive attack for the relevant appendix to the War Diary does not list them by name. The entry for 1 November is obviously not accurate and gives them as follows: Officers 1 killed, 2 wounded & 2 missing: other ranks 6 killed, 38wounded & 39 missing. The database "Soldiers Died" gives 23 men killed, but officers casualties for 1/Northumberlands are missing from

74 Captain St John was obviously not expected to live and left with the dead and dying in the church porch. Next morning, when they came to clear the dead, they found him still alive and put on the train to the base hospital.

the database. The 1/Lincolns lost 5 officers killed, 3 wounded and 294 other ranks killed, wounded or missing. At roll call the battalion numbered 175.

Monday 2 November

> *St John.* Next morning I was put on board an ambulance train and sent to Boulogne. I do not remember much about this journey except I occupied one side of a 1st class carriage and a man with a disabled limb occupied the other. Oddly enough I met this man some months later. I must have been pretty bad because I remember that the R.A.M.C. orderly who was looking after us thought it safe enough to go through my pockets and relieve me of £ 10 or £ 12 in gold and a few odds and ends as well[75]. I tried to call the medical officers attention to this when I got to Boulogne but I could not make myself heard. A strong feeling of furious indignation no doubt helped to increase my exhaustedness, at any rate when I was eventually was put to bed in No. 11 General Hospital I was past knowing anything and how I got through that night I do not remember.
>
> Of my wounds and how they progressed I do not intend to write much. Illness is mercifully easy to forget and is best forgotten but I cannot close a record of my war experiences without referring to those who have shown so much kindness to me during sickness and convalescence.
>
> To begin with I was badly hit. So badly so indeed that at the clearing hospital at Bailleul they did not think it worth while to move me from my stretcher to a bed which might be needed for someone else with more chance of living through the night.
>
> At Boulogne I was put into a ward with four other beds all full. Of the five of us I am now the only one alive. Three of the others died before my eyes and the fourth was sent over to England and died a few days after he arrived there. My life was saved chiefly by the devotion of Nurse Binns who spared herself no labour or fatigue to do all in her power to give me ease.

---

75 The £10-12 'lifted' from Captain St John would have a current value of about £600.

All through I was attended by an extraordinary series of pieces of good luck. At the very commencement I was lying on my face when hit in the neck. Had I been lying on my back I must have died at once. Then I suppose I am the only man who has been shot in the region where I was hit and whose throat the bullet had gone through without touching any of the three or four vital parts which are there grouped. About a fortnight after I got to Boulogne I developed septic Pneumonia. Had I got it 48 hours sooner nothing could have saved me as it was the skill of my doctors who where there. Sir Francis Makin, Sir John Rose Bradford and Mr Mears and Mr Warr the house surgeons combined with the splendid nursing of Nurse Binns and Sister Howe got me through it and also through an attack of Bronchitis which came on top of it.

One incident in my illness I must recall chiefly on account of its weird unpleasantness happened shortly after I got to Boulogne and before the wounds had healed much. It was at night and I must have coughed very hard or something at any rate the effect was that the air came through the wound and was forced up under my chin so my face was blown up like a balloon. I was terribly frightened and sent for the night surgeon who gave me an injection of something, I think digitalis which calmed things down for me. At first too I used to dream horrible dreams always the same thing that I was turned out and sent back to the trenches and couldn't find my company, but the awakening to reality in a nice safe hospital was distinctly good.

Tuesday 3 November

The battalion marched to Bailleul where they spent the next three nights in comfortable billets.

Wednesday 4 November

Capt. Gordon. Sir Horace Smith-Dorrien inspects the Regiment. The men turned out wonderfully clean and smart – which particularly struck Sir H. He spoke of the services the Battalion in words which will live for ever in the Regimental History. We got our valises last night, the first time for over a month. This morning I had a real hot bath and a change of clothing. Real luxury. Warmer tonight and raining.

Thursday 6 November

The battalion left Bailleul at 10 am and marched to Ypres, passing through the Menin gate and up the road to Hell Fire Corner. Here they remained in support until 11 pm when they relieved the 1st Cavalry Brigade in their trenches just south of the Menin road. In so doing came under the command of General Haig's I Corps.

As the fighting around Ypres intensified many battalions were reduced to almost company strength and to provide sufficient troops to act as an effective fighting unit many battalions were formed into *ad hoc* battle groups called after the name of their commander. The 1/ Northumberlands were in "Shaw's Group", loosely based upon the survivors of the 9th Infantry Brigade but with other units added on a piecemeal basis.

Capt. Gordon. Brigade marched from Bailleul at 10 a.m. I am sent to meet G.O.C. at Hooge at 12.30 p.m. ride on with Roderick – meet the armoured train at Ypres and come in for a dose of shrapnel and " Jack Johnsons " directed at the train. Wait all day at Hooge to take over trenches occupied by 1st Cavalry Brigade, at about 4 p.m. hurried back to rejoin Regt. then 1 mile W of Ypres. For several hours Brigade stands by to support a brigade in difficulties on our right.

Friday 7 November

The enemy were gearing up for another attack. Many of the trenches occupied by Shaw's Group had been deeply undercut beneath the parapet by previous occupants to provide "funk holes" and under the rain of high explosive many were to collapse, burying their garrisons, so that when the German infantry attacked, about 3 pm, they quickly overran many of the front line positions.

Captain Gordon's trenches jutted out slightly towards the enemy in a shallow salient and seemed to have escaped the worst effects of the bombardment but as the trenches either side of him had been overrun by the enemy he found himself in an almost identical predicament to the one at Neuve Chapelle ten days previously. With his right flank 'in the air' he had to throw back his right platoon and, in the midst of some

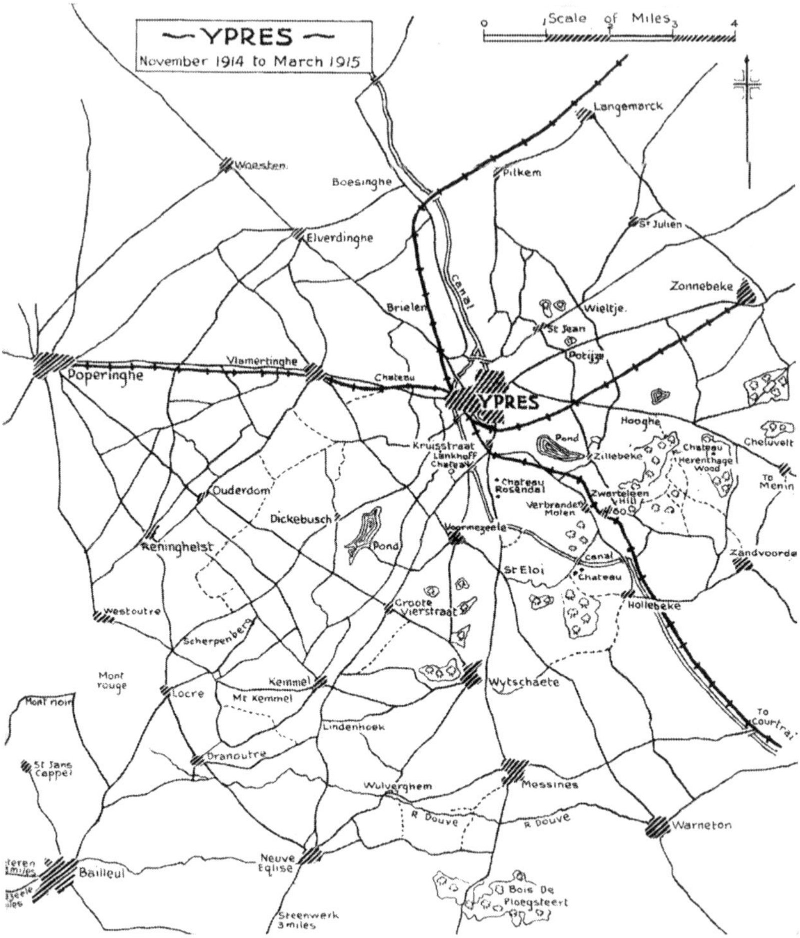

The Ypres Salient.

very bitter fighting, have them convert a communication trench into a fire trench facing the new enemy positions.

Meanwhile Captain Booth rallied the men of the Northumberland Fusiliers who had been driven from their trenches and with these, and two companies of the 1/Lincolns in support, mounted a counter-attack to recapture the lost positions but when Captain Booth fell wounded the attack faltered and the Lincolns , unable to make further progress, the dug a new fire trench about 300 yards to the right rear of Gordon's position leaving him, and his men, isolated.

> *Capt. Gordon.* At Herenthage Wood. relieve the 1st Cav. brigade in the trenches about 1 mile E of Hooge on the high

> ground above Herenthage Chateau. Enemy commences heavy bombardment of our trenches about 11 a.m. Trenches occupied by W, X, and Y suffered most severely, many parts being blown in and men buried. Right of my trench suffers similarly. About 3 p.m. trenches on my right are vacated and enemy take possession of them. Enemy also attack my right but we drive them off with some loss. Our Companies on right supported by 2 Coys of Linc. Regt. make unsuccessful counter attacks. Capt. Booth being wounded. This force now entrenches about 300 yards in my right rear and I throw my right back to meet the situation, converting my communication trench into a fire trench. Enemy now 30 yards on my right and about 250 yards in front entrenched.

Casualties, Ypres:
Wounded: 3095 Pte T. Cronford, Pte G Donohue, 7767 Sgt. F. Hall, 8775 Pte W. Bondes, 8708 Pte C Weston, 7093 Cpl. Lynch.(d.o.w. 9/11/14), 2214 Pte Rose.

Saturday 8 November
Brigadier-General Shaw came to the conclusion that further attempts to regain the lost trenches were unlikely to succeed, and only reduce his small force further. He ordered that the position dug by the Lincolns should be consolidated as the new front line. During the night Captain Gordon's trenches were re-supplied with water and ammunition during and he was ordered to hold their position at all costs.

> *Capt. Gordon.* Spend most of the night improving my trenches. Receive orders to hold line at all costs. Intermittent shells and rifle fire throughout the day. Enemy very busy with their entrenchments. At about 5.30 p.m. enemy left their trenches in my front and charged across to my right and we met them with heavy rifle and machine gun fire and repulsed them with heavy loss. Some of the enemy were killed on my parapet – one or two even succeeding in getting over it. Enemy left about 50 dead in my front and many wounded. Men behaved with great coolness and did splendidly.

Casualties, Ypres:
Killed: 271 Pte Popkin, 471 Pte T Toare, 8199 C.S.M. J Cameron.

Wounded: 9594 Pte D Ironke, 9460 Pte F Dawson, 1518 Pte A Brown, 3409 L/Cpl. Murray, 385 L/Cpl. Crawford, 1768 Pte Arnold, 1545 Pte Jarvis, 2594 Pte Wilson, 1523 Pte Beardsley, 3538 Pte B. Horan. Capt. R.M. St. J. Booth.

Missing: 9479 Pte A Donachy, 1413 Pte D Jukes. 8713 Pte E Smith, 9730 Pte D Kingsland, 1089 Pte T Loftus,1660 Pte J Patterson, 958 Pte H Chastney, 8033 Cpl H Jeffries, 9719 L/Cpl J Budd, 360 Pte W Wilson, 9315 Pte W Moore, 9102 Pte D Keeling, 5 Pte J Timmings, 2108 Pte A Grimes, 9742 L/Cpl J Hogg, 9219 Pte O Jackson, 9113 Pte H Powell, 3055 Pte E Crockford, 227 Pte A Breadshaw, 9348 Pte J Walters, 9168 Pte C Halliday, 3 Pte E Barber, 269 Pte J Mooney, 245 Pte T Abbott, 8885 Pte R Dawson, 2440 J Langley, 9253 Pte H Smith, 9332 Pte J Addam, 9592 Pte J Green, 314 Pte J White, 1318 Pte W Kelly, 9322 Pte S Noble, 8863 Pte A. Sharpe, 662 Pte D Reed, 9529 Pte O Casson, 2905 Sgt. Hamilton, 979 Cpl Wheeway, 3726 Pte W Malyon, 942 Pte F Coles, 625 L/Cpl J Crawford, 8878 Pte R Forster, 451 Pte J O'Connor, 1677 Pte F Dawson, 9901 L/Cpl H Tuffey, 9899 L/Cpl W Greatorex, 9835 L/Cpl W McKean, 1768 Pte A Arnold, 9485 Pte G Browning, 8871 Pte J Downey, 8836 Pte H Hudson, 9191 Pte A Fuller, 488 Pte B Finnett, 8722 Pte J Crindle, 9782 Pte G Hockley, 3667 Pte F Kingsbury, 1308 Pte G Mason, 138 Pte G Robinson, 1333 Pte J Walker, 641 Pte W Robins, 969 Pte G Winter, 182 Cpl S Kilvington.

Missing: (7 Nov.) Returned (8 Nov.): 9545 L/Cpl G Mooney, 9514 Pte W Atkins, 9215 Pte W Bestwick, 3740 Pte G Baithwaite, 3640 Pte J Blackbird, 975 Pte A Ford, 8755 Pte T Forrest, 9612 Pte H Pratt, 3511 Pte D Scales, 8646 Pte D Barker, 9737 Pte G Clarke, 529 Pte G Clarke, 9195 Pte W Hazlehurst, 9132 Pte W Hampson, 338 Pte J Peacock, 9550 Pte T Rush, 855 Pte R Sproat, 9464 Pte H Wright, 1103 Pte W Wiles, 9551 Pte M White, 3747 Pte Clements, 22 Pte Hammond, 8872 Pte Mustery, 3896 Pte Colls, 2090 Pte J Wilkins, 985 Pte G Watson, 1251 Pte C Austin, 9844 Pte J Cuddy, 8822 Pte F Kelly, 359 Pte J Horner, 8775 Pte J Burdis, 1136 Pte C Seabridge, 1934 Pte G Butler, 1 Pte A Smith, 9856 Pte A Major: 9614 Pte J Sinclair, 246 Pte W Burnbridge, 1192 Pte C Cater, 657 Pte W Stubs 9789 L/Sgt W Richardson, 9804 Pte N Burke, 2427 Pte G Bradley, 2075 Pte C Dickinson: 370 Pte W

Coote, 9330 Pte A Orange, 1024 Pte G Lampkin, 2306 Pte G Mustill, 1510 Pte L Smith, 1374 Pte G Simkins, 1488 Pte E Hudson, 959 Pte E Filby, 1890 Pte J Maloney, 1430 Pte W Crooke, 9799 Pte J Kemp, 720 Pte A Gill, 3536 Pte T Grimes, 443 Pte H Bell, 7749 Pte R Dunn, 726 Pte J Galbraith, 8708 Pte C Weston, 9819 Pte P Dalton, 9684 Pte J Marshall, 9846 Pte J Fishbourne, 2630 Pte C Simmonds, 9389 Pte P Ryan, 380 Pte H Pratt, 393 Pte T Patterson, 7745 Pte N Chapman, 1543 Pte M Wilkinson, 2761 Cpl H Reed, 4401 L/Cpl W Kimberley, 918 Pte H Shapley, 1511 Pte H Brown, Pte Martin, Lieut. K.G. William.

9/10 November.
During the next two days things were relatively quiet with only sporadic artillery and rifle fire and each night Gordon's men were re-supplied. Sergeant-Major Gillborn, a noted marksman, was especially effective in retaliating against enemy snipers that were such a nuisance during the day.

Casualties, 9 November:
Killed: 319 Pte Dodds, 8864 Pte Kearney, Lieut. R. St John Willans

Wounded: 9776 Pte White.

Casualties, 10 November:
Wounded: 3420 Pte G.A. Kilso, 516 Pte R Brittle, 8184 Pte D Ginn, 1409 Pte W Cope.

Tuesday 11 November
This was to be the critical day in the First Battle of Ypres for the Germans were to make a supreme effort to smash through the British and French lines using the last of their uncommitted troops, which included the famed Prussian Guard.

As usual the attack was opened with a bombardment of the Allied positions by every gun and trench mortar within range and this lasted for about ninety minutes before the infantry attacks began at about 8.30 am. In the Herenthage wood, close to the Menin road, Shaw's Group, supported by some field guns, beat off attacks the *4th (Queen Augusta's) Guard Grenadiers* from the *4th Guards Brigade*[76] inflicting heavy losses but their sister regiment, the *2nd Guard Grenadiers*, broke

76 This brigade consisted of six battalions and fourteen machine guns. The strength of a Guard's battalion was 26 officers and 1050 other ranks. The 4th guards Brigade were fresh troops and at full strength.

through the Allied line north of the Menin road and turned to attack the exposed flank of the 4/Royal Fusiliers forcing them, and the French 4th Zouave battalion next to them, to fall back.

General Shaw immediately counter-attacked with the 1/Royal Scots Fusiliers and two companies of the 4/Royal Sussex who drove the *Guard's Grenadiers* out of the wood to occupy what they though were the 4/Royal Fusiliers front line trenches. Unfortunately they were support trenches, which left the British two hundred yards short of their original front line. When two further attempts, one by the 4/Royal Fusiliers and the 1/Royal Scots Fusiliers in the late afternoon, and an even later one by the 1/Northumberlands failed to regain the old front line General Shaw was compelled to pull back several hundred yards in order to establish a new defence line leaving Captain Gordon, and his men, more isolated than ever.

> *Capt. Gordon.* Soon after daybreak enemy commenced a very heavy bombardment of our position and poured shells into the wood to search for supporting troops, this lasted for about 1½ hours – during which time we could see enemy working to the left along their trenches and collecting on the left. At 8.30 a.m. they left their trenches and attacked. My trench repulsed them with heavy loss but my trenches on my left occupied by R. Fusiliers were captured by the enemy, who held them within 15 yards of my left, exposing me to enfilade fire from which we suffered somewhat severely.
>
> Royal Fusiliers assisted by 2 Coys R. Scots Fusiliers counter attacked unsuccessfully and dug in on a line about 300 yards on my left rear. I was reinforced by 20 men of the R. Fus. – and preparations were made in rear to prevent further penetration into the wood by the enemy. At 4 p.m. a Company of the W. Riding Regt. were ordered to occupy the lost trenches on my left. This attack failed. I reported the seriousness of my situation frequently and ask what steps will be taken to relieve me. Am ordered to hold on at all costs. Prepare to do so.

Casualties:
Killed: 8726 Pte Alderson, 496 Pte Scott, 3678 Pte Fox, 291 Pte Glass, 446 Pte Scrivener, 88 Pte F Newsome.

Wounded: 1447 Dmr. A Sheffield, 672 Pte T Wood, 2630 Pte C Simmonds, 1339 Pte G Allsop, 94 Pte T Shippendale, L/Cpl A Millgate, 2197 Pte Underwood, Cpl Thorne, 1155 L/Cpl Hyde, 354 Pte Farquhar, 9645 Pte Wilson, 306 Pte Clark, 247 Pte Bird, 171 Pte Nichol, 216 L/Cpl Marchant.

Missing: 9268 Pte Heaton, 661 Pte Kelly, 1611 Pte H Brown.

Thursday 13 November

For the first time Gordon's men experienced the devastating effects of the *Minenwerfer,* the German short-range trench mortar which was methodically trying to destroy his trenches. In the evening Major Yatman, commanding the battalion, forwarded Gordon's latest report to Brigade headquarters with a note stating '*Captain Gordon and his men have had practically no sleep for five nights. Captain Gordon is quite worn out and his men fall asleep standing under fire*'. Major Yatmen urged that they should be relieved, but with no troops available the decision was made to abandon the trenches and the difficult and delicate task of withdrawing the men, unheard and unobserved by an enemy situated less than thirty yards away, was completed soon after 11 pm without a shot being fired.

> *Capt. Gordon.* A very quiet night. Still hold on and receive congratulations of the Brigadier and G.O.C. 3rd Division. During the day the enemy bombarded my trenches at unpleasantly frequent intervals and we suffer a good number of casualties. To add to our discomfort our own gunners on four occasions drop shell into us, causing us five casualties. Nothing could be more demoralising than this – and a few things more pleasant than to see our shells dropping into the enemy's trenches, this we also saw, but not at too frequent intervals. Enemy also bombed us to day – all bombs falling near the same spot outside our trench. These bombs appear to be fired from the enemy's trenches about 250-300 yards in front from a spring gun. The bomb is visible as it descends and bursts on impact with great force and much black smoke. Not pleasant. Darkness puts an end to an anxious day and at about 8 p.m. I am ordered to vacate the trench and withdraw to a prepared and re-adjusted line in the rear – the movement will start at 11 p.m.

Casualties:
Killed: 8792 Pte T Marsden.

Wounded: 554 L/Cpl J Marlow, 9555 Pte J Lake.

Friday 14 November
General Shaw's new defence line started on the Menin road and ran southwards passing just east of Herenthage Chateau.

Fortified as a strong point, about eighty yards from the Chateau, was a stable block with a short length of trench on either side and at about midday, in a surprise attack, the enemy captured it along with a section of the front line trench south of the Chateau. From here they could bring enfilade fire onto the main British positions so it was essential that they were evicted as soon as possible. A counter-attack by 1/The Royal Scots Fusiliers, supported by 'W' Company 1/Northumberlands (reduced to about 60 men by the recent fighting), succeeded in recapturing the trenches but not the stable block.

A second attempt, made just after dark, by Captain A.B. Smyth and 50 men of the King's Own Yorkshire Light Infantry, encountered an enemy prepared for an attack and most were killed or wounding before they were half way to the stables and in the resulting confusion of this failed attack the German infantry charged forward and captured the Chateau, and the trench running in front of it

> *Capt. Gordon.* Got my men out of the trenches at 11 p.m. last night without a shot being fired. It was a trying and very anxious operation and I was right pleased when it was over. Moved into dugouts in rear of wood in Brigade reserve. During the day my company dug support trenches in rear of the Chateau. Lose Corporal Fisk by sniper – a very useful N.C.O. The enemy were doing much damage by sniping from the stable and the two trenches at G[77]. At about 8 p.m. an assault on these trenches by the K.O.Y.L.I. failed and things remained " in status quo " and not too pleasant.

77 There are several references throughout the manuscript that suggest that it was originally illustrated with sketch maps.

Casualties:
Wounded: 1491 Sgt J Drayson, 814 Pte W Blackburn, 1096 Pte P Shoosmith, 658 Pte J Robinson, 1068 Pte W Schofield, 2476 Sgt Oliver, 9618 Pte A Holmes, 1509 Pte C Wilkie, 8824 Pte F Kelly, 2303 Cpl J Jordon, 761 Pte W Fuller,1073 Dmr F Sanders, 8778 Pte J Reevel, 347 Pte W Scott.

Saturday 15 November
The failure of the Yorkshire Light Infantry to recapture the stable block was bad news for the survivors of Captain Gordon's Company. At this moment they were the only troops in Shaw's battle group that were not actually serving in the front line and Captain Gordon was ordered to retake the stable block. During the night they had a field gun, its wheels well muffled to prevent any noise, manhandled up a ride in the wood until it was about fifty yards from the stables. As soon as it was light enough to see the outline of the building, four rounds of shrapnel were fired from the gun to suppress German defensive fire and the assault party charged forward.

> *Capt. Gordon.* At 5.45 a.m. this morning 50 of my company under C.M.S. Gillborn assaulted and captured in a most gallant manner the stable and two trenches, occupying the trenches during the remainder of the day. Loose Gillborn, my right hand man – and a most gallant N.C.O. Recommend him for recognition. Loose about 30 men in the assault and in holding the trenches. Shortly after dark the front trenches are relieved by the 5th D.G[78] and 2 companies of the Battalion march into billets at Hooge. The relief for my trenches not arriving I remain with W and Z Companies.

Casualties:
Killed: 8822 C.S.M. L Gilborn, 2200 L/Cpl A Lieth, 1562 Cpl A Fisk, 2235 Pte Anderson, 881 Pte Egan, 9494 Sgt Duke, 1361 Sgt. Butler.

Wounded: 179 Pte J Armstrong, 9313 Pte S Johnstone, 3519 Pte J Forster, 2616 Pte T Lumb, 1946 Pte W Spoors, 9541 Pte J Greenhalgh, 698 Pte J Hall, 1405 Pte C Chambers, 2357 Pte J Fraser, 229 Pte E

78 Dragoon Guards.

Lute, 1667 Pte F Evans, 2677 Cpl J Colby, 9500 Pte W Taylor, 970 Cpl C Breeze, 47 Pte J Haynes, 9576 Pte J Haynes, 407 Sgt Edmunds, 7 Pte J Lush, 9673 Pte F Baines.

Missing. 9790 Cpl S Rollins, 209 Pte S Churchill, 1639 Pte J Coulton, 9506 Pte W Elliott, 8778 Pte J Reevel, 347 Pte W Scott, Pte W Ball, 9342 Pte Baggaley, 9512 L/Cpl Skeys, 8782 Pte O'Connell, 9886 Pte Seaburg, 106 Pte Taylor, 598 Pte Mack, 1497 Pte Brown.

Sunday 16 November
The Northumberland Fusiliers move into reserve. It's strength is 170, all ranks, including transport and other Headquarter details.

> *Capt. Gordon.* Q.M.S. Gillborn awarded the medal for Distinguished Conduct in the Field, and no man thoroughly deserved it. Very sad he was not spared to wear it – he is a great loss to the Regt. At about 10 a.m. the Queens Bays arrived to relieve my 2 Companies. Carry out the relief by daylight and get shelled for our pains with a loss of two wounded (Bays). Report at Hooge at about 11.15 a.m. with no further worries. Wash and change my clothes – the first wash for 10 days. We hope we have seen the last of Herenthage wood – the Chateau, all buildings and trees are smashed to bits every yard of it has been shelled. It is 12 inches deep in slush, the result of rain during the last 3 days. The trenches are deep in water.

Casualties:
Died of Wounds: 7377 Pte A Bell.

Wounded: 8576 Pte C Knight, 9511 Pte H Nadin.

Monday 17 November
They are billeted in houses along the main road in Hooge. Two machine guns, with crews, are transferred from the Oxfordshire and Buckinghamshire Light Infantry to bring the battalion up to its new complement of four guns when it is serving in the trenches

> *Capt. Gordon.* Slept on a bed last night, very cold hard frost. During the day have to send 100 men to reserve back to the wood. These returned at nightfall.

Casualties:
Killed: 263 L/C T Bootle.

Died of Wounds: 3538 Pte P Horan.

Wounded: 1049 Pte Y Dodd, 8663 Pte C Thurton.

Tuesday 18 November

> *Capt. Gordon.* About 12 noon again send 50 men up to reserve in the wood and at about 3 p.m. remainder of the battalion moves back to the wood to relieve the Cavalry in the trenches. Take over the trenches without incident at about 6 p.m.

Wednesday 19 November.

> *Capt. Gordon.* Enemy shelled us in early morning, remainder of the day passing quietly. At 8.30 p.m. we are relieved by the Divisional cavalry and march back as reserve to 9th and 7th Brigades – through a sea of mud. It has snowed most of the day – about 1 inch of snow lying.

Casualties:
Killed: 9710 Pte C Clarke.

Died of Wounds: 407 L/Sgt T Edmonds.

Wounded: 9522 Cpl A Woodhead, 3834 Pte A Taylor, 159 Pte Leonard.

Thursday 20 November
The Battalion has been promised six days rest.

> *Capt. Gordon.* Very sharp frost. Spent most of the night crouching over a charcoal fire in a ruined cottage, sleeping on the floor after a stiff hot rum and water until 6 a.m. when we moved into dugouts for the day. Unmolested – but the 51st battery about 800 yards behind us came in for heavy shelling and suffer heavily. German aeroplanes over us all day.

Friday 21 November

French troops start relieving the exhausted and depleted ranks of the BEF who are withdrawn for rest and refitting.

> *Capt. Gordon.* French troops relieved us at 11 p.m. last night and we march back to billets near Westoutre, about 12 miles where we are promised a rest. Very chaotic arrangements have been made by staff for billets – 2 or 3 units being allocated the same billets. Eventually settle comfortably into a farmhouse about 8 a.m.. have real hot bath – luxury. During the day 300 reinforcements with 6 officers (Festing, Watkin, Dorman-Smith and three others). Stiff frost, roads very slippery.

Saturday 22 November

> *Capt. Gordon.* A day of rest. A communion service and a voluntary church service. Major Yatman and Q.M. proceed to England on leave.

Sunday 23 November

The day is spent in reorganising the Companies and training the new men in fire discipline and fire control. General Smith-Dorrien paid a short visit, followed by their new Divisional Commander Major-General Haldane who presented No 2558 Cpl Bentley and No 8473 Sgt Squires with the Distinguished Conduct Medal.

Monday 24 November

The reorganisation of the battalion continues. Braziers are provided for the trenches and they are given a demonstration on how to make charcoal by the Royal Engineers.

Tuesday 25 November

> *Capt Gordon.* Rifle practice in the morning and a demonstration of bomb (hand grenade) throwing in the afternoon. Thick fur waistcoats are issued leading to a debate on how they should by worn. If worn over the greatcoat they are very conspicuous, but if worn under interfere with the

men's movements during firing. Waiting instruction from Brigade before men wear them in the firing line.

Wednesday 26 November

Capt. Gordon. The C in C paid us a visit today and addressed the battalion on parade. 2nd Lieutenants Gatehouse and Parkinson with 111 men join. Am now able to reorganise my company into 4 platoons.

Thursday 27 November

The French troops holding the line west of Ypres are required to bolster Joffre's winter offensives and their trenches, facing the Messines ridge, were taken over by the 3rd Division with the Northumberland Fusiliers finding themselves once more in front of Wytschaete, the village firmly in enemy hands. During the previous week the Highland Light Infantry had relieved the French and, perhaps unwilling to do any unnecessary labour, had made no effort to improve the condition of the trenches. The 'front line' consisted of a series of unconnected pits, without communication trenches, and lined with thick layers of straw mixed with mud, human excrement and in some cases the bodies of the dead while other corpses, both French and German, carpeted the area in front and behind the trenches. The only redeeming feature about the position was that the trenches were so close together that neither side risked using artillery for fear of hitting their own men.

For each night of their five-day tour of duty the 1/Northumberlands worked steadily joining up the front line, digging communication trenches, and burying the dead. It was bitterly cold and, except for the odd sniper, they were almost totally unmolested by the enemy who seemed to be equally busy improving the safety and comfort of his own trenches. Colonel Anslie, still on sick leave, sent the battalion a private gift of two sets of telephones, which did much to improve communication between Brigade Headquarters and the trenches.

Friday 28 November

The battalion is supplied with steel plate loopholes to be built into the parapet to provide protection for the snipers.

Casualties at Kemmel:

Killed: 9837 Sgt Graham, 7940 L/Cpl Bonnington.

Wounded: 6004 Pte Dolan.

Saturday 29 November

During the night patrols discover that the enemy are constructing successive lines of trenches in the wood at the foot of the Messines ridge. This was reported to headquarters and the battalion had the satisfaction of seeing them destroyed by some well-directed artillery fire at first light.

Casualties:
Killed: 9602 Pte Murray.

Sunday 30 November

> *Capt. Gordon.* In the early morning the Companies in the trenches carried out a reconnaissance to ascertain the position of the German trenches, wire entanglements and strength of the enemy. French on our left attacked and captured 150 yards of German trench. Usual sniping. Relieved by R.I. Rifles at about 8 p.m. and the battalion marched to billets at Westoutre – arriving about midnight. I am granted leave till the morning of December 6th.

Casualties

The total casualties for the month of November were 1 officer and 33 other ranks killed; 3 officers and 138 other ranks wounded and 1 officer and 189 other ranks missing, a total of 366.

Monday 1 December

> *Captain Gordon* goes on leave.

> *Capt. Gordon.* Wash and shave and at 2 a.m. off in a wagon with Barrett and Jenner to Bailleul. Arrive there and report to Corps headquarters at 4.30 a.m. An hour later we set off on motor busses for Boulogne, a cold and somewhat shaky 70 mile drive. – these busses are not too good on the hills and heavy roads and we arrive in Boulogne only just in time to catch the 11.30 a.m. boat to Folkestone. We celebrate the occasion with a champagne breakfast – but crossing in a gale

it is wasted. Meet my wife at Victoria Station at 3.15 p.m. – a little more than 18 hours after leaving the firing line. Drive to 3 Brunswick Place.

Tuesday 3 December

The King visits his troops in the Field and the Northumberland Fusiliers are represented at the formal parade by a detachment of 1 officer and 50 men. The King presented the Distinguished Conduct Medal to 2558 Corporal Bentley[79]

Capt. Gordon. Am enjoying every minute of my leave. Buy lots of new outfits – see many friends. At 5.50 p.m. leave London for Salisbury and dine at Witley at 8.30 p.m.

Wednesday 4 December

The battalion moves to new billets at Locre and receives its first 'VERY' pistol to fire flares to illuminate No Mans Land at night.

Thursday 5 December

Capt. Gordon. At 10 a.m. meet sisters and sister-in-law with children at Selfridges toy fair and spend a small fortune on toys. At 12 noon Patty and I lunch at Victoria with Barratt, Gummer, Captain Herbert and Mitford. Leave Victoria at 1 p.m. Take sea sickness precautions with great success. H.M. King leaves Boulogne as we arrive. I feel like a schoolboy returning to School – very home sick. Find a motor bus not very comfortable to sleep in. Reach Bailleau at midnight. Here we find Lt. Col. Stoutbridge (5th) who is on the staff of 2nd Corps – he puts us up for the night.

Friday 6 December

Capt. Gordon. At 7 a.m. Stourbridge sent us in a car to Locre where we find the battalion in billets. A draft of 4 officers

---

79 Distinguished Conduct Medals had already been awarded to 8473 Sergeant J Squires for exceptional gallantry under machine gun fire at Vailly (Wounded and sent home.), 1822 Lance Sergeant J.G. Pickering for gallantry in the attack at Pont du Hem. (died of wounds received near Ypres on 7th Nov.), 8822 C.S.M. L Gillborn for gallantry in an attack near Ypres on 15th Nov. (killed in action.).

and men has arrived in my absence and my Company is now 178 strong. At 3.30 p.m. the Battalion paraded and marched to take over the same line of trenches as on the 27th November. This time my Company is in the firing line. The trenches are in an appalling state of mud and water. We take over from H.L.I. in heavy rain.

Saturday 7 December

The battalion returns to the trenches in front of Wytschaete.

> *Capt. Gordon.* It is difficult to adequately describe life in the trenches under these circumstances. The rain ceased last night at about 10 p.m. and we spent the entire night improving and draining the trenches. In many places the water is still 18 inches to 2 feet deep and the mud is often so deep and thick that one sticks and has to be helped out. Our clothes are caked in thick mud from head to foot. There is no dry spot where the men can possible lie down and sleep is practically out of the question. The men stick it splendidly but there is certain to be a great deal of sickness. It is raining again – I am sharing a dug out with Watkins who is in my trenches with the maxim guns. The dug out leaks like a sieve and the floor is covered with saturated straw on which we lie. We must work again all night – our rations and tea are brought up to us by night, tea usually stone cold – I find my new thermos invaluable. The enemy keep sniping all day and all night and bullets seem to come from every possible point of the compass.

Sunday 8 December

The War Diary records the fighting strength of the battalion as 678.

They are ordered to send out a patrol to investigate the enemy's trenches and if possible grab a prisoner, or two. A patrol of 2 NCOs and 12 men set out at 8.15 pm, returning at 9.15, to report that the enemy fire trench was held only by sentries, well protected by wire, but behind were support trenches that appeared occupied by the main trench garrison. This report apparently did not satisfy Brigade Headquarters who apparently still wanted their prisoners, and they ordered the 1/Lincolns to carry out a reconnaissance in force, employing two Companies.

This reconnaissance was a disaster from start-to-finish.

After two days of standing in ice-cold muddy water up to their knees the 1/Lincolns were too stiff to climb out of their trenches and had to be shoved and pulled up onto the parapet from where they shuffled their way across No Mans Land slithering in the slushy mud and falling into shell holes full of ice-cold water. Pulling the knife rests holding the enemy wire away from the front of the trench they saw that it was flooded and there was no sign of any sentries. Weighted down with kit and soaking greatcoats the Lincolns struggled across the flooded trench but as they attempted to clamber onto dry land on the other side they were met with a fusillade of rifle and machine gun fire that drove them back into the flooded trench. Fed up and dispirited the survivors made their way back to their own line as best they could having suffered four killed, eleven missing and nineteen wounded for no purpose at all.

Monday 9 December

The Northumberland Fusiliers spent most of the day shoring up and repairing those sections of their trench that were collapsing under the weight of water. With so many men reporting sick as a consequence of living for five days at a time, in what essentially an open ditch full of ice-cold muddy water, the tours of trench duty were reduced to three days. Even this was too long for many who, at the end of the three days, were too weak and stiff to carry their sodden blankets and greatcoats and it became standard practice that, on change over, the transport came up as close as possible to the front line to carry their kit and other trench gear back to their billets.

Casualties:

Killed: ***X Company.*** 7874 Pte. J Cassidy, Z Coy, 8480 Pte A McLachlan, 9157 Pte P Swinn

Wounded: ***X Company***. 7884 Pte J Douglas, 7793 Pte J Tweddel, 8270 Pte J Forster.
Y Company. 7375 Pte P Horan. 8153 Pte M Bartholomew.

Slightly Wounded: ***Y Company.*** 3496 Cpl W Bette.
2/Lieut. E.E. Doran-Smith.

Tuesday 10 December

It was decided that in future officer's servants would accompany sick or wounded officers to hospital to ensure that their kit is safely delivered.

Capt. Gordon. Am obliged to report sick with the "distressing and almost universal complaint". By motor ambulance at 7.30 p.m. to the Clearing Hospital at Bailleul, arriving about 8 p.m. and bedding down very comfortably in No 2 Clearing Hospital. It is established in a Grammar School.

11-13 December

On the 12th the battalion returned to the trenches to find them in a worst state than before and, by way of welcome, the enemy fired a single salvo at battalion HQ killing five men and wounding eight others.

On December 13th they reported to Brigade Headquarters that they were manning 530 yards of fire trench with 395 men. 130 yards of support trench with 50 and 200 yards of reserve trench with 110, and had 58 boxes of ammunition in reserve. It was also during the night of the 13th that the machine gun detachments of the 7th Infantry Brigade took up positions in their trenches in preparation for the Anglo- French attack on the Messines ridge as part of General Joffre's ambitious winter offensive, which was only very reluctantly supported by British GHQ.

While the main French effort was directed against the Messines Ridge the subsidiary attack by the British was to capture Wytschaete, a task allocated to the 8th Infantry Brigade. With little faith in the French plan, and aware of the condition of his army, Sir John French would only commit two battalions to the initial attack, the 2/Royal Scots to clear the enemy out of the Petit Bois, the wood in front of the village, and the 1/Gordon Highlanders to capture the enemy strong point of Maedestede Farm.

These assaults was to be made from the trenches held by the Northumberland Fusiliers who, on the 13th, were temporarily relieved by the attacking battalions, although leaving the machine gun section behind to provide additional fire support.

The attack was a complete failure. With insufficient artillery support the French made no progress against the heavily fortified of Messines at the top of the ridge, the 1/Gordons suffered heavily before becoming pinned down in No Mans Land, about 50 yards from the German wire, and the 2/Royal Scots, who were initially successful in clearing the wood, were stopped by heavy machine gun fire as they tried to exit from the cover of the trees.

Casualties:
Killed: ***X Company***. 9467 Pte T Royce, 7793 Pte T Sunderson.
W Comapny. 6137 Pte F Campbell, 6910 Pte J Mills.

Died of Wounds: ***Y Company***. 8487 Pte J Wileman.
X Company. 5232 J Thorburn, 48 Pte C Crudgington, 7098 Pte W Moses, 8106 Pte W Robertson, 5584 Pte T Walker, 371 Pte W Runson, Cpl Kennedy, 5491 Pte A Marley, 7733 Pte T Charlton.

Wounded: ***W Company.*** 9302 Pte J Crossley, 6910 Pte J Mills.
Y Company. 6010 Pte J Brusi, 7881 Pte T Gullaway. 8223 Pte J Lee.

Slightly Wounded: 2/Lieut. A.H. Gatehouse.

> *Capt. Gordon.* On arrival at Boulogne at 10 p.m. last night. We are told that all hospitals there are full up. We bed down in the train and at 8 o'clock this morning woke to find ourselves in Le Treport – and we are conveyed in motor ambulance to No 3 Base Hospital in the Trianon Hotel. A new comfortably fitted hotel on the top of the cliff. Am examined by the MO. and informed I am to be sent home for an operation.

Saturday 14 December
The battalion returned to re-occupy their trenches but also to face an enemy very nervous after the previous day's attack.

Casualties:
Killed: ***Y Company.*** 9637 Sgt. W Newell, 6888 Pte T McClelland.

Wounded: ***W Company.*** 6022 Pte J Lawson.

15-19 December
The Northumberland Fusiliers settling into the regular routine of three-day tours in the trenches. Except for the occasional sniping military activity was practically non-existent as both sides devoted most of their energy to attempting to relieve the unremitting misery of living in a trench in one of the coldest winters in living memory. Essential stores and equipment were in such short supply that each man had only one pairs of boots, and one uniform, so unable to change into

dry clothes either in or out of the trenches and although in the last two weeks of 1914 casualties from enemy action were light, at 8 killed and 12 wounded, dozens of men were invalided home with various illnesses resulting from the rigours of trench life.

Friday 20 December

St John. I stayed at Boulogne till the 20th December which was the first day I was not too ill to be moved to a ship and the sea was flat enough to allow me to travel on it with a reasonable hope of not being seasick. I have never been so important a person as I was on the voyage. Unlike ordinary wounded heroes I was not herded on board hours before the ship started but said goodbye to Miss Blakely, the matron and Nurses and proceeded in a chair to the ship just before it was about to sail. Nurse Binns came down to the ship with me and Sir Francis Makin and Sir John Bradford were both waiting to see me on the ship. Mr Mears was sent over with me all the way to Torquay to look after me.

Saturday 21 December

St John. When we got to Southampton next morning a Brigadier friend was waiting for me and I was the first off the ship and taken into a special Torquay train which left within half an hour.

We got to Torquay at about 7 0 that night and I was again the centre of attraction. I was to go to Mrs Burns' Hospital and Mrs Burns had got the idea that I could walk so had only brought a motor for me and no ambulance so that I had to wait amid a curious crowd of onlookers while an ambulance was procured. When I got to Stookley Knowle I was put in the drawing room until a room was got ready for me and I was there for a quarter of an hour among a number of officers one of whom was Norman Smith who had been one of my subalterns since March but who did not recognise me until I spoke to him !. I had been led to believe that once in Devonshire I would soon get all right again and was disappointed to find that instead I was getting worse. In fact I had quite made up my mind that I was going to die and as I found out afterwards the Doctors had similarly decided.

Tuesday 24 December

Capt. Gordon. Disembark at Southampton and proceed to London in Hospital train. Report to Sisters Agnes and am allowed to go on leave to Salisbury for Christmas. To Salisbury with P.

Casualties 24th-31st:
Killed: ***X Company.*** 8855 Pte T Carr, 8138 Pte J Patton.
Y Company. 2272 Sgt. H Bizeley.

Missing: 8037 Pte T Cook.

Wounded: ***X Coympany.*** 6330 Pte W Blakloch, 6437 Pte W Daniels.

Tuesday 31 December

St John. However my luck did not forsake me though it left matters pretty late. When it did come to my assistance it did so with a vengeance. Drs. Gillette and Green who were attending me had called in a laryngologist to consult but none of them had come to a definite diagnosis in my case. They decided therefore to call in a Mr Hill from London who said he would come in a week if possible. It was therefore decided to move me to a nursing home in Torquay where Hill could see me more conveniently and I was to go there on a Thursday. He was to come on Saturday. Now I quarrelled with a night nurse who had been got in to act as a special for me and who was some age and not very conversant with modern surgery etc. and who therefore did not trouble herself much about me. Mrs Burns had sacked her and on the Tuesday I got a new one whose name I forget so I called her Bo Peep all the time. She was an A1 nurse however and very good to me.

To cut a long story short I was a lot worse on the Wednesday night and Bo Peep went and woke up Mrs Burns. She woke up the house surgeon Dr Ward and two other nurses who all said I was in no danger though undoubtedly worse. Dr Gillette also agreed with this but remained at the hospital to have a look at me every half hour. In the meantime Mrs Burns had a cylinder of oxygen (which she got into the hospital at the beginning against everyone advice) moved into my room. After an hour of two Gillette became doubtful and sent for Dr Green who said at once that he must perform a tracheotomy immediately though he doubted it was too late.

Meantime I was slowly dying of suffocation but thanks to the oxygen I was kept alive long enough for injections of strychnine and ether to be given me and take effect. Dr Green operated without an anaesthetic and I nearly died on the table but was just able to cough in time and so get rid of a fine abscess as big as my two fists. Had I not changed my nurse, had Mrs Burns not insisted in watching me against the advice of her staff, had she not had the oxygen in the house also against advice, I should have died that night. Moreover had the climax postponed its arrival until next day I should have been moved and would have died for a certainty on the journey. From now onwards i never looked back though once again my luck served me in a minor way. This was when after having sat upright for three months I developed a bad boil on my tail just when I was once again able to lie down.

I stayed at Torquay till the middle of February during which time I managed to increase my weight from 7 st. 8 lbs. to 9 st. and on February 14th went up to London to King Edward VII Hospital for Officers where I stopped many months and have now visited the operating theatre some 27 times and which I expect to visit on several other occasions,

Captain Beauchamp St John's wounds were too severe for him to return to active service. He was invalided out of the army with the rank of Major in the middle of 1915 and for the rest of his long life he breathed through a tracheotomy tube inserted into his throat.

Appendices

Biographical Note

Beauchamp Tudor St. John (always known as "Tudor") was born on 17th July 1880, the second son of Edmund St. John, rector at Bletsoe in Bedfordshire, who was in turn the 3rd son of the Fourteenth Baron St. John of Bletsoe. Tudor's father had married Adeline Farquhar, (3rd Daughter of Admiral Sir Auther Farquhar of Drumnagesk, Scotland). Edmund St. John died when Tudor was five and he and three brothers were brought up by their widowed mother at Drumnagesk. After a spell at Aberdeen University he was commissioned into the Royal Northumberland Fusiliers, "The Fighting Fifth", in May 1900 and joined the recently raised 4th Battalion at York. Before they disbanded in 1910 he had served with them in Dublin and Limerick and it was there that he met and married Madeline Goodbody of Thornville (known as Madge) on 31st March 1910.

In 1910 he transferred to the 2nd Battalion at Dover and in 1911 became Adjutant of the 4th Battalion (Territorial Force) at Hexham. In 1914 Tudor was posted to the 1st Battalion at Portsmouth and went with the British Expeditionary Force to France August 1914 and was severely wounded during the First Battle of Ypres at Wytschaete on November 1st. He was promoted Major in 1915, and after many months in hospital was invalided out of the Army. For the remainder of his life he had to breathe through a tracheotomy tube in his neck – one of the very first patients on which this new technology was used.

While still recovering from his wounds in 1916, he volunteered to take over as editor of The St. George's Gazette (the Regimental magazine) and so continued to serve the Northumberland Fusiliers, and remained in this post for 31 years. It was said at the time of his death that he had given 47 years of faithful service to his Regiment. While at this post, a group of philanthropists, headed by Lord Wittenham secured him a position as HM Deliverer of The Vote on the Speaker's staff in the House of Commons. He was also provided with the Old Mill House on Wittenham's estate at Benson beside the Thames above Wallingford. When Lord Wittenham died his widow was compelled to sell the estate and so the family moved to Aboyne, Aberdeenshire. It was here that Major St. John died aged 84 in 1965.

Adapted form the Obituary in the St. George's Gazette, 31st May 1965.

The St. John Coat of Arms

Notes on Officers Died

Captain Alan Barnsley 4th Battalion, Lancashire Fusiliers. Was born in 1877 youngest son of Mr Arthur Barnsley of Southward Rd. Liverpool. Served in the South African War, twice mentioned in dispatches and awarded the Queen's medal with two clasps. He entered the 4th Batt Lancashire Fusiliers with rank of Lieutenant in December 1902. He became a highly competent Militia officer and promoted Captain in 1906. For active service he was attached to 1st Battalion of the Regiment

Lieutenant Edward Fenwick Boyd was born in 1890 and was the only son of the late Robert Fenwick Boyd of Houghton-le-Spring Co. Durham. Educated at Rugby and Oxford. He won football colours in 1912, played for Blackheath and the Army & Navy in 1912. He was commissioned into the Regiment in 1912. Mentioned in Dispatch 8 October 1914.

Lieutenant Donald M. Coles. Special Reserve appointed 2nd Lieutenant on probation in June 1913, promoted Lieutenant in Sept 1914. No known grave but is assumed to be buried in Aubers Ridge British cemetery where he is commemorated by a private memorial.

Captain Roland Sackville Fletcher. Born London 24 March 1882. Second son of Lionel Fletcher and Eleanor Mary (*nee* Stopford Fletcher). Educated Charterhouse. Joined the Regiment in 1901 from the Northamptonshire Militia and promoted Lieutenant in February 1902. From Nov. 1904 to Jan 1914 was seconded to North Nigeria Regiment. Promoted Captain 1912. Published on his experiences in Nigeria in 'Blackwoods Magazine. Sat examination for Staff College 1912

Captain Francis Gatehouse. Born 1875. 1913 married Evelyn May Gordon. Mentioned in Dispatched from Boer War. Buried plot II.D.8 Vauxbuin French National Cemetery.

Captain Everard Joseph Lamb. Aged 29. Only son of Robert & Helen Lamb of Hayton House, How Mill, Carlisle Cumberland and husband of Margery Lamb.
Secondary Regiment KOYLI. Entered 3rd Batt. Northumberland Fusiliers in October 1905, Lieutenant June 1910, Captain August 1914.

Captain John Mounsey Lambert 3rd Battalion. Born 21 Dec. 1883 at Beamish House, Alnwick, the only son of the late Maj. Gen. G.C. Lambert and Isabell Lambert. Educated at Wellington. Commissioned in the Militia in 1903, promoted Lieutenant in 1906 and Captain on August 1914. He was a keen sportsman and an excellent shot and followed the Badsworth Hounds. He joined the 1st Battalion in France at the end of August.

2/Lieutenant Alfred Victor Laws. Born in Gateshead 9 Aug. 1884. Educated at St. Johns School Gateshead. Enlisted in 1901 and attained Sergeant in 1904. Served in India and Africa. Commissioned on 1 October 1914. Mentioned in Dispatches 8 Oct. 1914.

Lieutenant Christopher Leather 3rd Battalion. Was the youngest of six soldier brothers and was 32 when killed. Educated privately he joined the 3rd (Militia) Battalion, Durham Light Infantry. In the South Africa War served with distinction, first in the mounted Infantry and after being commissioned in the Northumberland Fusiliers. He was awarded the Queen's medal with three clasps and the King's medal with two clasps. Joined the reserve in 1904, rejoining 3rd Battalion in August 1914.

Captain Malcolm Leckie, RAMC, Born 8 April 1880, son of James Blythe Leckie and his wife Salina. Educated at Blackheath Preparatory School, then privately abroad, he entered Guy's Hospital in 1899, graduating in 1907. He enlisted in the RAMC 4 February 1908. From 1910-1914 he was attached to the Egyptian Army, serving in the Sudan, Blue Nile and Upper Egypt. Promoted Captain 4 August 1914. Malcolm Leckie was one of the best hockey players of his day, playing for Blackheath, Kent and the Army. He was capped for England. On mobilisation was attached to the 1st Battalion Northumberland Fusiliers and was fatally wounded by shrapnel fire while attending "D" Company wounded during the battle of Frameries 24 August 1914 and died a prisoner of war five days later. He is buried in Frameries Communal Cemetery, the first of the 903 medical officers to die in the war. Mentioned in Dispatches 8 October 1914 and awarded a posthumous DSO for "Gallant and exceptional devotion to duty attending to wounded at Frameries where he was himself wounded.

Malcolm Leckie was the brother-in-law of Sir Arthur Conan Doyle. The two men were firm friends and Malcolm death affected Sir Arthur deeply and was partly influential in arousing his interest in Spiritualism.

Captain John Hubert Matthews was born 19 September 1878 at Walmer, Kent and educated at Charterhouse. Gazetted into the Northumberland Fusiliers in 1899 from the Militia. Served in South Africa and awarded the Queen's Medal and the King's Medal each with two clasps.

Lieutenant Charles Hylton Van Neck was born in 1893 and was the youngest son of the late Mr Charles Van Neck and Mrs Van Neck. Educated at Harrow and Sandhurst. Commissioned into the Regiment in October 1913 and promoted Lieutenant in September 1914. His eldest brother Lieutenant P Van Neck of the Grenadier Guards was killed in action at Kruiseik near Ypres six days after Charles on the 26 October.

Lieutenant Charles Francis Nunelley. 3rd Battalion. Born in Rennington vicarage Alnwick on 31 Dec. 1883, the youngest son of Rev. F.B. Nunelley M.D. Educated at Malvern College he joined the West Kent militia as Lieutenant in 1903 and transferred to the 2nd Battalion Northumberland Fusiliers in May 1905. Retired from the Army in March 1907. Rejoined 3rd Battalion in August 1914 and was attached to the 1st Battalion in October. His Commanding Officer wrote of his death " Lieutenant Nunelley met his death as follows at Neuve Chapelle on the 20th October 1914. The enemy had captured a trench in which was a gun. He attempted to recapture the trench by crawling through a wire fence, which was about thirty yards from the enemy. His men got hung up on the wire, and Lieutenant Nunelley calmly stood up, encouraging and directing them regardless of all personal risks, and was shot at close quarters by the enemy. "Mentioned in Dispatches 14 Jan. 1915.

Captain Beauchamp Henry Selby was born on 4 June 1882, son of Beauchamp Prideux Selby of Pawson Northumberland. Educated at Harrow and Sandhurst he was commissioned into the Regiment in March 1901, promoted Lieutenant in May 1902 and Captain in October 1912. He served on the North-West Frontier and took part in the engagement at Matta for which he received the medal and clasp. He never regained consciousness after being shot by a sniper.

2/Lieutenant Eric Harold Tottie died of wounds at Braisne He was born in 1895 and was the son of Mr. and Mrs. Tottie of Sherlocks, Ascot. Received his commission from Sandhurst on the 15 August 1914 and had been with the battalion only 4 days before he was fatally wounded. He was nineteen years old. It was a double tragedy for his family. His brother was killed in action with the fleet in the North Sea on Sept 22, the day Eric died.

Captain Harry Stanley Toppin was born on the 27 July 1874, the eldest son of General and Mrs Toppin. He was educated at Wellington and Sandhurst and commissioned into the regiment in February 1895, promoted Lieutenant in October 1896 and Captain in May 1900. He served in the Nile expedition of 1898 and was present at the battle of Khartoum. He also served in the Anglo- Boer war in the Transvaal and Cape Colony. He was mentioned in dispatches and received the Queen's medal with seven clasps. He was a trained French interpreter and mentioned in Sir John French's Dispatches (8 October 1914) and awarded the Croix de Chevalier of the Legion of Honour.

Lieutenant Robert St John Willans 3rd Battalion. Born 8th September 1877. After serving in the militia was gazetted 2nd Lieutenant in April 1900 and promoted Lieutenant in June 1901. Served with the battalion in the South African War and retired from the army in 1905. At the outbreak of the war was re-gazetted to the 3rd Battalion

A note about the named casualties

The War Diary of the 1st Battalion Northumberland Fusiliers is unusual in that it retains the appendices that list the daily casualties. These would have been recorded by the battalion adjutant after roll call and are therefore a snapshot of the men absent from their unit at a particular time and place, and should not be taken as the definitive listing of the casualties. For men killed in action (kia) the War Diary lists should always be checked against other sources such as the Commonwealth War Graves Commission database (free at cwcg.org) and 'Soldiers Died in the Great War'.
Even so great caution must be exercised. Below is a table of the soldiers of the Northumberland Fusiliers listed as killed at Mons on Sunday 23 August in the three databases.

War Diary	*CWGC database*	Soldiers Died Database
	9495 L/Cpl. W. Barraclough	9495 L/Cpl. W. Barraclough
	3309 Pte T.W. Buckingham	3309 Pte T.W. Buckingham
	9309 Pte T.W. Cairns. Z Coy.	9309 Pte T.W. Cairns. Z Coy.
1592 Pte J T Grey X Coy.		
8766 L/Cpl E. Hitchens. X Coy.	8766 L/Cpl E. Hitchens. X Coy.	8766 L/Cpl E. Hitchens. X Coy.
8658 Pte T Hughes. X Coy.		
1247 Cpl E.T. Johnson X Coy.	1247 Cpl E.T. Johnson X Coy.	1247 Cpl E.T. Johnson X Coy.
1931 Pte B.R Neave. Z Coy.	1931 Pte B.R Neave. Z Coy.	1931 Pte B.R Neave. Z Coy.
	2562 Pte F. Poole.	2562 Pte F. Poole.

	9463 Pte J. Saunders	
1188 Pte J.F. Thompson. X Coy.	1188 Pte J.F. Thompson. X Coy.	1188 Pte J.F. Thompson. X Coy.
898 Pte B.R. Tucker. X Coy.	898 Pte B.R. Tucker. X Coy.	898 Pte B.R. Tucker. X Coy.
1496 Pte H. Vines. X Coy.	1496 Pte H. Vines. X Coy.	1496 Pte H. Vines. X Coy.
755 Pte D Will X Coy.		

Notes:

1. The War Diary in the Fusiliers Museum of Northumbria is a carbon copy of a typescript of the original, now apparently lost. The copy in the National Archives appears to be the top copy.
2. When this typescript was made certain changes/corrections were made. In the War Diary casualties for 23 August are listed by Companies named "W", "X", "Y", "Z". This naming system was not introduced until 4 September 1914. Previous to that date the Companies were numbers "A","B","C","D" as they are in the War Diaries up to 1 October.
3. 1188 Pte John Francis Thomas is listed as kia 23 August 1914. Pte Thomas died 24 September 1915 and is buried in Wandsworth (Earlsfield) Cemetery London. In the absence of other information it may be assumed from wounds received at Mons.
4. 8658 Pte T Hughes; 755 Pte D Will and 1592 Pte J T Grey are listed as kia but were in fact POW.
5. 9495 L/Cpl W Barraclough was drowned in a bathing accident before the battalion moved forwards to Mons. Not listed as a casualty in the War Diary.
6. 8766 L/Cpl E. Hitchens is listed in the War Diary as wounded.
7. 9309 Pte T.W. Cairns is listed as wounded on 24 August in the War Diary.
8. The only soldier on the list with a known grave is 1247 Cpl. E.T. Johnson (I.D.10 Hautrage Military Cemetery).

Selected Bibliography

The Fusiliers Museum of Northumberland, Alnwick Castle.

The manuscript diaries of:

Captain Beauchamp Tudor St John.

Captain E B Gordon.

The diary of Lieutenant F E Watkins published in St. Georges Gazette.1914 and 1915.

Regimental War Diary. Aug. – Dec. 1914.

Books.

John Buchan. *Nelson's History of the War Vols, 1-VII* Nelson & Sons London (1915).

Craster, J. M *'Fifteen Rounds a Minute' The Grenadiers at War. August to September 1914.*Macmillan, London (1976)

J.E.Edmonds. *Military Operations. France and Belgium 1914.* Vols 1 & 2 MacMillan & Co London (1925 & 1928).

H. R Sandilands. *THE FIFTH IN THE GREAT WAR.* Facsimile copy of the 1938 original produced by The Naval & Military Press Ltd. (2002).

The Manchester Guardian History of the War. Vol. 1 Manchester (1914).